Britain and European Integration 1945–1998

Britain and European Integration 1945–1998 provides illuminating insights into a subject which has dominated the British political scene for much of the period since the Second World War. Through a wide and varied collection of documents complemented by detailed and perceptive analysis, this book explores Britain's reactions to the dynamics of European integration.

This comprehensive study gives an intelligent, informed survey of the most important stages in Britain's relationship with Europe since 1945. Key subjects covered include:

- European unity and 'missed opportunities' in the early post-war years;
- the Commonwealth dimension and the 'special relationship';
- Britain's belated attempts to join the EC in the 1960s;
- the challenges posed by the quickening tempo of European integration;
- the development of controversial issues such as the single currency.

This detailed volume examines a highly topical subject which embraces such diverse matters as grand political strategy, economic imperatives, national sovereignty, 'mad cow disease' and fishing quotas. Many of its numerous sources are made widely accessible here for the first time. It is an invaluable resource for all students of Politics, Modern British History and European Studies.

David Gowland is Senior Lecturer in History at the University of Dundee.
Arthur Turner is Lecturer in History at the University of Dundee.

Britain and European Integration 1945–1998

A documentary history

**Edited by David Gowland
and Arthur Turner**

London and New York

First published 2000 by Routledge
11 New Fetter Lane, London EC4P 4EE

Simultaneously published in the USA and Canada
by Routledge
29 West 35th Street, New York, NY 10001

Routledge is an imprint of the Taylor & Francis Group

© 2000 Selection and editorial matter, David Gowland and Arthur Turner

Typeset in Baskerville by
BOOK NOW Ltd
Printed and bound in Great Britain by
Biddles Ltd, Guildford and King's Lynn

British Library Cataloguing in Publication Data
A catalogue record for this book is available from the British Library

Library of Congress Cataloging-in-Publication Data
Britain and European integration, 1945–1998 : a documentary history / edited by David
Gowland and Arthur Turner.
    p.   cm.
    Includes bibliographical references and index.
    1. European Economic Community–Great Britain. 2. European Union–Great Britain.
3. Great Britain–Politics and government–1945– I. Gowland, D. A. II. Turner, Arthur.
    HC241.25.G7 B676 2000
    327.4104′09′045–dc21   00–020367

ISBN 0-415-17974-2 (hbk)
ISBN 0-415-17975-0 (pbk)

For Mary, Alison, Sally, Sarah, Paul and Adam

Contents

Tables

Acknowledgements

We should like to thank the following for permission to publish copyright material: the Controller of Her Majesty's Stationery Office for Crown copyright material from the Public Record Office, London, the Official Report of the House of Commons Debates, Command Papers and extracts from volumes of *Documents on British Policy Overseas*; I. B. Tauris and Co. Ltd for an extract from G. Urban, *Diplomacy and Disillusion at the Court of Margaret Thatcher*; Service de Presse et d'Information, Ambassade de France à Londres for the joint letter from M. Jacques Chirac, President of the Republic, and Mr Helmut Kohl, German Chancellor, to Mr Tony Blair, President of the European Council; the US Government Printing Office; News Group Newspapers Ltd for extracts from © *The Sun*; News International Newspapers Ltd for extracts from *The Times* for 15 January 1963 and 22 May 1963; © *The Economist*, London, for extracts from the issues for 25 December 1982 and 26 September 1993; statement signed by 74 Labour MPs in *Tribune*, 5 May 1967, reproduced with permission of *Tribune*; European Communities for texts and tables reproduced by permission of the publishers, the Office for Official Publications of the European Communities; the Peters Fraser and Dunlop Group Ltd on behalf of Nigel Lawson for permission to use an extract from N. Lawson, *The View from No. 11: Memoirs of a Tory Radical*; the Butterworths Division of Reed Elsevier (UK) Ltd; *The Spectator*; the Labour Party; Simon and Schuster UK for an extract from I. Gilmour, *Dancing with Dogma*; *Main Economic Indicators* (1970–80), copyright OECD, 1999; Routledge for an extract from U. Kitzinger, *The European Common Market and Community* (1967), pp. 33–7; David Higham Associates for an extract from B. Castle, *The Castle Diaries 1964–1976*; The Rt. Hon. Michael Portillo; Blackwell Publishers Ltd; the Democracy Movement; material quoted from *Understanding the Euro*, Federal Trust for Education and Research, London 1998, ISBN 0–901–57372–8; Assembly of Western European Union.

The publishers have made every effort to contact authors/copyright holders of works reprinted in this volume. This has not been possible in every case, however, and we would welcome correspondence from individuals or companies we have been unable to trace.

Introduction

This book consists of a selection of documentary extracts and commentary on the evolution of Britain's relationship with the process of European integration in the period 1945–98. Its principal purpose is to provide a wide-ranging, substantial collection of source material on the events, ideas and interests that have shaped and reflected British policy and attitudes towards the type of European integration associated with the European Community (EC) and – since the Treaty on European Union of 1993 (Maastricht Treaty) – the European Union (EU). The book does not pretend to offer comprehensive coverage of all aspects. It does aim to provide, however, a sufficiently representative cross-section of source material to enable the reader to acquire from contemporary accounts an understanding of a multifaceted subject.

British involvement in 'the building of Europe' figured as one of the most bitterly contested and enduring features of British politics during the second half of the twentieth century. No other issue in domestic politics has so dramatically and repeatedly exposed major faultlines within governments, or thrown into sharp relief deep divisions within and between the major political parties. Furthermore, few if any other fields of government policy have demonstrated the same capacity to damage, in some cases fatally, the authority of prime ministers and the careers of Cabinet ministers. At the time of writing, moreover, this highly inflamed varicose vein in British political life is assured of further prominence. The likelihood and timing of British membership of the single European currency remain unresolved questions, currently accounting for the formation of battle-lines in a contest which, whatever the outcome, will be as momentous as the original decision to join the EC.

Britain has occupied a distinctive position of deeply rooted ambivalence towards the construction of the highway of European integration since 1945. Its adjustment to the EC/EU has not been indicative of smooth, linear progression. Instead there has been an unpredictable trajectory governed by policy twists and turns subject to vacillation, unexpected decisions and unintended consequences. The first half of the period covered by this book, for example, witnessed a major reversal of British policy towards the EC and a protracted controversy over the merits of EC membership. During the later period of membership since 1973, when the principle of membership was still questioned in some quarters, British participation invariably attracted a high degree of equivocation among policy-makers and public alike. Governments in both periods frequently demonstrated a hesitant, reactive approach to the EC/EU, or 'procrastination on principle' as John Major recently described his preferred approach to new plans for Europe (J. Major, *The Autobiography*, London, HarperCollins, 1999, p. 273).

The uncertainty surrounding the precise nature and extent of British interest in the EC/EU has been one of the elements of continuity in the British approach to European integration. The following documents offer an insight into the roots, dimensions and implications of this uncertainty. They also provide source material for testing the validity of common observations about other long-standing features of the British engagement with the EC/EU: the emphasis on minimal goals; the quest for unconditional and preferably 'free rider' access to the economic benefits of membership; the preoccupation with reconciling Britain's European and extra-European interests and commitments; the projection of European integration as primarily an economic phenomenon; and antipathy towards the idea of a federal Europe.

Domestic and external influences have contributed to the making of policy and also to the combustible compound of competing perspectives, principles and interests concerning the meaning and value of European integration in British circles. A wide range of historical, strategic, political, economic and other forces has been responsible for determining policy and attitudes. The following documents cover domestic conditions such as the impact of economic, commercial and financial factors as well as the influence of party and electoral politics. They also focus on the changing external environment that has affected British perceptions of the EC/EU and the wider world. Neither the domestic nor the external context can be examined in isolation from each other. Policy and attitudes have been fashioned out of the interplay between domestic and external pressures. They have also been moulded by the interaction of long-term historical trends, like the end of empire, and short-term developments, like the failure of a government's economic policy.

The British debate about Europe since 1945 has ranged from the essential attributes of statehood in terms of national sovereignty and independence to the conduct of British foreign policy within and beyond Europe. Much controversy has turned on very different understandings of the 'national interest' and conflicting assessments of the advantages of and the relationship between economic and political integration. Given the magnitude of the issues at stake, the protagonists in this debate – the pro- and anti-marketeers of yesteryear and their Europhile and Eurosceptic descendants – have rarely allowed the *actual* workings and policy particulars of the EC/EU to interfere with their preconceptions and articles of faith concerning certain fundamental propositions. One such proposition, for example, is more or less to the following effect and consists of two parts: (1) a post-imperial Britain, reduced in standing from a global to a medium-range power and lacking any viable alternative to EC/EU membership, can secure economic benefits and enhance its power and influence in the international system as part of the EC/EU; (2) the consequential loss of national sovereignty and decisionmaking is outweighed by the advantages of membership. This proposition, as is evident in the documents, has attracted fiercely disputed claims about both the motives and objectives of British policymakers and the identity and long-term goals of the EC/EU.

The domestic discourse on European integration has taken a variety of forms, extending from fantasies demonising or defending the EC/EU to heavily nuanced language capable of different interpretations. The documents have been selected to capture some of the quintessential features of this discourse. In many of the documentary sections conflicting views and different accounts have been deliberately juxtaposed in order to facilitate examination of the underlying assumptions and contested ideas. Needless to say, however, the documents do not speak for themselves. They acquire meaning and significance when decoded and when placed in context. For example, policymakers' public representation of the EC/EU may shed little or no light on their private assessments, calculations and priorities. The Russian doll character of British politics concerning Europe has taken a number of forms. The EC/EU has regularly served several latent functions in British politics, most notably as a safety valve for deflecting attention away from domestic weaknesses, as a bogeyman for governments and parties under pressure on other fronts, and as a panacea at times of acute consciousness of national failure.

These functions, in turn, have been indicative of the absence of any long-term, national consensus concerning the value and purposes of European integration. Competition between the major political parties and the changing balance of forces within these parties have invariably put at risk any axiomatic assumptions about the issue. A broad consensus between the Conservative and Labour parties existed only in the period 1945–60 when British aloofness from the origins of the EC commanded widespread support. Since the first application for membership (1961), however, Europe has invariably served the purpose of differentiating between the Conservative and Labour parties. In the 1960s and 1970s the Conservatives were regarded as the 'pro-European' party, while the bulk of the Labour Party treated EC membership as anathema. By the 1990s these roles had been reversed, after each party had moved in opposite directions in the intervening period for a variety of reasons, some of which had little or nothing to do with EC/EU affairs.

The history of the EC/EU has itself had a marked impact on the British debate about Europe. A key element in this respect has been the continental European parentage of the European 'idea'. This has remained intact from the Schuman Plan for a coal and steel community in 1950 to the launching of the single European currency in 1999. In view of its absence from the formative stages of the EC, Britain had to come to terms with an organisation that was not of its own making, one that was forged in opposition to what British policymakers regarded (and continue to regard) as the superior merits of their own model of European cooperation, and that was based on 'foreign' notions of the divisibility of sovereignty and of multilayered political authority. Some of the British qualms about the EC/EU and the often dysphasic grasp of the mainsprings of European integration originate in the absence of a shared history between Britain and the founding member states of the EC. The consequence of this is that the historical foundations, language and rhythm of European integration have not been easily assimilated into mainstream British political culture.

The process of European integration has confronted successive British governments with a number of dilemmas, many of which have been based on a combination of fears about the cost of exclusion from and the price of inclusion in the organisation. At various stages in the evolution of the EC/EU, British policymakers have attempted to impose limits on European integration, often giving the impression of seeking to uphold Lord Salisbury's maxim in foreign affairs – 'Whatever happens will be for the worse, and therefore it is in our interest that as little should happen as possible' (A. Roberts, *Salisbury: Victorian Titan*, London, Weidenfeld and Nicolson, 1999, p. 841). This position, however, did not rest easily with the growing recognition in government circles in the 1950s and 1960s that Britain's 'national interest' was indissolubly linked to the fate of the EC/EU. It proved no less difficult to reconcile British reservations with the uncomfortable degree of dynamism exhibited by the EC/EU in the 1990s. At the formative stage of the EEC in 1956, one government minister (Peter Thorneycroft) commented: 'we cannot afford that the Common Market [EEC] should either succeed, or fail, without us' (Public Record Office, FO 371/122034). The documents shed light on why British governments over the past 40 years have shared this view, how they have sought to manage its ramifications, and why they have been vulnerable to persistent domestic controversy over the limits of British involvement in the EC/EU.

This controversy has become all the more intense over the years as a result of the changing boundary lines between foreign and domestic policy in the conduct of Britain's relations with continental Europe. At the beginning of the period covered by this book, continental Europe was widely perceived in British circles as belonging to the foreign policy sphere. Europe had long been the object of British policies of intervention and non-intervention and not the source of institutions and measures penetrating domestic affairs. EC/EU membership, however, has transformed this relationship, as EC/EU legislation has gradually impinged on many areas of national life. Shortly after delivering his judgement on the first case in the British courts concerning the application of EC law (see document 8.2), Lord Denning commented on the immediate and longer-term significance of the EEC Treaty of Rome: 'the Treaty is like an incoming tide. It flows into the estuaries and up the rivers. It cannot be held back' (*The Times*, 29 April 1978). The following documents indicate that the process has indeed so far proved irreversible. They also reveal, however, the extent to which the EC/EU has continued to figure as a bolted-on extra belonging to the external environment rather than as a widely acknowledged, integral feature of British public life.

Several caveats should be entered about the content and scope of this book. Historical treatment of the recent past bristles with problems. Proximity to recent events runs the risk of producing a study that lacks detachment and perspective and that provides an insecure basis for the exercise of historical judgement. At the time of the Irish treaty negotiations of 1921 Lloyd George claimed that the Irish question had not entered into history because it had not yet passed out of politics. This observation applies with equal force to the subject matter of this book. Documents covering the most recent developments such as the single European currency clearly belong to an unfinished chapter in the history of Britain's relations with mainland Europe. Yet source materials for this later period serve a number of important functions, not least in shedding light on how today's campaigners view earlier chapters in the story (see, for example, document 11.9). Certainly this selection of documents will fail to capture patterns and trends discernible to a historian in 10 or 20 years, but any form of historical work is always offered from a particular vantage point in time.

The choice of extracts inevitably reflects editorial views of the most appropriate texts for representing major developments and issues. The bulk of the source material is British. We have also included American and continental European documents where these have a direct bearing on the subject matter. Besides the unavoidably subjective element in the choice of items, our selection of primary source material has been governed by what is available in the public domain and especially by the operation of the 30-year rule concerning access to British government papers. Our coverage of the 1945–68 period is thus able to draw heavily on Cabinet, prime ministerial, Foreign Office, Treasury and other official papers that are unavailable for the post-1968 period. Whatever the nature of the source material, however, the historian's rules of engagement with and methods of interrogating a text apply in all cases for the purposes of analysis, explanation and interpretation. The historian of this as of any other period faces the task of forming a judgement on the basis of incomplete information and in the sure knowledge that no source offers either incontrovertible meaning or a 'definitive' picture. Each of the following documents places a particular construction on events and each account invites critical scrutiny in the light of other sources.

The historiography of this subject is still in its infancy. Much of the published work of historians has so far concentrated on the 1945–63 period and has made extensive use of government papers in the Public Record Office. Particular interest has focused on the failure of British governments to become involved in the origins of the EC at the time of the Schuman Plan of 1950 and the EEC treaty negotiations of 1955–57 – the period of 'lost opportunities' as it is designated in some of the polemical works of the time. There has also been exhaustive research into the first application for British membership of the EC in 1961. Such studies have provided a much fuller picture than was previously available. On the whole, however, they have generally tended to confirm rather than contradict what was previously known from contemporary accounts, some of which are still authoritative texts (for example, M. Camps, *Britain and the European Community 1955–1963*, Oxford, Oxford University Press, 1964). In some respects government papers for this period have often yielded so few major surprises that they lend weight to what A. J. P. Taylor once described as 'Taylor's Law' – 'The Foreign Office knows no secrets' (A. J. P. Taylor, *English History 1914–1945*,

Oxford, Oxford University Press, 1979, p. 603). In any event, such papers need to be scrutinised like any other source as part of a partial, fragmentary record.

Historians have continued to arrive at different conclusions on some of the major questions in this period. For example, the much-debated subject of the factors responsible for the decision of the Macmillan government to apply for EC membership receives contrasting treatment in two recent studies (W. Kaiser, *Using Europe, Abusing the Europeans: Britain and European Integration, 1945–1963*, London, Macmillan, 1996; J. Tratt, *The Macmillan Government and Europe: A Study in the Process of Policy Development*, London, Macmillan, 1996). As in the case of the following documents, the weighing and interpretation of the evidence, the innumerable combinations of data, and the significance attached to particular sources all contribute to the production of markedly different conclusions.

The documents are presented in a broadly chronological framework but with provision for a more thematic approach in some sections. The introduction to each set of documents deals with the historical context and also assesses the meaning, usefulness, significance and representativeness of each extract. The number of the document referred to in each introductory section appears in brackets ( ). Editorial additions to the text appear in square brackets [ ]. We have endeavoured to ensure that editorial abridgements (. . .) are kept to a minimum and that any omissions do not result in a misrepresentation of the views of the author(s).

1 Reconstruction and European unity: 1945–1949

During the early post-war years Britain occupied an indeterminate position within the international system. Although one of the 'Big Three' victorious allies, it did not possess the resources of the US and the USSR. Nor did it share the wartime experience of occupation, division and defeat of many continental European states. The documents in this section reflect the impact of these and other conditions on the evolution of British policy towards the idea of European unity during the period of post-war reconstruction.

In the immediate aftermath of war British policymakers believed that the country's status as an independent great power was best enhanced by leadership of a 'third force' comprising the west European states and their overseas possessions in a tripartite international system. This view was gradually undermined, however, as Cold War tensions formalised the division of Europe and of Germany and as the problems of post-war recovery in Europe impressed on British policymakers the dangers of overclose relations with states that appeared to offer a host of liabilities rather than assets. At the same time British financial weakness and the legacy of wartime debts of £4.7 billion resulted in heavy dependence on American assistance following the UK/US loan negotiations of September–December 1945 and the Marshall aid offer of June 1947. By 1949 the formation of the Atlantic Pact and British antipathy towards far-reaching plans for European integration resulted in a more defined and circumscribed view of British involvement in Western Europe among Whitehall policymakers than had earlier been the case. The emerging consensus on European policy remained substantially intact during the following decade when Britain refused to participate in the origins of the European Community.

Historians have offered different assessments of British policy towards Europe in this period. Particular attention has been paid to the main objects and motives of Ernest Bevin whose dominant personality and strong position in Clement Attlee's newly elected Labour government of July 1945 gave him much scope to determine policy as Foreign Secretary. Some accounts focus on the origins and impact of the Cold War and stress Bevin's role in shaping a Western bloc based on the restoration of the close wartime relationship between the UK and the US. This emphasis on the 'Atlanticist' strain in British policy is summed up in the view that the Atlantic Pact of 1949 was Bevin's 'crowning achievement'. Other studies, however, argue that Bevin was principally concerned to restore Britain's credentials as a world power on an equal footing with and independent of the US and the USSR. The formation of an American-dominated Western alliance was thus a second-best solution, which was indicative of British weakness. It marked the failure of Bevin's grand design to organise 'the middle of the planet' – including the west European states – as a power bloc comparable to the US and the USSR.

Britain's precarious position as a world power at the end of the Second World War highlighted the value of assuming a leadership role in the reconstruction of Europe and of developing close relations with the west European states (1.1 and 1.3). A principal reason for doing so was to enhance British power and influence in the conduct of relations with the US and the USSR (1.2). This primarily global emphasis in British policy meant that regional European cooperation was viewed in the context of Britain's great power relations and of global institutions for resolving international problems (1.3B). Bevin and senior Whitehall officials were convinced of the need to develop close relations with the Western European states and especially with France in the first instance. From the outset, however, they were conscious of the limited British assistance that could be offered to these states and also of the relative weaknesses of these states as an organised bloc (1.2 and 1.3B).

The cause of European unity attracted the support of British political leaders who, contrary to some accounts, were no less possessed of vision and imagination than their continental counterparts. Winston Churchill was a dominant figure on European platforms where his grandiloquent rhetoric sought to boost European morale and to encourage a new Franco-German partnership (1.4). Significantly, however, he portrayed Britain as a sponsor of rather than a full participant in the new Europe. In a characteristically more prosaic manner, Bevin also supported the idea of European unity, most positively in his Western Union speech of January 1948 at a time when four-power cooperation in Germany had collapsed and the economic division of Europe had hardened following the offer of American (Marshall) aid in June 1947 (1.5). This speech marked both the apogee of Bevin's third force thinking and also his growing recognition of the importance of American assistance in addressing the problems of economic recovery and security in Western Europe. It also demonstrated that his interest in European unity lay principally in the fields of defence and security and economic cooperation: he was far more circumspect about detailed plans for the political unification of Europe.

The immediate consequence of Bevin's speech was the formation of a mutual security pact – the Brussels Treaty Organisation (BTO) – in March 1948, comprising Britain, France, Belgium, the Netherlands and Luxembourg. Earlier interest in constructing a European bloc of states to contain post-war Germany was here overtaken by growing anxiety with what was perceived as the greater Soviet threat to Western Europe. At the same time the Organisation for European Economic Cooperation (OEEC) was founded to supervise the distribution of American aid among 16 west European countries. Both organisations were shaped in accordance with British support for the principle of intergovernmental cooperation. They also established the foundations for a British-led Western Europe with a proprietorial attitude in Whitehall towards the functioning of such organisations.

By the time of Bevin's Western Union speech there was a rising tide of interest in continental, and especially French, circles in far-reaching forms of economic integration. Most notably the idea of a west European customs union, which came to fruition 10 years later in the EEC Treaty of Rome, began to take root, especially as France made an unsuccessful attempt to forge a customs union with Italy and the Benelux states. Initially, Whitehall opinion was divided about the advantages of British membership of a European customs union. Bevin was a long-standing supporter of this project. He was also concerned to give some economic substance to his Western Union grand design. As in other areas, however, his strong preference for a Western Union bank at this time depended on American backing in the absence of sufficient British reserves to underwrite such a venture. Immediately after the Western Union speech a Foreign Office paper presented the case for British member-ship of a European customs union and thus for a course of action which would have fundamentally changed Britain's role in Europe in later years (1.6). In characterising Whitehall's attitude towards the idea, the author of this paper touched on a feature that was also evident in official British reactions to advances in European integration in later years: 'the short term complexities and adjustments loom more largely in the minds of departments than the problematical (though generally conceded) long term advantages'. In the event, the Treasury under Stafford Cripps, the recently appointed Chancellor of the Exchequer, and the Board of Trade under Harold Wilson successfully opposed the idea. Bevin's particular interest in fostering close economic relations with France made little impact on the Treasury view that a dollar-starved European customs union was unlikely to serve the dollar-earning and dollar-saving principles underlying Britain's foreign economic policy at this time. In his rejection of the idea of British membership of a customs union, Cripps advanced a potent mix of arguments that concentrated on the preservation of national economic sovereignty, the long-term dangers of a customs union and the vital importance of maintaining a protectionist com-mercial policy (1.7).

By late 1948 Bevin's interest in European unity began to wane, especially as mounting support for a federal Europe found a platform at The Hague Congress of Europe (May 1948) and as the idea of a European parliamentary assembly was subsequently taken up by the French government in the BTO. In the course of negotiations resulting in the formation of the Council of Europe in 1949, Bevin was greatly irritated by federalist ambitions that accompanied the formation of this organisation (1.8). He was thus all the more disposed to define the limits of British interest in Europe. Cripps and Bevin eventually forged a common position on the general question of British involvement in the economic recovery of Western Europe. Their paper of January 1949 was approved by the Cabinet's Economic Policy Committee (1.9). In preparing this paper, Foreign Office and Treasury officials had urged that British assistance to Western Europe should be governed by the concept of limited liability and should avoid any surrender of national sovereignty. This position more sharply defined and qualified British policy towards Europe than at the time of Bevin's Western Union initiative. It also registered an increasingly pessimistic view in British circles about political and economic conditions in the continental European states.

At the same time support for a federal Europe among the continental states confirmed the weaknesses of these states in British eyes, justifying British scepticism about the idea and also reinforcing the importance of British guidance and leadership (1.10). The prevalent attitude of British policymakers was often based on a mixture of condescension, arrogance and insularity arising out of the continuing influence of Britain's exceptional wartime status as compared with the altogether different experiences of the continental European states. British policymakers also demonstrated a deeply ingrained consciousness of the qualititative difference between Britain and the continental states in the post-war international system. Many of the factors accounting for post-war interest in European integration had far less application in Britain than on the continent (1.11).

Document 1.1

The following extract is from a memorandum of 11 July 1945 by Sir Orme Sargent, a senior Foreign Office official who became Permanent Under-Secretary of the Foreign Office in 1946.

STOCKTAKING AFTER VE-DAY

The end of the war in Europe leaves us facing three main problems, none of which has any resemblance to the problems with which we were faced at the end of the last war. They are (*a*) the military occupation by Soviet troops of a large part of Eastern Europe and the Soviet Government's future policy generally; (*b*) the economic rehabilitation of Europe so as to prevent a general economic collapse; and (*c*) the task of administering Germany and deciding on her future institutions in agreement with the Soviet, United States and French Governments.

2.   Our own position, too, in dealing with these problems is very different from what it was at the end of the last war, when we and France shared and disputed, and eventually lost, control of Europe. This time the control is to a large degree in the hands of the Soviet Union and the United States, and neither of them is likely to consider British interests overmuch if they interfere with their own and unless we assert ourselves.

3.   Thus it suits us that the principle of cooperation between the three Great Powers should be specifically accepted as the basis on which problems arising out

of the war should be handled and decided. Such a co-operative system will, it is hoped, give us a position in the world which we might otherwise find it increasingly difficult to assert and maintain were the other two Great Powers to act independently. It is not that either the United States or the Soviet Union do not wish to collaborate with Great Britain . . . But the fact remains that in the minds of our big partners, especially in that of the United States, there is a feeling that Great Britain is now a secondary Power and can be treated as such, and that in the long run all will be well if they – the United States and the Soviet Union – as the two supreme World Powers of the future, understand one another. It is this misconception which it must be our policy to combat.

4.   We have many cards in our hands if we choose to use them – our political maturity; our diplomatic experience; the confidence which the solidarity of our democratic institutions inspires in Western Europe; and our incomparable war record. Unlike our two great partners we are not regarded in Western Europe either as gangsters or as go-getters. But we must do something about organising our side or we shall find our friends gradually drifting away from us. Time is not necessarily on our side. For this reason and because we are numerically the weakest and geographically the smallest of the three Great Powers, it is essential that we should increase our strength in not only the diplomatic but also the economic and military spheres. This clearly can best be done by enrolling France and the lesser Western European Powers, and, of course, also the Dominions, as collaborators with us in the tripartite system. Only so shall we be able, in the long run, to compel our two big partners to treat us as an equal. Even so, our collaboration with the Soviet Union, and even with the United States, is not going to be easy in view of the wide divergence between our respective outlooks, traditions and methods.

Source: Public Record Office [hereafter PRO], FO 371/50912

Document 1.2

The following extract is taken from the minutes of a meeting of Foreign Office, Treasury and Board of Trade officials on 25 July 1945, the day before the announcement of the general election results. It reveals some of the main features of Whitehall opinion concerning economic relations with France and Western Europe.

Sir Wilfred Eady [Treasury] said that in general terms the Treasury regarded a close association with the Western European powers as clearly in the economic interests of our country . . .

Development of association, both politically and economically, with Western Europe involved three considerations, that the scheme was within the framework of the San Francisco ideas [United Nations Charter], that any plan did not involve transferring to the United Kingdom some of the political and financial weaknesses of the other partners, and that both politically and economically the association could not be regarded as designed in opposition to policy of economic cooperation with the United States . . .

Sir Percivale Liesching [Board of Trade] said that there could be a great improvement in our trading relations with Western Europe, but that progress towards such an improvement was held up by the absence of a Cabinet decision on our commercial policy. In any case, the idea of a Customs Union in Western Europe or between this country and France was much too ambitious to aim at as the first objective of our policy. A Customs Union between two such equal powers as the United Kingdom and France was a very difficult proposition. It would in any case presuppose a strong political tie and, even with such a tie, it would under the current philosophy of full employment imply concrete mobility of labour between the two countries and this was difficult to visualise. It would be very difficult to find remedies for the various problems which a Customs Union would bring in its train for the Government of each of the countries concerned. Moreover a Customs Union would involve a common level of tariffs suitable both to the highly developed metropolitan countries and to their colonial dependencies whose economic circumstances were very different. This was a formidable difficulty. We should also have to reckon with the fact that the Dominions might suffer and that there might be a re-orientation on their part towards the United States . . .

Mr. Harvey [Foreign Office] said that the Foreign Office favoured the formation of a Western bloc in order that both we and our Western European Allies should carry more weight in the counsels of the Big Three. So far, however, we had had nothing much to offer to the other Western European countries. The Foreign Office had never thought it would be necessary to have anything so provocative as a Customs Union. What they looked forward to was a regional group on the lines contemplated at San Francisco the other potential partners in such a group being just as anxious as we were to be covered by the formula of the United Nations Charter. Until such a regional group could be formed we should do whatever we could for these countries on the economic side.

Source: PRO, T 236/779

Document 1.3

The general election of 5 July 1945 resulted in the formation of a Labour government under Clement Attlee. Ernest Bevin served as Foreign Secretary throughout the lifetime of this government and until ill health ended his period of office in March 1951. The following extracts reveal Bevin's thinking about Europe and wider international developments in the early post-war period. Extract A is taken from a record of a meeting between Bevin and Foreign Office officials on 13 August 1945. Extract B is part of a memorandum (8 November 1945) by Bevin.

A

2.   The Secretary of State explained that his long-term policy was to establish close relations between this country and the countries on the Mediterranean and

Atlantic fringes of Europe – e.g. more especially Greece, Italy, France, Belgium, the Netherlands and Scandinavia. He wanted to see close association between the United Kingdom and these countries – as much in commercial and economic matters as in political questions. It was necessary to make a start with France, and he was therefore very anxious to put relations between this country and France on to a better footing as soon as possible. As a first step in this direction it seemed essential to endeavour to reach some agreement with the French Government over the question of the Levant States . . .

5.   As regards the further steps to be taken to improve relations with France, the Secretary of State explained that while he was anxious, as he had already said, to work towards a closer association between this country and the countries on the fringe of Europe, more particularly France, he did not wish to take any active steps towards the conclusion of a Franco-British alliance or the formation of a Western group until he had had more time to consider possible Russian reactions. He was anxious, however, that in the meantime everything possible should be done to improve our commercial and economic relations with France – and also if practicable with the other liberated countries in Western Europe. Unfortunately, just at the present time it was very difficult for the United Kingdom to help France and the other countries in this direction to any very substantial extent . . .

Source: PRO, FO 371/49069

B

Instead of world co-operation we are rapidly drifting into spheres of influence or what can be better described as three great Monroes.

7.   The United States have long held, with our support, to the Monroe Doctrine for the western hemisphere, and there is no doubt now that notwithstanding all protestations that have been made they are attempting to extend this principle financially and economically to the Far East to include China and Japan, while the Russians seem to me to have made up their mind that their sphere is going to be from Lubeck to the Adriatic in the west and to Port Arthur in the east. Britain therefore stands between the two with the western world all divided up, with the French and British colonial empire separated and with a very weak position in what is called the western group . . . If this sphere of influence business does develop it will leave us and France on the outer circle of Europe with our friends, such as Italy, Greece, Turkey, the Middle East, our Dominions and India, and our colonial empire in Africa: a tremendous area to defend and a responsibility that, if it does develop, would make our position extremely difficult . . .

I have reviewed the whole position in the light of the above and have reached the conclusion that with the present deadlock between the Big Three, we shall not accomplish very much. Therefore, I propose, in dealing with all these problems, to proceed in the light of the obligations which will be assumed by all under the United Nations Organisation and to assure myself that the decisions I reach will ultimately fit in with the procedure, constitution and obligations of that body...

In my view, therefore, the only safe course for this country is to stand firm behind the United Nations Organisation and, in carrying out our policy there, to rely on our right to maintain the security of the British Commonwealth on the same terms as other countries are maintaining theirs, and to develop, within the conception of the United Nations, good relations with our near neighbours in the same way as the United States have developed their relations on the continent of America.

Source: *Documents on British Policy Overseas* [hereafter *DBPO*] (1986), series I, vol. III

Document 1.4

Extracts from a speech by Winston Churchill at the University of Zurich, 19 September 1946. In the early post-war years Churchill was a prominent supporter of European unity and called for a new Franco-German partnership with Britain as one of the sponsors.

And what is the plight to which Europe has been reduced? Some of the smaller States have indeed made a good recovery, but over wide areas a vast quivering mass of tormented, hungry, care-worn and bewildered human beings gape at the ruins of their cities and homes, and scan the dark horizons for the approach of some new peril, tyranny or terror. Among the victors there is a babel of jarring voices; among the vanquished the sullen silence of despair . . .

Yet all the while there is a remedy which, if it were generally and spontaneously adopted, would as if by a miracle transform the whole scene, and would in a few years make all Europe, or the greater part of it, as free and as happy as Switzerland is today. What is this sovereign remedy? It is to re-create the European family, or as much of it as we can, and provide it with a structure under which it can dwell in peace, in safety and in freedom. We must build a kind of United States of Europe . . .

There is no reason why a regional organisation of Europe should in any way conflict with the world organisation of the United Nations. On the contrary, I believe that the larger synthesis will only survive if it is founded upon coherent natural groupings. There is already a natural grouping in the Western Hemisphere. We British have our own Commonwealth of Nations . . .

I am now going to say something that will astonish you. The first step in the re-creation of the European family must be a partnership between France and Germany. In this way only can France recover the moral leadership of Europe. There can be no revival of Europe without a spiritually great France and a spiritually great Germany. The structure of the United States of Europe, if well and truly built, will be such as to make the material strength of a single state less important . . .

Our constant aim must be to build and fortify the strength of UNO [United Nations Organisation]. Under and within that world concept we must re-create the European family in a regional structure called, it may be, the United States of Europe. The first step is to form a Council of Europe. If at first all the States of Europe are not willing or able to join the Union, we must nevertheless proceed to assemble and combine those who will and those who can . . . In all this urgent work, France and Germany must take the lead together. Great Britain, the British Commonwealth of Nations, mighty America, and I trust Soviet Russia – for then indeed all would be well – must be the friends and sponsors of the new Europe and must champion its right to live and shine.

Source: U. Kitzinger, *The European Common Market and Community*, London, Routledge and Kegan Paul, 1967, pp. 33–7

Document 1.5

Extracts from a speech by Ernest Bevin in the House of Commons on 22 January 1948 in which he pressed the case for a Western Union and for the consolidation of Western Europe.

The conception of the unity of Europe and the preservation of Europe as the heart of Western civilisation is accepted by most people. The importance of this has become increasingly apparent, not only to all the European nations as a result of the post-war crises through which Europe has passed and is passing, but to the whole world. No one disputes the idea of European unity. That is not the issue. The issue is whether European unity cannot be achieved without the domination and control of one great power. That is the issue which has to be solved. I have tried on more than one occasion to set forth in this House and at international conferences, the British policy which has been carefully considered in connection with Europe.

This policy has been based on three principles. The first is that no one nation should dominate Europe. The second is that the old-fashioned conception of the balance of power as an aim should be discarded if possible. The third is that there should be substituted Four-Power co-operation and assistance to all the states of Europe, to enable them to evolve freely each in its own way. . .

It is easy enough to draw up a blueprint for a united Western Europe and to construct neat looking plans on paper. While I do not wish to discourage the work done by voluntary political organisations in advocating ambitious schemes of European unity, I must say that it is a much slower and harder job to carry out a practical programme which takes into account the realities which face us, and I am afraid that it will have to be done a step at a time.

But surely all these developments which I have been describing point to the conclusion that the free nations of Western Europe must now draw closely together. How much these countries have in common. Our sacrifices in the war, our hatred of injustice and oppression, our parliamentary democracy, our striving for economic rights and our conception and love of liberty are common among us all . . . I believe the time is ripe for a consolidation of Western Europe.

First, in this context we think of the people of France. Like all old friends, we have our differences from time to time, but I doubt whether ever before in our history there has been so much underlying goodwill and respect between the two peoples as now. We have a firm basis of co-operation in the Treaty of Dunkirk, we are partners in the European recovery programme . . . We are not now proposing a formal political union with France, as has sometimes been suggested, but we shall maintain the closest possible contact and work for ever closer unity between the two nations.

The time has come to find ways and means of developing our relations with the Benelux countries [Belgium, Luxembourg and the Netherlands]. I mean to begin talks with those countries in close accord with our French Allies . . .

I hope that treaties will thus be signed with our near neighbours, the Benelux countries, making with our Treaty with France an important nucleus in Western Europe . . .

Our formal relations with the various countries may differ, but between all there should be an effective understanding bound together by common ideals for which the Western Powers have twice in one generation shed their blood. If we are to preserve peace and our own safety at the same time we can only do so by the mobilisation of such a moral and material force as will create confidence and energy in the West and inspire respect elsewhere, and this means that Britain cannot stand outside Europe and regard her problems as quite separate from those of her European neighbours.

> Source: *Parliamentary Debates (Hansard) House of Commons Official Report* [hereafter *H.C.Deb.*], vol. 446, cols. 389–90, 397–9, 22 January 1948

Document 1.6

In January 1948 a Foreign Office working party was convened to consider the arguments in favour of a European customs union. The following extracts are from a draft paper that was considered by the working party at its meeting on 25 February 1948. The paper was written as if authorised by the Foreign Secretary.

The case for a Customs Union: Argument.

23.   To summarise I submit

(a) that it is essential to find an economic support for my policy of Western Union;

(b) that a Customs Union provides the most satisfactory method of providing such support;

(c) that the United Kingdom should take an early lead in sponsoring such a Union;

24.   I base my case on the following grounds:-

(i) No other solution is likely to bring about the same political and economic strengthening of Western Europe;

(ii) No other solution has the same promise of stability and permanence;

(iii) A Customs Union is likely to lead in time to full Economic Union, with a substantial measure of industrial integration and financial assimilation. This is the best guarantee of security in Western Europe;

(iv) It is essential for all countries in Western Europe to know where they stand economically over the next ten or fifteen years. A decision to form a Customs Union would provide the firmest basis for planning.

(v) A Western European Customs Union is already the subject of intensive study by an International Group set up during the Paris Conference. Within a few months much useful data should be available.

(vi) The immediate effects on U.S. opinion of a decision to form such a Union would be favourable, and might make a substantial difference to the volume of aid voted in the ensuing year (say 1949). No less far reaching proposal would have the same effect.

(vii) A number of proposals for Regional Unions – Benelux, France and Italy, Scandinavia, Greece and Turkey – are under consideration. Such unions, particularly if they were to amalgamate, would operate to the economic disadvantage of the U.K.

(viii) It is quite possible however that other countries will content themselves with forming regional unions, and that they are not doing more than paying lip service to the broader concept. We could not consider joining a regional European Union ourselves. Unless we are to be left outside, we must therefore not merely favour but *advocate* a wider union.

(ix) Thus we may have an opportunity of making more far reaching proposals, which are relatively to our advantage, than any other country is prepared to make. This is doubly to be welcomed, since it puts us in the lead and may enable us to exercise a corresponding influence upon the details of the arrangements (e.g. in relation to Imperial Preference).

(x) In the long run our capacity to survive will be based on our competitive efficiency. This will be enhanced by our joining a Union of industrial powers. If we are unable to make use of this opportunity, then no amount of sheltering behind a protective tariff would have helped us; we should not have deserved to survive.

(xi) It is indeed our national survival which is at stake. The crisis in our affairs calls for radical solutions. For better or worse, our fate is in large part inextricably bound up with that of Western Europe. Our policy should frankly recognise this fact, and set about devising the most effective methods by which we can survive together. Our policy to this end must be underpinned in the economic field. A Customs Union provides immeasurably the most secure method in that field.

Source: PRO, FO 371/71766

Document 1.7

In the early post-war years the idea of British membership of a European customs union encountered strong opposition in the Treasury and the Board of Trade. The following extracts from a memorandum of 7 September 1948 by Sir Stafford Cripps (Chancellor of the Exchequer) outline some of the main arguments against British involvement in a customs union.

At present the real obstacle to expanded trade among European countries is not tariffs, but the quantitative restriction of imports. In view, however, of the current balance of payments difficulties of many European countries it would be difficult to secure the removal of these restrictions at the present time. If such obstacles are to be removed by the European countries as far as their mutual trade is concerned, we must be willing to remove our own tariffs and quota restrictions. Immediately, however, such removal, and the other action implicit in full economic co-operation, would mean the abandonment of many policies which in existing economic circumstances we regard as vital. The system of Imperial Preference would, to some extent at any rate, be weakened. Our policy for home agriculture with all that implies strategically, politically and economically, would have to be profoundly modified . . .

A Customs Union under which trade continues to be hampered by quantitative restriction of imports would be a sham, and if this country were to contemplate entering a Union it would have to be a reality and not a sham. A Customs Union which is a sham would give us the worst of both worlds. We could not develop our protected agriculture and industries because there would be a constant risk of the home market being invaded by European competition. But we could not rely on an assured market for our exports, because at any time these might be held up by import restrictions imposed (and necessarily imposed) owing to balance of payments difficulties. Also any Union, even if it were confined to tariffs, would raise serious difficulties in relation to Commonwealth preference.

European economic co-operation, whether starting from a Customs Union or otherwise, might entail a considerable measure of common action among the members in fiscal, financial and other economic fields, which would only be workable if the members gave powers of decision in these fields to a central body . . .

We consider that such arrangements would involve a measure of Union control over exchange rates combined with a system of Union rationing of 'hard' foreign currencies and with inter-member credit facilities going some way, but not necessarily the whole way, towards a pooling of monetary reserves and a possible right for the Union to intervene in domestic policy in the event of substantial inflationary or deflationary developments in the economies of particular members having severe repercussions on the economies of other members. They would also involve some degree of Union control over the use of subsidies, Union right to require the discontinuance or scaling down of any internal tax which discriminated against imports from other countries in the Union, and of any consumption tax which bore severely on Union imports of which there was no home production . . .

It may be doubted whether democratic Governments would be willing, in spite of the economic advantages which the Union might bring with it, to give to any international body the ultimate power to suggest or enforce the devaluation of their currencies . . .

If this is so, there is a strong presumption that if the Customs Union were to survive it would, in the present conditions of economic disequilibrium in Western Europe, have to move towards a full economic union with a single economic and financial policy. Experience of past Customs Unions goes to show that in themselves they represent only an impermanent half-way measure and that they have always either passed on to the stage of political fusion or else broken up.

Source: PRO, CAB 134/219, E.P.C. (48) 78

Document 1.8

The Council of Europe was formed in 1949 comprising a Committee of Ministers and a Consultative Assembly. While this arrangement was consistent with the British emphasis on European cooperation, Bevin initially had no wish to create such a body and was greatly irritated by French-inspired plans for a stronger and more federal organisation. The experience reduced Bevin's interest in European unity, and the early proceedings of the Consultative Assembly confirmed his worst fears about creating a hothouse for federalist opinion. The following extract is taken from a memorandum by Bevin (19 October 1950) dealing with the origins and early development of the organisation.

3.   There have always been two conflicting views of the nature and purposes of the Council of Europe. To the majority of Governments which set it up the Council of Europe was not an instrument for the immediate political unification of Europe, but part of the general material and moral build-up of which other aspects are represented by the O.E.E.C. [Organisation for European Economic Cooperation], the Brussels Treaty and the North Atlantic Pact. Their object was merely, as the Preamble of the Statute puts it, to bring 'European States into closer association.' They had no intention of conferring the powers of a European executive upon the Committee of Ministers, still less on any body emanating from the Consultative Assembly. Nor had they any intention of allowing the Assembly to become a responsible parliament. The Committee of Ministers was intended to be an organ of inter-governmental co-operation, covering fields, and including countries, not dealt with by other organisations. The Consultative Assembly was intended to be a forum of opinion and a forcing-house of ideas, broadly representative of political tendencies in the countries concerned but not so closely bound to governmental policies as to be unable to discuss European problems from a reasonably detached point of view.

4.   From the outset this conception has broken down. The idea of a European Assembly had been launched by the European Movement and the Assembly has from the first been dominated by that organisation. The driving force behind the Assembly's actions has thus been an energetic and able pressure group dedicated to the objective of transforming the Consultative Assembly into a European

parliament and the Council as a whole into a European political authority. Secondly, the Assembly has tended naturally to consist largely of enthusiasts for European federation. It is therefore biased in favour of federal solutions to an extent which wholly invalidates its claim to represent European opinion as a whole. In consequence, the Assembly has from the first refused to be content with a purely consultative rôle, and has attempted by every means to secure its transformation into a European parliament from which a European executive would derive authority. . .

6.   A number of Governments, led by His Majesty's Government, have made it clear that they do not accept this aim, and the result has been a running conflict between the two organs of the Council. The Committee of Ministers have been represented as a tyrannical and reactionary 'executive' thwarting the wishes of a democratic and progressive 'legislature' and standing in the way of the universal desire for federation . . . The matter is further complicated by the unwillingness of certain Governments – and particularly the French – to take a firm line with the Assembly enthusiasts, or to apply a critical judgment to idealistic schemes. Thus, apart from the cleavage between the Committee of Ministers and the Assembly, there is a latent cleavage within the Committee of Ministers between the Latin continental Powers, who favour European federation, and the rest led by His Majesty's Government, who are very much more cautious.

Source: PRO, CAB 129/42, C.P. (50) 236, 19 October 1950

Document 1.9

In 1949 a consensus emerged in Whitehall about the nature and extent of British participation in European economic cooperation as institutionalised in the Organisation for European Economic Cooperation (OEEC), the European body responsible for supervising the four-year European Recovery Programme. In the following extracts from a memorandum of 25 January 1949 approved by the Cabinet, Bevin and Cripps subscribed to a common position on British involvement in the economic recovery of Western Europe.

The framework of our defence policy is being built up in the Atlantic Pact, which seeks to bring together the United States, Canada, the United Kingdom and the principal countries of Western Europe. This policy can only come to fruition in its entirety if economic stability is restored in France and the Benelux countries and if they come into the pact, Italy, Portugal, Norway and Denmark. A policy of economic help to those countries is, therefore, in accord with our own vital interests and we should be ready to make considerable sacrifices and run risks to bring it about. On the other hand, we must take a realistic view of the risks to be run and of the sacrifices to be made; the degree of assistance offered must not jeopardise our chances of survival, or of economic viability . . .

It is clear that we are now reaching a critical moment in the affairs of O.E.E.C. The original impetus that brought it into being and enabled it to reach agreed allocations in the first year's aid is now largely lost. The discussions about integration and specialisation and so forth have proved sterile and are unlikely to lead to practical results within the next few critical years. The Customs Union project is, as expected, turning out to be no talisman or open sesame but an unusually difficult and complex affair which would take many years to bring about, and could only indeed come to pass as part of a larger scheme.

If no new idea is injected, there is a real risk that O.E.E.C., and with it the whole E.R.P. programme, will break down. An effective new lead can only be provided by this country, which alone of the countries of Western Europe, has the necessary standing and technical capacity to work out a scheme which can give new life to the O.E.E.C. conception.

We must not, however, lose sight of the risk that, in taking this lead, and attempting to put Western Europe on its legs, we may be led into courses which would make this country no longer a viable unit apart from the rest of Western Europe; and that should the attempt to restore Western Europe fail we should then find that we had deprived ourselves of things necessary to our economic survival.

The extent of the risks which we should run and of the sacrifices which we should make in order to restore Western Europe is not, however, a question which can usefully be discussed in the abstract . . . We can, however, lay down firmly the principle that, while we must be ready to make temporary sacrifices in our standard of living, and to run some degree of risk in the hope of restoring Western Europe, we must do nothing to damage irretrievably the economic structure of this country. The present attempt to restore sanity and order in the world depends upon the United States and the British Commonwealth and the countries of Western Europe working together. If, however, the attempt to restore Western Europe should fail, this country could still hope to restore its position in co-operation with the rest of the Commonwealth and with the United States. But in these circumstances we could not look for continued United States military, political and economic support if, in the endeavour to re-establish Western Europe, our economic structure had been hopelessly impaired.

Source: PRO, CAB 134/221, E.P.C. (49) 6, 25 January 1949

Document 1.10

Sir Edmund Hall-Patch served as official representative of the United Kingdom on the OEEC for four years. On his retirement from this post in July 1952, he reflected on the experience in a note to the Foreign Secretary (8 July 1952). The following extracts focus on British leadership in Europe and the weaknesses of the continental states.

5.   The Europeans look to us for leadership; they are delighted when we are able to give it; they respond to it in a remarkable manner.

6.   During the past four years when we have given any firm lead in the economic field it has invariably been followed. We may not always have secured all of our objectives, but we have always secured the greater part without undue difficulty, and there has been an increasing understanding of our world-wide responsibilities and the burdens and difficulties which these responsibilities entail. The developments of the Schuman and Pleven Plans do not mean that

Europe is irresponsive to any lead we may give; the fact is that in the fields covered by those Plans we did not give any lead, and, after a period of hesitation, Continental Europe, with American encouragement, commenced to think in terms of 'integration', supranational authorities and finally federation.

7.   There is a deep malaise in France, Germany and Italy; the post-war Governments have been weak and divided and there is no outstanding leadership. This situation has led to a search for supra-national solutions to difficulties for which no immediate remedy seems possible on a national basis. These Governments grope with supra-national or even federal solutions, but they take this path reluctantly and seek at every turn to ensure that ways are left open to enable the United Kingdom to associate itself, insofar as this is possible, with the new developments.

8.   The other three partners in the supra-national camp are even more hesitant and doubtful, but with no clear alternative open to them, resign themselves reluctantly to follow in the steps of their more powerful partners.

9.   This tendency to partial European federation is not an urge to European brotherhood on a healthy basis. It is based on uncertainty and fear. If federation meant at some fairly early date a cohesive Western Europe with which we could work, with a federal authority for which continental Europe would fight and pay taxes, its importance would be enormous. But this is hardly possible . . .

25.   Although part of Europe, the United Kingdom has strong links with the Commonwealth and enjoys a special relationship with the United States. In these circumstances we can, if we so wish, guide Europe in searching for a solution in common with the United States, and it is the hope of many of our European partners that we will give that guidance.

26.   Unless we do so, the forces of disruption and decay may well increase in Europe. On the one hand there will be an increasing tendency to dependence on the United States going, in some cases, almost to the point of mendicity. On the other hand, there will be a tendency to establish economic autarchy in Europe which, while probably doomed to failure in the long run, would disrupt multi-lateral trade and payments and do great damage to the objectives we have in view. The move to a partial federation in Europe masks a desire in some quarters for European economic autarchy and this is one of the dangers of the present situation.

27.   It is quite clear that there is no purely European solution, as there is no purely American solution, for the present difficulties. The solution can only be found by the Western World as a whole and we may be able to provide the connecting link . . .

Source: *DBPO*, series II, vol. I, no. 466

Document 1.11

The following extract from a Foreign Office memorandum of 12 December 1951 indicates the perceptions of British officials concerning the origins of continental interest in European integration during the early post-war years.

The desire for closer integration in Western Europe has been much stimulated by the defeat and humiliation suffered by many European countries in the last war. These experiences, combined with the obvious failure of the old system of alliances, drove many to conclude that separately the nations of Europe can neither maintain peace nor, if war comes, protect their citizens.

The post-war policy of the Soviet Union has stimulated the desire for integration. The size and unity of the Soviet *bloc* in themselves emphasise the weakness and disunity of Western Europe. The existence of the Red Army is a constant threat. Soviet hostility to the United States brings home to Europeans the dangers of their position between the two Great Powers.

The desire for integration has from the first been encouraged by the United States. The basic reason for this is the American belief that union can help Europe as it has helped the United States. A European Union would, in the American view, be stronger militarily and economically than separate States and thus better able to resist communism.

The experiences of the war years, Russian policy and American backing have thus given impetus to the movement for closer integration. This movement has supporters in every country in Western Europe. Their motives are varied and complex; some derive from idealism, others from self interest, although the two naturally exist side by side, so that it is not always possible to distinguish between them, nor to diagnose which type of motive predominates in any given country.

The idealistic motives, broadly speaking, spring from the belief that European culture and civilisation have a vital contribution to make in the shaping of world affairs and that they can only effectively do so if the European idea supersedes the old national loyalties.

The motives which derive from self-interest are those which see in the integration movement a means of gaining sectional or national advantage. Such, for instance, is the belief, held notably by the Christian Democratic Parties, that integration would make it possible to unite Europe under increased Christian – mainly Catholic – influence (although they could, of course, only hope to ensure this as long as they all retained power in their own countries.) A different type of self-interested motive is the belief that certain countries (*e.g.* Dutch exporters) will benefit economically from integration. Yet another form of self-interest is the thought, springing from defeatism in some circles in Europe, that integration might make easier the pursuit of a 'neutralist' policy, and so avoid the effects of a war.

Idealism and self-interest, however, combine in the motive which, in France and Germany at least, provides the driving force for the integration movement – namely, the desire to end the Franco-German conflict. It is not merely that most Frenchmen and many Germans have been convinced by the experiences of the last war that the old order cannot offer peace or security to the peoples of Europe, and have thus been led to put their faith in a wider community. It is rather that some form of integration alone can provide a framework within which France and Germany can live in peace while remaining separate, if not entirely independent, States.

There are also Nationalist motives behind the desire of both France and Germany for integration. France believes that in a direct conflict German strength would be too much for her. She therefore hopes to build an integrated Europe after the pattern of her own making in which German strength will be effectively controlled. Germany, on the other hand, is intent at present in regaining her lost place as an equal member of the European community. No doubt she believes that given formal equality the size and strength of her resources will confer advantages upon her not enjoyed by all her 'equal' partners. If nationalism grew in Germany, she would naturally be tempted to exploit these advantages within the European community. France hopes that progress towards this community will itself stifle the rebirth of German nationalism.

Source: *DBPO*, series II, vol. I, no. 414

2   'Lost opportunities': 1950–1957

This section deals with key turning points in Britain's relations with the emerging European Community in the period 1950–57. The extracts focus on some of the main considerations accounting for the British refusal to join Belgium, France, Italy, Luxembourg, the Netherlands and West Germany (the Six) in launching the EC. They also cover British attempts to develop forms of association with the EC that fell short of full membership. More detailed treatment of several aspects is provided in sections 3 and 4.

Some studies of British policy in this period portray British governments as short-sighted and unimaginative in their response to the formation of the EC. Governments missed the European bus/train/boat, according to the over-worked metaphors of such literature, and their successors paid dearly for this failing when they sought membership of an EC that served the interests of the founder member states. Certainly the landscape of European integration changed faster than the perceptions of British policymakers and in ways that confounded their expectations. At the same time, however, policymakers were convinced that their approach to European unity and cooperation best served British interests in and beyond Europe and was in accord with public opinion.

The founding Community of the EC originated in the proposal of Robert Schuman, the French Foreign Minister (9 May 1950), to place French and West German coal and steel production under a supranational High Authority open to the participation of other European countries (2.1). Some of the distinctive features of this plan, as outlined by its its author Jean Monnet (head of France's Modernisation and Re-equipment Plan), were the emphasis on establishing a new basis for Franco-German relations and insistence on commitment to the supranational principle prior to detailed negotiations between interested states.

The prior commitment requirement was cited by the Attlee government as the major stumbling block to its participation in negotiations about the plan (2.2A). The government's formal position was based on a desire to avoid either acceptance or rejection of the plan's principles in advance of detailed discussions. While officials claimed to be open-minded about the supra-national principle, neither ministers nor officials were prepared to engage in negotiations on French terms (2.2B). Besides this formal objection, however, the main obstacle to participation was the surrender of national sovereignty to a High Authority empowered to act independently of the governments of the member states. This possibility was judged to exceed the limits of the British commitment to European cooperation as defined by the Cabinet in the previous year, and it was all the more keenly resisted in Labour circles as coal and steel were an integral part of the government's nationalisation programme. Furthermore, Britain as Western Europe's largest coal and steel producer did not share French concerns about arrangements to safeguard access to German coal following the removal of occupation controls and the beginnings of economic recovery in the western occupation zones (2.3).

British policymakers welcomed the Schuman Plan as a breakthrough in Franco-German relations. Yet they doubted the seriousness of French intentions and also the usefulness of forming another European organisation. At this time, as in later years, the British did not subscribe to the French view of European integration and the partial loss of national sovereignty as a necessary price for containing Germany. The Western alliance was adequate for this purpose in the British view. French policymakers, however, were sceptical of the longer-term commitment of Britain and the US to continental Europe and wanted a more tightly knit European system to curb Germany. As Cold War conditions intensified with the outbreak of the Korean War (June 1950), moreover, British attention was directed primarily towards strengthening the Western alliance with the close UK/US relationship at its apex. In this context the Schuman Plan was viewed more as a complicating factor than an invaluable element in projecting Britain as the centre of the three great interlocking circles of Europe, the Commonwealth and North America.

The Schuman Plan negotiations between the Six resulted in the Treaty of Paris (April 1951) and the formation of the European Coal and Steel Community (ECSC). At the same time the Six were engaged in a more ambitious and ultimately unsuccessful scheme for a European army. This initiative, launched by René Pleven (the French Prime Minister) in October 1950 and originally known as the Pleven Plan, subsequently formed the basis for the proposed European Defence Community (EDC). It aimed to apply the Schuman Plan principles of supranationalism and sector integration to the military field. This French response to the American call for West German rearmament (September 1950) was born out of strong opposition to the principle of German rearmament and to the prospect of a new German national army within NATO, which was then emerging as the executive machinery of the North Atlantic Treaty of 1949. From the outset the British government had no intention of joining the Six in this venture. French schemes for European integration were by now anathema to Bevin, who had deep misgivings about the viability of this project and its detrimental effects on efforts to develop an integrated NATO force (2.4). Herbert Morrison, Bevin's successor, appeared more accommodating in his advocacy of the closest possible association between Britain and the Six.

The policy of association with the proposed EDC was maintained by Churchill's Conservative government on winning power in October 1951.

Continental supporters of the project had expected a more positive attitude from the Conservatives in view of Churchill's pronouncements on European unity and his Council of Europe proposal (August 1950) for a European army. Churchill, however, did not envisage British absorption into an integrated Europe and privately expressed contempt for the EDC (2.5). His characterisation of Britain's relations with a united Europe – 'a separate closely – and specially – related ally and friend' – was fairly representative of the conventional wisdom of British policymakers at this time. Anthony Eden as Foreign Secretary eventually negotiated a UK/EDC treaty of association (April 1954) which was joined shortly afterwards (December 1954) by a UK/ECSC treaty of association. These measures appeared to safeguard what Whitehall regarded as some of the ideal (and enduring) features of British policy towards European integration, most notably the preservation of a position of influence without full commitment and the emphasis on embedding an integrated Europe in the more important framework of the Atlantic community (2.6). At the same time, however, some attempts like the Eden Plan of 1952 to forge institutional links between Britain and the Six fell by the wayside (2.7).

The rejection of the EDC treaty by the French National Assembly (30 August 1954) presented an opportunity to reassert British leadership in Western Europe after five years of defensive responses to the Six's initiatives. Eden was primarily responsible for devising the means whereby a fully sovereign, rearmed West Germany entered an enlarged BTO known as the Western European Union (WEU) and also joined NATO (2.8). The accompanying commitment of British forces to the continent was surrounded by escape clauses and the institutional arrangements for the WEU were governed by the principle of intergovernmental cooperation. This outcome took full account of the British aversion to any federal arrangement. The failure of the EDC project, in fact, strengthened the British impression that the Six were unlikely to embark upon or to succeed in more adventurous schemes for integration, especially in view of French objections and anxieties. There was therefore much complacency in British policymaking circles, which in turn contributed to some fundamental miscalculations when the foreign ministers of the Six met at Messina (June 1955) and undertook to consider plans for a common market and a nuclear energy community. A preparatory Brussels-based committee under the chairmanship of Paul-Henri Spaak, the Belgian Foreign Minister, was commissioned to work out detailed proposals that formed the basis of the Treaties of Rome which were signed by the Six (March 1957) and established the European Economic Community (EEC) and the European Atomic Energy Community (EAEC).

The Six invited Britain to join the Spaak committee without any of the preconditions that had been attached to the Schuman Plan negotiations. Nevertheless, British membership of any resulting organisation appeared unlikely, and British representation in the early proceedings of the Spaak committee was based on the principle of association without any commitment to the outcome. In November 1955 the Eden government decided to withdraw from the committee (2.9). Ministers took the view that the British-led OEEC offered the best forum for discussing trade matters and, by implication, for emasculating the Six's plans for the creation of a tariff-free bloc with a common external tariff. The issue of tariffs had been kept off the OEEC agenda since its formation in 1948, largely due to British distaste for any exclusively European arrangement that put at risk a global approach to international trade and payments (2.10).

As British expectations of the likely failure of the Six's plans proved increasingly ill-founded, a greater sense of urgency and occasional panic prompted attempts to safeguard British trading interests in the growing European markets. A Treasury/Board of Trade proposal for a free trade area in manufactured goods comprising the Six and the other OEEC member states was drawn up in the first half of 1956, announced in November 1956 and accepted as a basis for OEEC negotiations (February 1957). These negotiations commenced under the chairmanship of Reginald Maudling, Paymaster General, in October 1957.

The free trade area proposal was viewed in London as marking a major shift in British commercial policy towards Europe, especially in view of the willingness to consider tariffs in a European framework. Maudling was not one of the 'pro-European' members of Harold Macmillan's recently formed government (January 1957). Nor was he optimistic about the likelihood of success. Other ministers and officials, however, were inclined to overestimate British bargaining strength and to underestimate the Six's commitment to a customs union and their suspicions of a British sabotage operation.

Some of the main obstacles to reaching an agreement on British terms were the exclusion of agriculture from the proposed free trade area and the problem of combining a free trade area with a customs union. France, in particular, was unlikely to support the exclusion of trade in agricultural goods in view of its large agricultural surpluses that accounted for the inclusion of a common agricultural policy in the EEC treaty. In French circles, the free trade area proposal was therefore viewed as an objectionable arrangement whereby British manufactured goods had favourable access to the European market while French agricultural goods were denied comparable access to the British market. The other major French criticism of the proposal was that it enabled Britain to derive maximum trading benefits without jeopardising its importation of cheap food and raw materials from non-European sources and without submitting itself to the disciplines of a common market. There was therefore ample scope for France to wreck the negotiations (2.11).

Document 2.1

On 9 May 1950 Robert Schuman, the French Foreign Minister, announced a plan to place French and West German coal and steel production under a common High Authority. Other European countries were invited to participate in this scheme. Schuman's announcement below explains the purpose of the initiative that resulted in the formation of the European Coal and Steel Community comprising Belgium, France, Italy, Luxembourg, the Netherlands and West Germany.

World peace cannot be safeguarded without the making of creative efforts proportionate to the dangers which threaten it.

The contribution which an organised and living Europe can bring to civilisation is indispensable to the maintenance of peaceful relations. In taking upon herself for more than 20 years the role of champion of a united Europe, France has always had as her essential aim the service of peace. A united Europe was not achieved and we had war.

Europe will not be made all at once or according to a single plan. It will be built through concrete achievements which first create a *de facto* solidarity. The coming together of the nations of Europe requires the elimination of the age-old opposition of France and Germany. Any action which must be taken in the first place must concern these countries. With this aim in view, the French Government proposes that action be taken immediately on one limited but decisive point. It proposes that Franco-German production of coal and steel as a whole be placed under a common High Authority, within the framework of an organisation open to the participation of the other countries of Europe.

The pooling of coal and steel production should immediately provide for the setting up of common foundations for economic development as a first step in the federation of Europe, and will change the destinies of those regions which have long been devoted to the manufacture of munitions of war, of which they have been the most constant victims. The solidarity in production thus established will make it plain that any war between France and Germany becomes not merely unthinkable, but materially impossible. The setting up of this powerful productive unit, open to all countries willing to take part and bound ultimately to provide all the member countries with the basic elements of industrial production on the same terms, will lay a true foundation for their economic unification.

Source: *Europe – A Fresh Start: The Schuman Declaration, 1950–90*,
Office for Official Publications of the European Communities, 1990

Document 2.2

The British decision not to participate in the Schuman Plan talks was formally taken by the Cabinet on 2 June 1950. The following extracts reveal the particular reasons for refusing to engage in talks on French terms and also some of the general considerations that influenced this decision. Extract A refers to the Cabinet meeting which was chaired by Herbert Morrison (Lord President of the Council) in Attlee's absence. Kenneth Younger, the Minister of State at the Foreign Office, spoke on behalf of Bevin who was also unable to attend this meeting. Extract B is from a report (2 June 1950) by a committee of officials appointed by Attlee to consider the Schuman Plan.

A

The Minister of State said that, in spite of the numerous diplomatic exchanges which had taken place during the past few days, it had proved impossible to reach agreement with the French Government about the terms on which the United Kingdom could join in the examination of the French proposal for the integration of the coal and steel industries of Western Europe. The French Government were insisting that all Governments participating in the proposed examination of this proposal should commit themselves in advance to accepting the principle of the scheme before it was discussed in detail. Since the matter had last been mentioned at the meeting of the [Cabinet] Economic Policy Committee on 25th May, a further attempt had been made to overcome the French scruples by suggesting that the position of the United Kingdom Government should be explained in a final paragraph to be added to the proposed communiqué announcing the initiation of the discussions. This paragraph . . . would have stated that the United Kingdom Government would participate in the proposed conversations in a constructive spirit in the hope that, as a result of the discussions, there would emerge a scheme in which they would be able to join; but it would have made it clear that the United Kingdom Government could not at this stage enter into any more precise commitment. This suggestion had, however, been rejected by the French Government . . . The French Government had stated that, if we were unable to assure them by 8 p.m. that day [2 June] that we would join in the discussions on the basis which they now proposed, they would feel compelled to go forward without United Kingdom participation . . .

In discussion there was general agreement that the United Kingdom could not participate in the proposed discussion of the French proposal on the basis of the communiqué suggested by the French Government . . . This would commit us to accepting the principle of the French proposals before any of its details had been made known to us. No British Government could be expected to accept such a commitment without having had any opportunity to assess the consequences which it might involve for our key industries, our export trade and our level of employment . . .

Other points made in the discussion were:

(*a*) The bulk of public opinion in this country, as reflected in Parliament and in the Press, was likely to support the view that the Government could not be expected to commit themselves in advance to accepting the principle of this proposal before they knew what practical shape it would take and what it was likely to involve. There would doubtless be some criticism from groups which were disposed to favour almost any scheme for European integration; but most people would think that the course now proposed was not unduly cautious . . .

(*e*) Although the other European Governments invited to participate in the discussions had accepted the latest French formula, some of them had done so with reservations. It would, however, be undesirable for the United

Kingdom to take this course; for nothing would be more likely to exacerbate Anglo-French relations than for us to join in the discussions with mental reservations and withdraw from participation at a later stage.

(*f*) Our position was different from that of the other European countries by reason of our Commonwealth connections, and we should be slow to accept the principle of the French proposal without consultation with other members of the Commonwealth, especially as it appeared to involve some surrender of sovereignty.

Source: PRO, CAB 128/17 C.M. (50), 34th Conclusions

B

In our view this latest French proposal is basically no different from the earlier one. It essentially seeks to commit us in advance of negotiations to the principle of pooling European steel and coal resources and to the surrender to an independent authority of sovereignty over an important sector of our economy. We think it wrong to commit ourselves in this way, not because we necessarily preclude any possibility of some measure of pooling or some surrender of sovereignty, but because we think it wrong to pledge ourselves on these matters without knowing more precisely the nature of the commitment we are being invited to accept . . .

Our provisional view is that the economic arguments in favour of coming in or staying out of an international association of the kind contemplated by the Schuman plan are not conclusive one way or the other, and on this score there need be no cause for alarm if at this stage the French decided to proceed without us.

The main issues are really political. The exchanges with the French Government have brought out that their proposals, which started in a Franco-German context, have now been given a wider application. It is not merely pooling of resources, but also, in the first place, the conception of fusion or surrender of sovereignty in a European system which the French are asking us to accept in principle. M. Schuman's original memorandum said in terms that his plan would be a step towards the federation of Europe. It has been our settled policy hitherto that in view of our world position and interests, we should not commit ourselves irrevocably to Europe either in the political or the economic sphere unless we could measure the extent and effects of the commitment. It is a commitment of this kind which in essence the French Government is now seeking, and at the very moment when the decision has been taken to develop and give greater meaning to the Atlantic community.

5.   The most important aspect of the French proposal is that it represents a new and constructive approach to the problem of Franco-German relations. This is very much in our interest, from the political, as also the defence point of view. If we abstain from the present phase of the negotiations the possible effects of our action on the progress of Franco-German rapprochement will have to be borne in mind.

Source: PRO, CAB 129/40, C.P. (50) 120, 2 June 1950

Document 2.3

At the time of the announcement of the Schuman Plan, Britain had a commanding lead over the Six as a coal and steel producer. The following figures are taken from the report of a Whitehall working party which examined the French proposal.

Table 2.3 Coal and steel production 1938 and 1949 (millions of metric tons)

	Production of coal [a]		Production of crude steel	
	1938	*1949*	*1938*	*1949*
UK	231.8	218.6	10.6	15.8
West Germany	153.8	120.9	17.9	9.2
France and Saar	61.2	66.0	8.8	11.0
Belgium and Luxembourg	29.6	27.9	3.7	6.1
Netherlands	13.6	11.8	0.1	0.3
Italy	1.9	1.5	2.3	2.1
Total	491.9	446.7	43.4	44.5

[a] Hard coal and lignite in terms of hard coal equivalent.

Source: PRO, CAB 134/293, FG (WP) (50) 38, 16 June 1950.

Document 2.4

In October 1950 René Pleven, the French Prime Minister, proposed the formation of a European army including German forces. This plan was based on the Schuman Plan principles of supranationalism and sector integration. It represented the French response to an American proposal a month earlier for the rearmament of West Germany within NATO. The following extract is taken from a memorandum (28 October 1950) by Bevin to Sir Oliver Franks (UK ambassador in Washington). Bevin had strong reservations about the plan and its likely effect on attempts to create an integrated NATO force.

2.   The Pleven Plan is objectionable on two main grounds. It is important to distinguish between these and to appreciate that both raise difficulties:

(*a*)   it delays the moment of German rearmament and the participation of Germany in the defence of Europe;

(*b*)   quite apart from the above, it introduces delay and complication into the setting up of the integrated N.A.T.O. force, i.e. the force comprising the European countries (less Germany), Great Britain, the United States and Canada.

3.   As regards the delay, it is true that the French apparently contemplate that, while the European army is being created, existing national armies will be available for the N.A.T.O. integrated force, and have stressed that their plan will

not lead to delay in creating the latter force. But quite apart from the question whether the United States would be prepared to go ahead with the plan for a N.A.T.O. force until they know whether there will be a German contribution such as will make that force a reality, it is obvious that, in practice, delay would ensue, if only because two complicated sets of negotiations would be running concurrently, one for the N.A.T.O. integrated force on the basis of national contributions, and the other for the setting up of a European Army eventually to be merged as a federal unit with the N.A.T.O. force . . .

5.   The question then arises whether the Pleven Plan represents, in its federal aspects, a fundamental attitude on the part of the French Government, or whether it has been devised largely for electoral and tactical reasons. It is true that the federal conception underlying the Plan responds to a widespread feeling in France that some form of federalism is the best safeguard against a revival of German aggression but if the start of German rearmament were put off until the French were stronger themselves and provided it were surrounded with sufficient safeguards, they would probably not die in the last ditch for their specifically federal solution.

6.   The key to the problem therefore seems to lie in convincing the French that the proposed N.A.T.O. system of Combined Atlantic Force provides, or can be made to provide, sufficient guarantees in the short term and the long term against the German dangers which they fear. This may require a little time. We have to reckon with the French fear (which however unreasonable is genuinely and deeply felt) that under present N.A.T.O. plans a national German army with its Chief of Staff and Ministry of Defence is likely to emerge whatever safeguards may be devised; and that as soon as the Germans have acquired a substantial military strength they will abuse it. At the same time, the safeguards which we introduce must not be such as to invite a German refusal to make any contribution to Western Defence at all.

7.   I am not, at this stage at any rate, prepared to urge on the Americans any modification of their views on the timing and form of a German contribution. For the present I think that we should all be guided by two considerations:

(a) We ought not to take the French plan for a European Army too seriously. We should allow it to be discussed as a long-term plan provided that this does not in any way interfere with progress on the immediate problems of N.A.T.O. defence planning. Mr. Acheson's [US Secretary of State] mind appears to be moving on the same lines.

(b) Secondly, it is much to be hoped that we can assume tacitly that the French have agreed to the principle of a German contribution (though not on the manner in which it should be brought about), and that this being so, it is unnecessary to press them for the moment to commit themselves to it more openly.

Source: *DBPO* (1989), series II, vol. III, no. 89

Document 2.5

The return to power of a Conservative government under Churchill in October 1951 was welcomed by federalist opinion on the continent as likely to lead to greater British involvement in the process of European integration. The following extracts from a Cabinet note by Churchill (29 November 1951), however, indicate his opposition to British inclusion in a federal Europe. They also reveal his contempt for the Pleven Plan which formed the basis of the abortive proposal for a European Defence Community (EDC) involving the six Schuman Plan states.

1.　At Zurich in 1946 I appealed to France to take the lead in Europe by making friends with the Germans, 'burying the thousand-year quarrel,' &c. This caused a shock at the time but progress has been continual. I always recognised that, as Germany is potentially so much stronger than France, militarily and economically, Britain and if possible the United States should be associated with the United Europe, to make an even balance and to promote the United Europe Movement.

I am not opposed to a European Federation including (eventually) the countries behind the Iron Curtain, provided that this comes about naturally and gradually. But I never thought that Britain or the British Commonwealth should, either individually or collectively, become an integral part of a European Federation, and have never given the slightest support to the idea. We should not, however, obstruct but rather favour the movement to closer European unity and try to get the United States' support in this work . . .

I should doubt very much the military spirit of a 'sludgy amalgam' of volunteers or conscripts to defend the E.D.C. or other similar organisations. The national spirit must animate all troops up to and including the divisional level. On this basis and within these limits national pride may be made to promote and serve international strength.

5.　France does not seem to be playing her proper part in these arrangements. France is not France without 'L'Armée Française.' I warned MM. Pleven and Monnet several times that 'a Pleven Army' would not go down in France. The French seem to be trying to get France defended by Europe . . .

6.　On the economic side, I welcome the Schuman Coal and Steel Plan as a step in the reconciliation of France and Germany, and as probably rendering another Franco-German war physically impossible. I never contemplated Britain joining in this plan on the same terms as Continental partners. We should, however, have joined in all the discussions, and had we done so not only a better plan would probably have emerged, but our own interests would have been watched at every stage. Our attitude towards further economic developments on the Schuman lines resembles that which we adopt about the European Army. We help, we dedicate, we play a part, but we are not merged and do not forfeit our insular or Commonwealth-wide character. I should resist any American pressure to treat Britain as on the same footing as the European States, none of whom have the advantages of the Channel and who were consequently conquered.

7.   Our first object is the unity and the consolidation of the British Commonwealths [*sic*] and what is left of the former British Empire. Our second, the 'fraternal association' of the English-speaking world; and third, United Europe, to which we are a separate closely- and specially-related ally and friend.

Source: PRO, CAB 129/48 C. (51) 32, 29 November 1951

Document 2.6

The following extract from a Foreign Office memorandum of 12 December 1951 considers future British policy towards the process of European integration. It subscribes to a view of Britain's role in Europe and of Western Europe in the Atlantic community that was to remain largely intact until the late 1950s.

The United Kingdom cannot seriously contemplate joining in European integration. Apart from geographical and strategic considerations, Commonwealth ties and the special position of the United Kingdom as the centre of the sterling area, we cannot consider submitting our political and economic system to supranational institutions. Moreover, if these institutions did not prove workable, their dissolution would not be serious for the individual countries which would go their separate ways again; it would be another matter for the United Kingdom which would have had to break its Commonwealth and sterling area connexions to join them. Nor is there, in fact, any evidence that there is real support in this country for any institutional connexion with the continent. Moreover, although the fact may not be universally recognised, it is not in the true interests of the continent that we should sacrifice our present unattached position which enables us, together with the United States, to give a lead to the free world.

But while it is neither practicable nor desirable for the United Kingdom to join the integration movement, there would seem to be advantage in encouraging the movement without taking part in it. This is, in fact, the policy which the United Kingdom is now following. In the past the United Kingdom has been criticised for being not merely disinterested but hostile. This reputation did us some harm both in Europe and the United States. But more recently it has been generally accepted that the British attitude was due to caution and not to hostility.

It may be desirable from time to time to issue a general statement clarifying our attitude and emphasising our sympathy with the aims of the integration movement . . .

Another method of showing encouragement without taking part in schemes for integration is the appointment of observers, on the lines of the United Kingdom representatives at the European Army conference. Such observers provide a means of influencing the development of integration schemes at an early stage, while not committing the United Kingdom to taking part. Indeed, it seems probable that, unless we are so represented, there may be serious danger of confusion and our vital interests may get overlooked.

But while emphasising our support for European integration, we must at the same time take every opportunity to propagate the idea of the Atlantic community and, in particular, to point out that the N.A.T.O. is not merely a short-term body set up to organise the defence of Western Europe. We should therefore do all we can to further the development of the economic, social and cultural sides of the N.A.T.O. and should, where possible, focus attention on Article 2 of the treaty, which, briefly, binds the member states to 'contribute toward the further development of peaceful and friendly international relations' by means such as these. We may well make use of the Council of Europe for this purpose, since it is in any case probable that, if a working union of the Schuman Plan countries is set up, the council will be subject to less pressure than formerly for concerning itself with schemes of integration, and propaganda for the idea of unity will be its main rôle. Thus, by giving encouragement and support to the integration movement on the continent, we shall be in the best position to prevent it becoming exclusively European and to ensure that it develops as part of the Atlantic community.

Source: *DBPO* (1986), series II, vol. I, no. 414

Document 2.7

In 1952 the Eden Plan unsuccessfully attempted to establish institutional links between the European Community of the Six and the rest of Western Europe via the Strasbourg-based Council of Europe. It was also designed to counter federalist opinion in the Council of Europe's Assembly. The following memorandum of 15 February 1952 from Foreign Secretary Anthony Eden contains the main features of the plan.

The movement for unity in Europe, which led to the creation of the Council of Europe, is now flowing along two main streams: the Atlantic Community, a wide association of states which, without formal surrender of sovereignty, is achieving increasing unity of purpose and action through the machinery of the North Atlantic Treaty Organisation; the European Community, a small group of states which are moving towards political federation by the progressive establishment of organisations exercising supranational powers in limited fields.

The Council of Europe is stranded between these two streams. Many members of the Assembly feel despondent about the future of Strasbourg and some are prepared to admit that, in its present form, the Council of Europe is out-of-date and superfluous. In an attempt to acquire 'limited authority but real powers', the Assembly has produced a draft new statute of the Council of Europe, which will be on the agenda at the next session of the Committee of Ministers. This transforms what is now a purely consultative body into a quasi-federal institution with legislative and executive powers and the right to be consulted by member Governments on certain matters within its competence. It would therefore be difficult for us to remain in the Council of Europe if the new statute were adopted.

A more promising future for the Council of Europe would lie in a remodelling of the organisation so that its organs could serve as the institutions of the

Schuman Plan, the European Defence Community and any future organisations of the same structure and membership. The advantages would be:

(a) the Council of Europe would be given valuable work to do;
(b) the reduplication of European bodies would be avoided;
(c) the Schuman Plan and the European Defence Community would be provided with ready-made machinery.

The position of the members of the Council of Europe who are not members of the Schuman Plan and the European Defence Community would have to be worked out between all Governments concerned.

Recommendation

I therefore suggest that I should be authorised:

(*a*) to propose to my fellow Foreign Ministers on the Committee of Ministers that the Council of Europe should be reconstituted to permit the Committee of Ministers and the Assembly to become institutions of the Schuman Plan, the European Defence Community and any future organisations of the same structure and membership;
(*b*) to discuss the position in the reconstituted Council of Europe of countries which are not members of the organisations mentioned in (*a*) above.

Source: PRO, CAB 129/49 C. (52) 40

Document 2.8

After the failure of the French National Assembly to ratify the EDC treaty in August 1954, Eden took the initiative in convening a conference of Western powers, for which he devised a plan for the entry of a rearmed, fully sovereign West Germany into the BTO and NATO. In the following note to Churchill (27 September 1954), Eden set out the substance and implications of his plan.

If we produce a workable plan, the Americans are unlikely to allow it to fail through the lack of the essential American support. If, however, we are to do this it will be necessary for the French to face some unpleasant realities. They will have to accept German sovereignty and German membership of N.A.T.O., and withdraw or drastically reduce their safeguard proposals. If they are to do this, they must be given some striking *quid pro quo*. The assurance most likely to strike French opinion is the continued presence of British troops in France . . .

In my opinion, the key to the success of the conference will be a new commitment by the United Kingdom to maintain our present forces on the continent, and not to withdraw them against the wishes of the majority of the enlarged Brussels Treaty powers. This would not give France a veto, but we should no longer be able to withdraw our forces at our sole discretion, and would have to obtain the consent of the majority of the seven expanded Brussels Treaty partners . . . It would be necessary to provide for certain exceptions to the general rule: an overseas emergency so acute that there was no time to go through the process of consultation, or balance of payments difficulties which made it financially impossible for us to maintain the strength of our forces on the continent.

I realize that this would be an unprecedented commitment for the United Kingdom, but the hard fact is that it is impossible to organize an effective defence system in Western Europe, which in turn is essential for the security of the United Kingdom, without a major British contribution. This situation will persist for many years to come. By recognizing this fact and giving the new commitment, we may succeed in bringing in the Germans and the French together, and keeping the Americans in Europe. If we do not, the conference may fail and the Atlantic alliance fall to pieces.

Source: A. Eden, *The Memoirs of Sir Anthony Eden – Full Circle*,
London, Cassell, 1960, pp. 165–6

Document 2.9

At a meeting of the ECSC foreign ministers held at Messina on 1–2 June 1955, it was agreed to appoint a Brussels-based preparatory committee under the chairmanship of Paul-Henri Spaak, the Belgian Foreign Minister, to consider plans for a European common market and a nuclear energy community. While represented in the early sessions at Brussels, the British government eventually decided to withdraw from the project. This decision was taken by the Cabinet's Economic Policy Committee on 11 November 1955. The extract is from the minutes of that meeting.

The Chancellor of the Exchequer [R. A. Butler] said that the impulse for a common market arose from the desire of certain sections of opinion in Europe for greater political integration. The Brussels proposals for a common market would infringe the wider interests of O.E.E.C. As the holder of the leading position in O.E.E.C., it should therefore be the concern of the United Kingdom to divert as far as possible the activities of the Brussels Conference into the wider framework . . .

The Chancellor of the Exchequer said that it seemed clear that the United Kingdom should avoid joining a European common market, at any rate for some time to come. He therefore recommended that we should accept an invitation to attend the meeting of Brussels Conference Ministers which would be held in December, and should at that meeting explain plainly our inability to join a common market. We should also then issue a warning against the danger that the common market project, instead of fostering European co-operation, might result in dividing Europe . . .

The following were among the main points made in discussion:

(a) The United States was following two contradictory policies about European integration; on the one hand there was idealistic support for the political integration of Europe, while on the other hand there was the pressure for multilateral trade with no discrimination against the United States. Her Majesty's Ambassador in Washington should be instructed to explain the views of the United Kingdom on the question of European integration and a common market to the United States Government, so that we should be ensured of their support in O.E.E.C.

(b) In our endeavours to persuade the Brussels Conference countries to maintain closer relations with O.E.E.C. we should be careful not to damage that Organisation by over-emphasising its advantages ...

(c) It was noted that officials had set on foot an examination of the possible elements in a United Kingdom initiative for further progress in the reduction of barriers to trade in Europe, on an all-European basis. When the studies were complete they would be reported to the Committee. It was important not to expect too much from this examination. There were limitations to the extent to which we could offer tariff reductions, and we were in any case about to enter a further round of tariff discussions in the G.A.T.T. ....

(d) There was a probability that the plan for a common market might collapse without our opposition being pressed too hard. In the first place, the French, even if they subscribed to the project on paper, were unlikely to take any positive action in its support. The fear of German economic domination might well lead the other Brussels Conference countries to abandon the plan.

(e) Part of the impetus for a supra-national European organisation had come from the coincidence of Catholic leadership in France, Germany and Italy. This element had virtually gone.

(f) Although Germany was taking part in the Brussels Conference, a substantial body of opinion was not in favour of joining in a common market. If we were to give them a lead, the Germans might decide not to join a common market and to concentrate on co-operation through O.E.E.C.

Source: PRO, CAB 134/1226 E.P. (55), 11th Meeting

Document 2.10

The following extract from a Treasury paper of 1956 deals with British policy towards global trade and payments, here referred to as 'the collective approach' and sometimes described as the one world approach'. All the elements described in this paper had an enduring influence on the making of British foreign economic policy.

The collective approach to freer trade and currencies is a policy for freeing and expanding world trade and its main features, as set out in February 1953 in a memorandum submitted to the United States Administration, may be summarised as follows:

'On the financial side the objective is the convertibility of sterling and other currencies and the gradual removal of restrictions on payment. On the trade side it is to bring about the removal of trade restrictions and discrimination in a way which will encourage the expansion of world trade on an economic and healthy basis. Progress must be made towards both objectives by stages; it will be some considerable time before the objectives can be reached. The first aim must be to create the conditions in which the process can begin.

The proposals envisage collective action by the United States, the Commonwealth and Western Europe to secure the adoption of policies, by creditor and debtor countries, which will restore balance in the world economy on the lines of "Trade, not Aid" and will, by progressive stages and within reasonable time, create an effective multilateral trade and payments system covering the widest possible area. The main elements are:-

(a) Freer currencies: the provision of satisfactory conditions, including adequate financial support, for the convertibility of sterling and other important currencies.
(b) Freer trade: the progressive removal of import restrictions and discrimination by the debtor countries, together with action by the United States to improve other countries' opportunities to earn dollars.
(c) Development: the creation of conditions, both by creditor and by debtor countries, which will foster adequate international investment and the sound and rapid development of the resources of the free world.
(d) Organisation: the active constructive use of international institutions (the International Monetary Fund (I.M.F.), the General Agreement on Tariffs and Trade (G.A.T.T.) and the International Bank) to promote these policies, and the provision of a forum where effective discussion of major economic policy can yield fruitful results.

The United Kingdom Government regards these proposals as a comprehensive whole; the speed of advance which is possible must be judged in the light of the progress made under each of these heads.'

Source: PRO, CAB 21/3323

Document 2.11

In October 1957 the OEEC opened negotiations on a British-inspired plan for a European free trade area in manufactured goods comprising the six EEC states as a single entity and the 11 other member states of the OEEC. The following extracts are from a memorandum of 4 October 1957 by Reginald Maudling, the Paymaster General and chairman of the intergovernmental committee appointed to study the plan. The memorandum focuses on two of the most problematical issues that were to account for the protracted and ultimately unsuccessful negotiations.

There is a wide divergence still between our views and those of the Six. We regard the Free Trade Area as an extension of the type of co-operation between independent states achieved in the OEEC and we are thinking in terms of achieving the elimination of tariffs and quotas on the lines of the familar OEEC process of liberalisation. This practical objective of abolishing tariffs and quotas, coupled with the establishment of a system of rules to ensure fair competition, is about the full extent of our concept of the Free Trade Area.

The European Economic Community, on the other hand, is as much a political as an economic project. It is designed to achieve genuine unification of the economies of the Six countries and many of its most enthusiastic supporters regard it as part of the progress toward ultimate political unification. The Treaty provides for a substantial surrender of national sovereignty in economic matters and it embodies in its provisions a carefully worked out balance between the economic interests of the various participants. Clearly it will not be easy to establish working arrangements between two economic systems based on such different principles. Yet we cannot subscribe to the European doctrines of integration; nor will they abandon the Treaty of Rome.

Agriculture

. . . The Europeans are realists. They know we cannot abandon, or compromise on, the Commonwealth position, and, though they will grumble and haggle, in the end they will accept the fact. They will be less amenable about the protection of our own agriculture (and they know full well that they have a good deal of Commonwealth support in this). They do not expect us to drop all our barriers or to abandon our support policy – any more than they would themselves – but they feel that if they are to open their markets to our industrial products they must be able to show to their exporters of agricultural products something in the nature of a *quid pro quo* . . .

Problems of origin

Agriculture is the most difficult political problem. Questions of origin pose the toughest technical problem. The difficulty arises from the fact that the members of the Free Trade Area will not have a common tariff against countries outside the Area. British traders will be able to sell their goods, for example, in France in competition with French manufacturers, but in many cases the British manufacturers will have been able to obtain their raw materials duty-free whereas the Frenchmen will have had to pay the tariff charged by the members of the Common Market. The degree of difficulty which this problem will present in negotiation depends on the extent to which the Six countries propose to impose high tariffs on raw materials. It seems likely that the Germans, the Dutch and the Belgians will want to have low tariffs on imported raw materials, while the French, on the other hand, supported by the Italians, will wish to have high tariffs

3 The 'special relationship': 1945–1963

The documentary evidence in this section concentrates on the relationship between British policy towards European integration and Anglo-American relations from the end of the Second World War to the failure of the first British application for EEC membership in 1963. During this period the US was the most influential supporter on the international stage of British involvement in an integrated Europe. This influence was in turn a measure of British dependence on the US which was initially most evident in the form of financial assistance and later in the sphere of nuclear weapons delivery systems. Throughout much of this period British governments emphasised what they regarded as Britain's unique, invaluable role as a bridge or intermediary between the US and Western Europe. They were particularly concerned to stress the importance of the Atlantic Alliance, or Atlantic community which was their preferred description, as the principal forum for the conduct of relations between the Western states.

This heavily 'Atlanticist' complexion of British foreign policy involved a keen determination to uphold the notion of a UK/US 'special relationship' and to safeguard the British position as America's foremost ally in Western Europe. The British attempt to straddle the Atlantic and European worlds, however, gave rise to continental, especially French, doubts about Britain's European credentials. It also intensified suspicions of British plots to thwart European integration by stressing the Atlantic dimension. The British emphasis on maintaining close relations with the US eventually contributed to the making and the failure of the first British application for EEC membership.

The striking imbalance of power between the two countries at the beginning of this period was most marked when the termination of American wartime credits to Britain via the Lend–Lease system exposed the grim realities of Britain's overseas balance sheet. The US emerged from the war as the world's strongest economic and military power with some 50 per cent of total world production, two-thirds of the world's gold stock and exclusive possession of the atomic bomb. Britain, however, faced 'a financial Dunkirk' according to Keynes, the government's chief economic adviser. In August 1945 Keynes reported a deficit of £2.1 billion on the country's overseas balance sheet for 1945 and warned the newly elected Labour government that the bleak alternative to an American loan was 'Starvation Corner'. In spite of a seemingly weak bargaining position, British policymakers were confident that American power could be made to serve British interests and that the US could be guided by Britain's diplomatic experience and wisdom (3.1). By the Anglo-American Financial Agreement (December 1945), Britain obtained a loan of $3.75 billion (plus $650 million to write off Lend–Lease debts). This loan, however, was so rapidly used up and so diminished in value as a result of price inflation that only some $400 million remained after the sterling convertibility crisis of July/August 1947. At this point the British need for further dollar aid, together with American support for an integrated Europe, resulted in diverging views between London and Washington over American plans for integration and the extent of British involvement.

Immediately after the Marshall aid offer (June 1947), British policymakers ideally wished to negotiate another bilateral loan without any commitment to European cooperation. They strongly resented the American refusal to acknowledge Britain's role as a major player in the world economy and to offer special treatment for Britain outside the proposed four-year European Recovery Programme (ERP). Furthermore, the British argued that a European dollar aid programme failed to address the world dollar shortage that was adversely affecting Britain, which had a far more substantial interest in trade outside Europe than within it (3.2A and 3.2B). In the event British policymakers were able to capitalise on the American view that British leadership in Western Europe was essential for the success of the recovery programme. Britain received 25 per cent of the total aid disbursed under the ERP, which was the largest amount of aid to any single recipient, and also successfully resisted American attempts to give stronger powers to the European organisation responsible for supervising the aid programme (OEEC).

The aid programme was instrumental in giving sharper definition to British policy towards West European economic cooperation in the period 1947–49. British ministers and officials were keen to demonstrate support for European cooperation, especially to impress the US Congress which voted the annual ERP appropriations. At the same time, however, they were determined to withstand American pressure for British involvement in far-reaching forms of European integration. It was feared that this latter course of action would afford the Americans an opportunity to withdraw from Europe and leave Britain with a host of insupportable commitments there. There were problems in striking a balance between these considerations. In American circles it became commonplace to criticise the British for 'dragging their feet' on European unity (3.3 and 3.4). The British response to such criticism was assisted by what Whitehall perceived as the absence of American agreement on a detailed plan for European integration (3.6).

More importantly, the making of the North Atlantic Treaty (April 1949), UK/US cooperation in managing the devaluation of sterling (September 1949), and the dominant American and British presence in the emerging infrastructure of NATO a year later, all convinced British policymakers that the wartime 'special relationship' had been restored. There was also the additional bonus of American recognition that Britain's economic problems and financial ties could not be dealt with exclusively or primarily within a European context. Consequently, by 1950 the US was less disposed to exert pressure on Britain to take the lead in European integration and was more inclined to acknowledge the existence of a 'special relationship' (see 3.5). British political leaders thereafter frequently cited the 'special relationship' as a major impediment to closer involvement in European integration. This argument never carried much weight in American circles where Britain's long-term future was still envisaged as part of an integrated Europe.

During the 1950s American support for European integration and British interest in consolidating the 'special relationship' inhibited British policymakers from engaging in any overt attempt to undermine the Six's plans. Throughout this period, however, the Eisenhower administration (1953–60), and especially Secretary of State John Foster Dulles, harboured strong suspicions about British interest in sabotaging the process of integration. Dulles held Britain responsible for the collapse of the EDC project, and shortly after the British decision to withdraw from the Spaak committee in November 1955 (see section 2) he moved swiftly to head off any British action to stymie the Six's post-Messina deliberations. In a despatch to Foreign Secretary Harold Macmillan he emphasised the importance of encouraging the Six at a time when the Foreign Office was about to mount a diplomatic offensive against the Six's plans (3.7).

While the term 'special relationship' passed into disuse in the later 1950s, the concept of interdependence as employed by Macmillan, who succeeded Eden as Prime Minister in January 1957, conveyed the continuing strategic importance of Britain's relations with the US. Macmillan was intent on repairing the damage to Anglo-American relations caused by the Suez crisis (October/ November 1956). He was rewarded for his efforts in July 1958 when Britain was America's only ally to benefit from the repeal of the MacMahon Act of 1946 which had banned the transfer of American nuclear know-how to other states. The higher priority given to Britain's relations with the US than with Europe at this juncture, however, carried the danger of a diminishing British influence in Europe and a consequential reduction in Britain's standing in Washington as the leading West European power (3.8). While aware of this dilemma, British ministers and officials were slow to appreciate the extent to which political considerations outweighed commercial concerns in American policy towards the emerging EEC. They clung to the view that American support for the EEC as a political project assisting the integration of West Germany into the Western international system would be tempered and eventually overridden by Washington's adherence to a multilateral trading system based on GATT and thus opposed to a regional common market discriminating against American exports.

The primarily trade-oriented view of European developments in Whitehall meant that British policymakers increasingly faced an uphill and ultimately unsuccessful struggle to convince the Americans of the value of a European free trade area and subsequently of an EEC/EFTA agreement (3.9). Mistaken British assumptions about American policy were finally exposed at a meeting between Macmillan and Douglas Dillon (US Under-Secretary of State) in December 1959 (3.10). Dillon left so little doubt about his preference for the EEC rather than the EFTA and his objections to any EEC/EFTA agreement that Macmillan described the outcome as 'a considerable setback to our policy'.

American opposition to the idea of an EEC/EFTA agreement prompted a reappraisal of British policy. In Whitehall there was mounting concern about the incipient threat of an EEC power bloc to Britain's standing in Washington. British policymakers reaffirmed the importance of the Anglo-American partnership, which was now considered all the more vital in view of the declining importance of the Commonwealth as a British power base in the wider world (see section 4). They were also determined to avoid making a strategic choice between the United States and Western Europe (3.11). This definition of the parameters of British policy, however, did not address the American case for British membership of the EEC. Macmillan was increasingly anxious to accommodate American wishes in this respect, largely with a view to preserving Britain's value as Washington's principal ally: his publicly expressed anxieties about the disastrous effects of a European trade war on Western unity convinced neither the Americans nor the Six. At this time, moreover, Macmillan was not best placed to resist American pressure, especially in view of his agreement with Eisenhower (March 1960) that American-built Skybolt missiles, which were still at the development stage, should be provided for British nuclear weapons.

The incoming Kennedy administration of January 1961 quickly dashed any lingering British hopes of a more sympathetic American regard for British interest in a close and primarily commercial association with the EEC short of full membership. Vigorous American support for British membership of the EEC was forthrightly expressed by George Ball, an Under-Secretary of State who was primarily responsible for shaping the new administration's policy towards European integration. This view was endorsed by Kennedy at his first major meeting with Macmillan in April 1961 (3.12 and 3.13). Immediately after this meeting Macmillan felt sufficiently emboldened to seek Cabinet approval for an early application for EEC membership.

This period in Anglo-American relations culminated dramatically in two events that had a direct bearing on the fate of Britain's first application for EEC membership. As a result of negotiations between Kennedy and Macmillan at Nassau (19–21 December 1962), Britain was offered American-built Polaris missiles instead of the recently cancelled Skybolt. A month later de Gaulle vetoed the first British application for EEC membership. In the context of Anglo-American relations these events highlight the Macmillan government's view of the constraints and the advantages of Anglo-American cooperation in the nuclear weapons field. Before and during the UK/EEC negotiations of 1961–63, Macmillan considered the possibility of assisting the French nuclear weapons programme in return for obtaining de Gaulle's agreement to British membership of the EEC. The US, however, was the major stumbling block to a deal. The Kennedy administration supported the non-proliferation of nuclear weapons, opposed the idea of rewarding de Gaulle for his increasingly un-cooperative behaviour in NATO, and was sensitive to German complaints about exclusion from the Western powers' nuclear club. Immediately prior to the opening of the UK/EEC negotiations, Kennedy bluntly informed Macmillan that a tripartite US/UK/France arrangement to enhance France's status as a nuclear power was out of the question. Thereafter, the possibility of Anglo-French cooperation fell foul of British assessments of the terms and conditions of Anglo-American nuclear weapons cooperation (3.14).

During the Nassau negotiations Macmillan presented the case for British possession of Polaris missiles and insisted that an agreement would not adversely affect either America's relations with its other Western European allies or Britain's EEC application (3.15). This last claim was correct at least in so far as Macmillan was aware of de Gaulle's objections in principle to British membership of the EEC following their meeting at Rambouillet (15–16 December 1962) on the eve of the Nassau meeting. Whether de Gaulle expected Macmillan to propose Anglo-French cooperation on nuclear missiles development in exchange for French agreement to British membership of the EEC following the cancellation of the Skybolt project has long been a matter of speculation. Given the British emphasis on the importance of the 'special relationship', however, it is difficult to contest the view that British policy-makers had no wish to strike an agreement with de Gaulle that jeopardised close Anglo-American relations in defence matters (3.16).

Document 3.1

The following extracts from a Foreign Office memorandum of 21 March 1944 entitled 'The essentials of an American policy' examine the principles and objectives of British policy towards the United States, focusing especially on how American power might best be used to serve British interests.

. . . it is essential to recognise the relationship which exists between the United States and this country. The special quality of this relationship can no more be denied than can the nature of our relations with Soviet Russia . . .

. . . in the long run, the nature of the relationship does compel national collaboration between ourselves and the Americans, no matter what friction may occur. And it should be noted that more often than not this means that the Americans follow our lead rather than that we follow theirs. Fortunately, we are not confronted with the alternatives of pleasing them or standing up to them. They have enormous power, but it is the power of the reservoir behind the dam, which may overflow uselessly, or be run through pipes to drive turbines. The transmutation of their power into useful forms, and its direction into advantageous channels, is our concern.

Many Americans are now thinking for the first time about taking part in world affairs, and to most of them this means collaborating with us . . . It must be our purpose not to balance our power against that of America, but to make use of American power for purposes which we regard as good. The process of calling in the new world to redress the balance of the old is still incomplete, and the ability to evoke the new world's immense resources is stronger in these islands than elsewhere. We should be throwing away one of our greatest assets if we failed to evoke it, or if we were to credit the people of the United States with having developed their own ideas of the world's future to such a point of clarity that they were uninfluenced by ours. If we go about our business in the right way we can help to steer this great unwieldy barge, the United States of America, into the right harbour. If we don't, it is likely to continue to wallow in the ocean, an isolated menace to navigation.

A strong American policy must therefore be based not on a determination to resist American suggestions or demands, but on an understanding of the way in which their political machinery works, and a knowledge of how to make it work to the world's advantage – and our own. Instead of trying to use the Commonwealth as an instrument which will give us the power to outface the United States, we must use the power of the United States to preserve the Commonwealth and the Empire, and, if possible, to support the pacification of Europe . . .

The fundamental factors in such a policy [British policy towards the United States], under these circumstances, seem to be:-

(*a*) that we must pursue an economic policy aimed at the expansion of markets, of trade, and of employment;

(*b*) that we must be prepared to take the initiative in dealing with and settling issues with the United States Government which seem likely to become causes of contention before they have time to do harm;

(*c*) that we must seek every opportunity for public political initiative which will enable us to demonstrate that our policies are in the public (*i.e.* the world) interest, as well as our own, and that they are not harmful to the United States. That is, we must make the running ourselves, rather than leaving it to them;

(*d*) that when we are considering the content of any policy the success of which may depend in any way on American action, we should consider simultaneously its timing and presentation . . .

These principles are offered as a guide to the conduct of day-to-day business with the United States and not merely for occasional application, or in relation to major issues. In applying them we shall need a wise tolerance of American modes of thought, a recognition of their ways of doing business and, above all, a conviction that our age, wisdom and experience in international affairs not only enable us to afford but demand that we should display that magnanimity in the conduct of foreign affairs which can be our greatest asset in this field of human activity.

Source: PRO, FO 371/38523

Document 3.2

On 5 June 1947 US Secretary of State, George Marshall, offered American aid to assist the economic reconstruction of Europe. While Bevin promptly organised a European response, UK/ US differences immediately emerged over the usefulness of a European-centred dollar aid programme. Extract A is part of a memorandum by the British embassy in Washington to the Department of State (18 June 1947). It indicates that the British attached more importance to a global than to an exclusively European aid programme. The memorandum also highlights the rapid loss of British dollar reserves and anticipates further deterioration following what proved to be the short-lived convertibility of sterling in July/August 1947. Extract B is taken from the record of a meeting (25 June 1947) of British ministers and officials with Will Clayton (Under-Secretary of State for Foreign Affairs in the State Department). Bevin strongly urged the Americans to recognise Britain's special standing and interests, while Clayton emphasised the importance of a European response.

A

19.   The importance to us of world recovery is threefold:-

(1) The failure of primary production is a basic cause of world price inflation. Moreover it is keeping us short of food and raw materials; the cereals crisis of the last two years has prevented us from restoring our own livestock, and forces us to choose between doing without bacon, eggs and meat or importing them at high prices.

(2) We are unable to get enough supplies from our traditional suppliers and are therefore compelled to depend to a far greater extent upon Western Hemisphere supplies than we can afford.

(3) We have difficulty in getting acceptable payment for our exports to European and Asiatic countries. Our economy is the bridge between the Western and Eastern Hemisphere. Traditionally we have deficits with the West which are financed by surpluses with the East. The effect of the world supply crisis is that our deficit with the West is inflated to quite unmanageable proportions, while we are unable to get full benefit, in goods or in gold, from our surplus with the East . . .

III. THE WORLD DOLLAR SHORTAGE

23.   This is the crux of our problem. The increase in our dollar drain from less than dollars 100 million a month in the second half of 1946 to over dollars 300 million a month in April and May, corresponds with the rapid growth in the United States surplus of exports over imports from less than dollars 400 million a month in the second half of 1946 to over 700 million dollars a month in the first quarter of 1947 and nearly dollars 800 million in April . . . The dominating consideration for us is the appearance of a world dollar shortage. This is critical for the United Kingdom for the following reasons:-

(1) It hampers the growth of production in Europe and the East and thus prevents us from reducing our huge import bill with the American continent.
(2) It prevents us from securing enough dollars from the rest of the world to finance our deficit with the American continent.
(3) It threatens to make convertibility a serious drain upon our resources. If countries are short of dollars they will conduct their affairs so that they can earn sterling from us and convert it into dollars and so pass their dollar difficulties on to us.
(4) Our interests lie in the expansion of multilateral world trade which is impossible if the world is short of dollars.

Source: *Foreign Relations of the United States* [hereafter *FRUS*], 1947, vol. III, pp. 21–2

B

Mr. Bevin as the next point sought elucidation of Mr. Clayton's belief that the UK problem must be lumped into the problem of Europe . . .

Mr. Bevin said that if the U.S. took the line that the UK was the same as any other European country this would be unfortunate because the UK could contribute to economic revival. The UK held stocks of rubber and wool and 'we, as the British Empire', could assist materially. The British did not want to go into the program and not do anything – this would sacrifice the 'little bit of dignity we have left'.

Mr. Clayton did not quite see how the UK position was different from that of other European countries. The whole trouble arose from a shortage of dollars but this in turn represented failure of Europe to produce. The production bottleneck should be eased in a few years – perhaps by 1951. The UK had a dollar shortage the same as other European countries and if the US could do something to ease this shortage he wondered where the difference in impact upon the UK arose . . .

Mr. Bevin then asked for a somewhat more concise statement of the present American attitude toward Europe and the Marshall program. In response Mr. Clayton said that he foresaw the following phases: (1) Europe should explain why more progress has not thus far been made since the cessation of hostilities with the help already received; (2) European countries should set forth in a concrete and substantial way a statement of what they proposed to do to help themselves, how long it will take and by what steps – what minimum assistance is required from the US, why it is necessary and when the load on the US would be reduced – presumably on a sliding scale. Mr. Clayton again stressed it would not be easy to sell the idea in the US. There was much in the press of what the US 'has got to do' and much about American needs for export markets. Mr. Clayton knew the US need for export markets but many of his fellow citizens had other views and in order to put the program across the US must know when Europe will be able to get on its own feet. To supplement this, if possible, the US would like some proposals regarding a closer integration of European economy. He did not assume that anything in great detail could be provided in a short time and cited his conversation with Senator Millikin [chairman, Senate Finance Committee] as an example of why a firm plan for Europe including European integration was necessary to convince Congress on the necessity of additional assistance by the US.

Source: *FRUS*, 1947, vol. III, pp. 276–8

Document 3.3

The Marshall aid programme was accompanied by growing American support for European political unity which did not coincide with more modest British plans. In a memorandum of 23 October 1948, Sir Oliver Franks, UK ambasssador in Washington, stressed the importance of taking account of American opinion in the formulation of British policy towards European integration.

Mr. Attlee's frequently quoted statement that 'Europe must federate or perish' and your [Bevin's] own initiative at the beginning of this year in advocating 'Western Union' confirmed many Americans in their conviction that the United Kingdom could alone provide the leadership necessary to bring about closer political unity in Europe . . . When, therefore, you [Bevin] felt obliged to point out the difficulties in the way of early implementation of any 'United Europe' and the hard work before anything practical could be accomplished, the disappointment was correspondingly great, and it was perhaps understandable that Americans, who are never slow to criticise the United Kingdom, gained the impression that His Majesty's Government were at best losing interest in the cause of European unity and generally 'dragging their feet', or at worst acting as some sort of international Luddite trying to spoil or slow down the machinery of European integration for selfish or shortsighted ends . . .

If, as I assume, European federation is in fact not immediately attainable or practicable, or if it is considered undesirable as the ultimate objective, then, if we are to succeed in maintaining American faith and support for Western Europe, including economic and military aid, we shall have to succeed in convincing Americans that we are moving towards the same basic idea of closer political integration, though perhaps in a somewhat different form and in our own, and what we consider a better, way . . .

It will not be sufficient for us, while continuing to give support to some form of European unity as a long term aim, merely to repeat the difficulties in the way of implementation and the impracticability of embarking upon such steps at the present time. Nor shall we be able to satisfy the Americans' urge for political integration in Europe simply by telling them of the far-reaching measures of economic co-operation which have already been carried out under the O.E.E.C., of the studies which are now being made of the possibility of a Customs Union, or of the other steps which are being taken to bring about closer economic collaboration between the Western European countries . . . I, myself, am convinced that in attempting to meet or rather forestall American pressure in favour of the idea of federation, we must put forward an idea of our own, more practicable in application, and not less effective in result.

To formulate such an idea must take time. In the meantime, of course, it is important that during the next few months everything possible should be done to continue to stress the concrete, even though limited, measures of co-operation which can be taken by the European governments within the scope of the existing organisations such as the O.E.E.C. and the Committees set up under the Brussels Pact. This would not satisfy American opinion, but it would serve to smooth the passage of the second E.R.P. appropriation through Congress.

Source: PRO, FO 371/73065

Document 3.4

By 1949 British policymakers increasingly distanced themselves from the idea of a British-led integrated Western Europe but were sensitive to and often puzzled by American views on the subject. The following extract is part of a Foreign Office dispatch (8 November 1949) to the British embassy in Washington.

The general impression here of United States opinion is one of confusion . . .

Perhaps part of the difficulty is that the Americans have now realised that they themselves do not know what they mean by unification or integration, and are faced with the prospect of defining their position. The United Kingdom has taken the lead in the most important step towards unification which has so far been made, i.e. liberalisation of trade. The United Kingdom has not put forward a scheme for Regional Groupings, although they have undertaken to examine any such scheme sympathetically and are now, in fact, considering a possible arrangement with Scandinavia. It is clearly difficult for us to take the lead in making proposals for Regional Groupings of which we do not propose to be members. But there is as yet no concrete scheme in the field, all the talk about greater Benelux having failed to materialise in any identifiable plan. In Paris, the Dutch seemed disposed to run out at one end, and the French, although the main protagonist, declined to be pinned down to any definite proposals.

In the result the Americans, while not having any clear ideas themselves and while recognising that the United Kingdom is in a special position, seem disposed to blame us because the O.E.E.C. countries which have been calling for closer regional groupings have not made any proposals, Perhaps they doubt whether if neither the United States or the United Kingdom take further steps anything will really happen or happen in time or on a scale adequate for Congress. There may be substance in this fear, but it is clearly difficult to reconcile the United Kingdom special position with leadership in Europe for the adoption of specific schemes for integration through regional groupings.

Source: PRO, FO 371/78023

Document 3.5

By 1950 British policymakers increasingly emphasised the special relationship between Britain and the United States and also the extent to which this relationship placed limits on British involvement in European integration. The following extracts from a US State Department paper of 19 April 1950 reveal American thinking on the subject.

The salient points to bear in mind in determining our relations with the British are the following:

(a) To achieve our foreign policy objectives we must have the co-operation of allies and friends. The British and with them the rest of the Commonwealth, particularly the older dominions, are our most reliable and useful allies, with whom a special relationship should exist. This relationship is not an end in itself but must be used as an instrument of achieving common objectives.

(b) We cannot afford to permit a deterioration in our relationship with the British. We must strive to get agreement on the identity of our objectives and reaffirm the fundamental identity of our interests.

(c) British capabilities are limited by the British financial position. We are affected as well by limits on our financial and other capabilities. The British appear to be giving an overriding priority to these steps which will terminate their need for outside aid and reestablish sterling as a strong international currency by mid-1952. Concentration on this financial goal may be seriously prejudicing other more important world objectives . . .

(d) We should reassure the British that we do not advocate their political merger with the [European] Continent, but that we are convinced that closer economic and political, as well as military, ties between them and the Continent are essential. In this connection we would be glad to support British leadership (in conjunction with the French), and we must face the implication for us, i.e. what action must be taken to enable closer U.K.– Continent association to develop?

(e) While we recognize and support the British in their role as leader of the Commonwealth and their attempts to strengthen it, we do not believe that, except in very special cases, this role is incompatible with close association with the U.S. or with Europe.

(f) We recognize the special close relation between us and it is one of the premises of our foreign policy. It is not, however, a substitute for but a foundation under closer British (and perhaps U.S.) relations with the Continent. In dealing with other Europeans, however, we cannot overtly treat the British differently and they should recognize that the special US– UK relation underlies US–Europe relations, and that we do not consider close UK–European relations as prejudicial to the US–UK relation.

Source: *FRUS*, 1950, vol. III, p. 878

Document 3.6

In the wake of the French-inspired Schuman and Pleven Plans of 1950, British policy towards European integration was criticised in American and especially Congressional circles. The following extracts are from a Foreign Office brief (20 December 1951) for Churchill on his first visit to Washington after his return to power in October 1951. They deal with the Foreign Office's view of and response to American criticism.

European integration is the panacea favoured, for varying reasons, in certain United States quarters, ranging from internationally-minded liberals to former isolationists, who believe, or affect to believe, that united Europe would shortly be able to manage without either United States armed forces or United States dollars . . .

Among America's Western European allies, Britain has been subjected to special criticism. This has been due, in part, to American disappointment at the reluctance of her staunchest ally to take any prominent share in schemes allegedly designed to strengthen European powers of resistance. The United Kingdom attitude has been contrasted to our disadvantage with the initiative shown by the French . . .

European integration, with or without United Kingdom participation, is only an immediate objective if it can be shown that it would promptly and effectively strengthen the capacity of Europe to resist aggression. But during a transitional and experimental period leading towards federation the defence effort of Western Europe would certainly be at its weakest. From this point of view the question whether Britain participates is largely irrelevant . . .

The attitude of those Congressmen who seek to make further military aid conditional upon quicker progress towards political and economic unity is an inconsistent one. The test for granting more military aid should be the effective use made in Europe, especially for rearmament, of aid already received. Judged by this standard, His Majesty's Government can hold their heads high; the formidable British rearmament programme should certainly be emphasised.

Britain has a unique position at the heart of three interlocking communities: Commonwealth, Atlantic and European. A mistake frequently made in the United States is to regard Britain exclusively as a European Power . . .

In private, if not in public, the question may be put whether the American people are wise to interfere so flagrantly in the political destinies of another country. By doing so the Americans vindicate only too clearly the allegations of Soviet propaganda that they seek to dominate Europe and do not scruple to apply economic pressure to this end.

The American attitude gains emotional strength from an historical analogy which does not bear examination. It does not follow that, because the United States flourish under federal Government, to establish the United States of Europe would at once solve the problems of this continent. The Americans would do well to recall that their own federal unity arose from a war of liberation and was only upheld in the following century at the cost of civil war. The obstacles to federation are real and have not been invented by His Majesty's Government to jusify slow progress . . .

Source: DBPO (1986), series II, vol. III

Document 3.7

The US strongly backed the post-Messina attempts of the Six to form a common market. In a letter (10 December 1955) from Dulles (US Secretary of State) to Foreign Secretary Macmillan, Dulles expressed support for the Six's approach as the most promising model of European integration. He aimed to ensure that Britain, which he held responsible for the collapse of the EDC project in the previous year, did not impede the Six's efforts.

At present, there are two trends discernible in Europe, both directed toward goals of increased unity. One is the six-nation approach which has had one signal success in the Coal and Steel Community and one signal defeat in the European Defense Community. This, as we know, is essentially a supranational approach. The other is the OEEC approach, a co-operative effort which has accomplished much in reconciling conflicting national interests. The United States Government has enthusiastically supported both of these concepts. In my opinion, they seek to accomplish different but not conflicting purposes. As we look toward the future it seems to me that the closer community of interests that Europe can build, the more hope Europe will have of realizing its potential for security, prosperity and influence in world affairs. To my mind, the six-nation grouping approach gives the greatest hope of achieving this end because of the closer unity which is inherent in that Community and because of the contribution which it will make to the strength and cohesion of the wider European grouping. It may well be that a six-nation community will evolve protectionist tendencies. It may be that it will show a trend toward greater independence. In the long-run, however, I cannot but feel that the resultant increased unity would bring in its wake greater responsibility and devotion to the common welfare of Western Europe.

It is for these reasons, and with the companion determination to cooperate with the OEEC, that the President [Eisenhower] and I have been anxious to encourage in every appropriate way the current revival of initiative by the six nations in their search for new forms of integration in the fields of nuclear and conventional energy, a common market and transportation. We hope that progress will be swift, but we should be satisfied if there is sustained and real advance toward the practical ideal inherent in the supranational principle.

I hope that you will let me have your reaction to these views on this matter and that we can count upon your Government's support. I hope to discuss this matter with you at the NATO meeting in Paris [15–16 December, 1955]. Should it then appear desirable, perhaps we could arrange for further discussions between our two staffs with a view toward assuring that, despite any differences of emphasis between us, we do not give conflicting advice to the Continental Europeans with respect to the movement toward closer unity.

Source: FRUS, 1955–57, vol. IV, pp. 363–4

Document 3.8

Following the damaging impact of the Suez crisis on Anglo-American relations, Macmillan gave higher priority to restoring close relations with the US than to cultivating Britain's relations with Europe. His emphasis on interdependence in Anglo-American relations, however, ran the risk of diminishing British influence in Europe and in the US. The following extract is taken from a Foreign Office paper (27 January 1958) on this subject.

(iv) The danger of exclusive Anglo-American interdependence

19.   Since our interests and those of the United States do not in fact much diverge, there is relatively little danger of a situation arising in which we have to choose between breaking away and becoming an American satellite. But the danger of seeming to become one is greater. If we give the impression we shall suffer on two counts:

(a)   we shall damage our relations with our friends particularly the Europeans;
(b)   we shall lose influence with the Americans themselves, because this depends upon the extent of our influence elsewhere . . .

Western Europe

. . . there is already a widespread feeling in Europe that there are two alternative policies for the United Kingdom, to enter Europe and to stand outside it in an 'Anglo-American' clique, and that, by adopting the policy of interdependence, we have plumped for the second. This is a misconception of 'interdependence' which was invented as an expanding rather than as an exclusive idea, but there are good reasons for its appearance. The suspicion that Britain is standing aloof from Europe and is indifferent or even hostile to European unity is an old one. The fact that we, along [*sic*] of the Western European Powers, have made the hydrogen bomb, joined the American nuclear directorate and are now seeking to prevent any 'fourth country' from possessing it, implies to many Europeans, especially the French, that we are seeking to establish and maintain a two-level power system in the free world, with Britain and America in command and the rest in the ranks. There is also the suspicion that the United Kingdom is trying to edge out of her commitment to maintain troops on the Continent . . .

Although suspicions of too close Anglo-United States solidarity will probably always exist especially in France, the present extreme manifestation of this feeling may prove to be comparatively short-lived, provided we recognise its dangers and act accordingly. For it would indeed be dangerous for the United Kingdom and for the Western world as a whole if this impression were allowed to grow and to persist. As far as the United Kingdom is concerned, we cannot afford to build up a position as the First Lieutenant of the United States if this is done at too great an expense to our position in Europe. As the leader of Europe we should be an invaluable ally to the United States. Isolated from Europe, our value, and therefore our influence, would fall away disastrously. Unless we are careful, it is possible that a situation might arise in which, if Britain were isolated from the political leadership of Europe, the United States might, in spite of inter-dependence, deal direct with Europe over our heads. Further, the danger that the Anglo-American partnership may one day break up is relevant. If in the meanwhile the United Kingdom has lost the confidence of Europe by seeming to withdraw into an exclusive partnership with the United States, she may find herself without either.

Source: PRO, FO 371/132330

Document 3.9

The United States showed little enthusiasm for the British plan for a European free trade area. In a dispatch of 13 November 1958, immediately prior to the French veto on further free trade area negotiations, Sir Harold Caccia (UK ambassador in Washington) advised the Foreign Office on how best to present British views to a largely unsympathetic American audience.

It is a great help to us here that our main object should at this stage be limited to getting the Americans to understand fully our views on the seriousness of the present situation. If we are to succeed we shall have to bear certain things clearly in mind.

The first is the importance which the United States Government attach to the political as well as the economic advantages of the Common Market from the point of view of the integration of Europe. Politically the Free Trade Area is less attractive to them. They would be alarmed at the prospect of anything which threatened to undo the Treaty of Rome.

In the second place they are likely to be extremely suspicious of our motives. The past history of European integration makes them inclined to doubt our protestations of support for the European idea. They will be much more prone to believe that since we may not be able to obtain the Free Trade Area on our terms, and since we cannot join the Common Market, we are out to destroy the latter.

Thirdly, the Americans with whom we have to deal are tough traders, but they know that General de Gaulle can be extremely obstinate. They realize that they will have to be at odds with him about his plans for reorganizing the Western alliance, and they will not want to seek any more trouble with him than they can avoid. I need hardly add that the French Embassy here are active in warning the Americans to keep off the grass. They will therefore take a lot of convincing that we can be as awkward as the General.

Consequently in dealing with the Americans it will be desirable to say in the clearest possible terms what the results of a break-down will be. The points which will be likely to tell most are:

(a) the prospect that the Common Market itself will break down if not accom-panied by a Free Trade Area. No doubt it is difficult to give chapter and verse for this. It is an argument that must be used with caution if we are to avoid the accusation that we want such a breakdown.

(b)   What we and the other non-six are prepared to do in the way of retaliation.

(c)   What we mean by a reappraisal of our role in European organisations. In this it would be desirable to go as far as we can, though no further than we mean . . .

I repeat that in view of the various American complexes referred to above, it is helpful that we have some time in which our objective should be to educate the United States Government rather than to try to persuade them to rush in.

Source: PRO, FO 371/134513

Document 3.10

British hopes of an EEC–EFTA association to reduce the degree of discrimination between the two trading blocs were dealt a major blow by the United States. At a meeting with Macmillan on 9 December 1959, Douglas Dillon (US Under-Secretary of State) confirmed American opposition to an EEC–EFTA deal.

The Prime Minister said that the Six were now explaining that if there was discrimination it would only be very small and this was satisfactory so far as it went. In general the United Kingdom felt that the Six had a certain value particularly in tying Germany into the European system. Certainly the United Kingdom would prefer to see a strong France and a flabby Germany rather than the opposite.

Mr. Dillon said that he agreed. The only thing that had alarmed the United States was the suggestion that there might be some arrangement between the Six and the Seven which would discriminate against the rest of the world. This would be bad for the United States but he was glad to learn that there seemed to be no present intention of making such an arrangement. In general he felt that the United States ought to take a closer and more continuous interest in European trade policies.

The Prime Minister enquired if the United States accepted that the Six would discriminate against them.

Mr. Dillon said that the United States of course realised this. There was also discrimination against the United States in the Seven. The United States had accepted the economic disadvantages to them of the Six as part of the political price for tying Germany into Europe. The United States hoped that the greater economic strength of the Six would enable them in due course to be more liberal, and they also took the view that in the long term the total volume of United States trade with the Six would not decrease although this volume might become a smaller proportion of the Six's trade; in other words the Six would become economically stronger . . .

The Prime Minister enquired whether the United States had been prepared to accept the idea of a European Free Trade Area. **Mr. Dillon** said that they had accepted this but it did not seem now to be a practicable possibility . . . **Mr. Dillon** said that the United States had always recognised the political importance of the Common Market but felt that the Seven had no political importance but were purely an economic organisation.

The Prime Minister said that the working out of an accommodation would be a long business. The great thing to do was to moderate the harmful effects of discriminatory arrangements. The United Kingdom would use every opportunity, such as GATT, to get tariffs down . . .

Source: PRO, PREM 11/2870

Document 3.11

In June 1959 Macmillan set up an interdepartmental body of officials in Whitehall to consider the British position in world affairs over the next ten years. The following extracts from the resulting report ('Future Policy Study, 1960–1970') illustrate the importance attached to relations with the United States and Britain's standing in both the Atlantic Alliance and Western Europe.

Our partnership with the United States is an existing source of power and is capable of still further development. It is our first interest that it should remain as close as possible. In many cases, the United States will be the only Power capable of supporting our interests in the world outside Europe. We shall become increasingly dependent on their support, as perhaps they will on ours, and our status in the world will largely depend upon their readiness to treat us as their closest ally. They will be the more ready to do this, if we play our full part in the international groups to which we belong.

But Anglo-American partnership is not a law of nature . . .

One basic rule of British policy is clear: we must never allow ourselves to be put in a position where we have to make a final choice between the United States and Europe. It would not be compatible with our vital interests to reject either one or the other and the very fact that the choice was needed would mean the destruction of the Atlantic Alliance. The continued cohesion of that alliance, though not necessarily in its present form, is essential. We must therefore work to ensure the continuation of the United States presence in Europe and the development of a wide economic and political community of interests embracing both the United States and Western Europe. In so far as the United Kingdom can help to keep Western Europe steady in the alliance we shall enhance our own standing in American eyes.

This is the core of our policy and we must be prepared to adapt our plans and actions to it. If we can uphold it successfully, our influence on the United States will be considerable and we shall not need slavishly to follow their line, though we should always consider their susceptibilities before making policy decisions. In particular this is true where no essential interests of our own are involved . . . Even where essential interests are involved we should never ignore the American point of view. Similarly to secure our position *vis-à-vis* Western Europe, as well as the United States, we must continue to maintain our military contribution to NATO at a level acceptable to our Allies even if this means a disagreeable strain on our military and economic resources. And we must be prepared to adapt our traditional trading and domestic policies if, by failing to do so, we should run a serious risk of being isolated from the rest of Western Europe.

Source: PRO, CAB 134/1929, FP (60) 1, 24 February 1960

Document 3.12

At a meeting with Edward Heath (Lord Privy Seal) and Sir Frank Lee (Joint Permanent Secretary to the Treasury) on 30 March 1961, George Ball (Under-Secretary of State) was the first senior member of the Kennedy administration to indicate strong American backing for British membership of the EEC. His views helped to convince British policymakers that Washington was unlikely to approve any UK/EEC arrangement such as close association or 'near identification' that fell short of full membership.

Mr. Ball said that the United States deeply regretted that the United Kingdom had not yet felt able to accept the Rome Treaty commitments. They had a great admiration for the United Kingdom's political genius and qualities of leadership. British membership of the Community would represent a contribution of great importance to the cohesion of the Free World. In 1958 the United States had feared that the free trade area proposals might dilute and weaken the political integration of the Six, while at the same time increasing trade discrimination against the United States. The Lord Privy Seal had suggested that there had been a considerable evolution of United Kingdom policy. The United States certainly hoped that, within a wider O.E.C.D. [Organisation for Economic Cooperation and Development] framework, an arrangement might be made whereby the United Kingdom came much closer to joining the E.E.C. than had hitherto been contemplated . . .

Mr. Ball said that, from what they knew of United Kingdom thinking generally and from what the Lord Privy Seal had said, he did not think that the kind of solution at present envisaged by H.M.G. would be satisfactory to the United States. He hoped, however, that United Kingdom thinking would continue to evolve and that there might be further discussions of all these problems in the O.E.C.D., or in some other forum where the United States could be represented. He wished to repeat that the American Administration were fully persuaded that it was a misfortune that the United Kingdom was outside the Community.

Sir F. Lee said that he would be grateful for any further indications as to the direction in which the United States would like to see United Kingdom policy evolve. Was Mr. Ball suggesting that the United Kingdom should join the E.E.C.? **Sir F. Lee** did not see how this could be done unless the United Kingdom were to be given some derogations from the Rome Treaty. If this were not the case the effects on the Commonwealth would be too divisive; moreover the United Kingdom would not favour a solution which would involve placing a tariff on imports of American wheat, as would be the case if they accepted the common tariff without derogations.

Mr. Ball said that the United States would certainly like to see the United Kingdom join E.E.C. They recognised that the United Kingdom had special problems with regard to agriculture and the Commonwealth and that there might have to be derogations. These would have to be considered on their merits . . .

Summing up the United States position, he [Ball] said that the concept of a United Kingdom *association* with E.E.C. was very difficult for them: it would enable the United Kingdom to benefit from the commercial aspects of the Rome Treaty while at the same time eroding the political content of the Community. On the other hand the United States would applaud British *membership* of the Community, which they would regard as a great contribution to the cohesion of the Free World.

Source: PRO, FO 371/158162

Document 3.13

At his first major meeting with President Kennedy in April 1961, Macmillan was left in no doubt about American support for a British application to join the EEC. At the very least this American position tipped the balance in favour of an immediate bid for membership and finally persuaded Macmillan to seek Cabinet backing for an application. The following extract is taken from a British record of this meeting.

President Kennedy then asked how the problem of the Six and the Seven stood. Did Mr. Macmillan think a more prosperous Europe would come out of it, with opportunities not only for the United Kingdom but also for the United States and Canada, or would the problem of the Six and the Seven be solved in such a way as to cause difficulties for all of us?

Mr. Macmillan said that there were both economic and political aspects to this problem. Modern technology demanded that markets should be larger; and, the larger a trading association was, the more useful it would be. His own dream was that the Six and the Seven might ultimately form part of a wider Atlantic union. The widest possible trading area would thus be created. His own feeling was that the United Kingdom and some of their partners in the Seven would have to find a means of association with the Six. He believed that it was in the interests of the free world that Europe should be re-united and should ultimately look to an Atlantic union. Otherwise the Six might constitute themselves a third force and that would cause difficulties both for the United Kingdom and for the United States. At present the main obstacle might be General de Gaulle, who saw in the Six a political entity which would allow Europe to be free from what he regarded as the domination of the Anglo-Saxons. But, if he went, the leadership might pass to Germany and it might not be Dr. Adenauer's Germany. The temptation to set themselves up as a third force would be very strong.

Mr. Macmillan therefore thought that it would be to the advantage of the Western world that the United Kingdom should be associated with the political institutions of the Six. The United Kingdom could provide a stabilising element which would prevent either France or Germany from dominating Europe. He would like to see this come about provided it was supported by the United States.

Mr. Macmillan added that it was sometimes suggested that the choice for the United Kingdom was between Europe and the United States. He did not accept that. He thought that we should all try to work together and that the United Kingdom could use its influence to make a bridge between Europe and North America. That is why, provided he was sure of United States support, he would like to get into the Six.

President Kennedy agreed that the arguments that Mr. Macmillan advanced in favour of United Kingdom participation in the Six were valid. He thought that if the United Kingdom took such steps now, when conditions were favourable, the effect would be to tie Germany more closely to the West. This would be to the common good. But if the United Kingdom remained aloof from this European association until after Dr. Adenauer and President de Gaulle had gone, the situation would be very much more difficult. He added that it would also be in the economic interests of the United States and of the Commonwealth for the Six to be broadened. It was true that the United States and some of the less developed countries, particularly in Latin America, would have to face certain problems, but the free world in general would be strengthened.

Source: PRO, CAB 133/244, P.M. (W) (61), 1st Meeting, 5th April 1961

Document 3.14

Anglo-American cooperation in the nuclear weapons field was a major constraint on the Macmillan government in its handling of the possibility of assisting the French nuclear weapons programme in return for de Gaulle's agreement to British membership of the EEC. Macmillan strongly suspected that de Gaulle would fail to keep his side of the bargain. In any case there were likely to be formidable American objections to any substantial agreement between London and Paris. The following extract is taken from a record of a meeting of Macmillan, Lord Home (Foreign Secretary) and Edward Heath (Lord Privy Seal) on 19 May 1962 to review the UK/EEC negotiations.

The Foreign Secretary said that after discussion he wondered whether it might be possible to envisage arrangements on the following lines:-

(a) The U.K. and France could declare themselves the European trustees of nuclear weapons within the framework of NATO.

(b) As part of this arrangement we would have a joint targeting policy.

(c) The U.K. and France would jointly approach President Kennedy suggesting that the time had come to put France on a par with the U.K. in these matters.

(d) An arrangement on the above lines would re-introduce an element of tripartitism which might flatter de Gaulle and would prevent his isolation from the Americans and the concept of nuclear trusteeship might also be attractive not only in the United States but in Europe.

The possibilities of practical co-operation with the French in this field seem to be as follows:-

(a) The supply of fissionable material. In the past the difficulty here had been that the Canadian price was too high but this had recently been re-negotiated and it might be possible to offer something to the French in this field.

(b) The U.K. might be able to co-operate with France and perhaps other European countries in the manufacture of launchers for nuclear weapons; an organisation similar to ELDO [European Launcher Development Organisation] might come into existence. There had, however, been considerable difficulties with the Americans even about ELDO and they would be much more hostile to any arrangement specifically designed to provide nuclear carriers. It was therefore not clear how far such an organisation could be entered into without American agreement.

(c) European targeting. It should in theory be possible to arrange for an Anglo-French plan for the co-ordination of nuclear strikes against the Soviet Union, presumably in circumstances in which the United States would not be involved. At the moment there was close U.K./U.S. planning of joint targeting but there was no reason why we should not also have joint targeting with the French provided we did not tell the French what the American plans were. However, the Americans were likely to become alarmed if they heard that Anglo-French planning was going on since they would assume that the British contribution would be made in the light of our knowledge of U.S. plans.

(d) The arrangements would leave on one side the question of manufacture of nuclear weapons. Here the U.K. would still have a privileged position.

(e) The Anglo-U.S. targeting arrangements would presumably be unaffected. Here too the U.K. would maintain a special relationship with the United States.

(f) It must therefore be recognised that the French might not be satisfied with limited arrangements such as the above but would ask for a full degree of nuclear knowledge and possibly for the abandonment of any special U.S./U.K. joint targeting arrangements.

Source: PRO, PREM 11/3775

Document 3.15

At their Nassau meeting of 19–21 December 1962, Kennedy and Macmillan reached an agreement that provided Britain with American-built Polaris missiles instead of the recently cancelled Skybolt. The following extracts from the official British and American records of this meeting deal with Macmillan's views about the impact of this agreement on Britain's negotiations for EEC membership and also the reasons for maintaining Britain's status as a nuclear power.

A

Mr. Macmillan thought that it was worth considering what the effect would have been on the French, Germans and Italians if the SKYBOLT project had been successfully developed. He did not think that they would have been upset. They were all fully aware of the history and of the co-operative arrangements which had made Britain with America a founder member of the nuclear club. They knew about the special arrangements under the McMahon Act and the tradition, which had been renewed – but not started – at Camp David [Eisenhower/Macmillan meeting of March 1960 resulting in the offer of Skybolt missiles to Britain]. There would, therefore, have been no problem. Now that Skybolt had failed the question arose of the effect of an American decision to continue to help the United Kingdom in some other way on the possibility of larger groupings in Europe on which so much depended. As regards the Common Market negotiations he [Macmillan] could frankly see no objection. The truth of the matter was that the French felt that they had made a very good deal with the Germans about agriculture and the real problem was whether they would be ready to abandon this. There was of course a division between the French concept of the Six building up a somewhat autarchic agricultural structure and reducing imports almost to nothing and the British view that it was the duty of the Europeans, not just to the Commonwealth but to the whole outside world, to accept a reasonable degree of imports, thereby promoting economic stability, preventing political upheavals and fulfilling their moral duty. But the outcome of the Common Market negotiations would not be affected by decisions about nuclear delivery systems . . .

He [Macmillan] would like to make one point about the alleged difference between POLARIS and SKYBOLT. It seemed to him that these weapons were not fundamentally different but merely varying ways of delivering ballistic rockets. Whether these were fired from the air or from the sea was just a difference in method.

Lastly, the difficulties which had been mentioned about the allies would be as nothing to the difficulties which would follow if the United States seemed to be using the SKYBOLT decision as a means of forcing Britain out of an independent nuclear capacity. This would be resented not only by those who were in favour of the British independent deterrent but even by those who opposed it and yet felt that abandonment of this United Kingdom force should come about because of a decision made by Britain and not by others.

President Kennedy feared that any co-operation between the United Kingdom and the United States would add further force to all President de Gaulle's arguments, which he used to some effect round Europe, about the United States' intentions to dominate Europe. And it would certainly have a further effect on the Germans. It might be possible to overcome these pressures and it might be necessary to face them. But in the United States' view it was not true to say that the supplying of POLARIS would make no difference at all. It would represent a change in the British position and would be exploited as such by the French.

Source: PRO, PREM 11/4229

B

'Actually', said the Prime Minister, 'the whole thing is ridiculous.' What do seven or eight UK units add to the existing nuclear strength, which is enough to blow up the world? So why does the UK want it? It is partly a question of keeping up with the Joneses', which is human. We have not yet reached the point of a melting pot of nations. So countries which have played a great role in history must retain their dignity. This area is not merely a question of difference of degree, but of order. The UK does not want to be just a clown, or a satellite. The UK wants a nuclear force not only for defense, but in the event of menace to its existence, which the UK might have to meet; for example: when Khrushchev waved his rockets about the time of Suez, or when that fellow Qassim got excited and Kuwait was threatened. The UK, the Prime Minister went on to say, wants to do three things: to contribute to NATO, to contribute to the strength and unity of Europe, and to retain an element of strength in its foreign policy in order to maintain the valuation given by other countries to the UK's advice.

Source: *FRUS*, 1961–63, vol. XIII, pp. 1109–10

Document 3.16

Immediately after de Gaulle vetoed British membership of the EEC in January 1963, Sir Pierson Dixon, British ambassador to France and the leading official on the British negotiating team in Brussels, wrote a detailed account of Anglo-French exchanges in the course of the UK/ EEC negotiations of 1961–63. During this period Dixon had more dealings with de Gaulle than any other British minister or official and was closely involved in meetings between de Gaulle and Macmillan. The following extract from this account (dated 18 February 1963) deals with his assessment of de Gaulle's views about the possibility of Anglo-French cooperation on nuclear weapons and the importance of Anglo-American ties in this field.

54.   I now come to the complicated and opaque subject of General de Gaulle's views about the relationship between defence matters and our entry into Europe. In this whole affair nothing is more difficult than to establish whether or not General de Gaulle really expected to make a nuclear deal with us and if so on what terms ... After the Rambouillet meeting [de Gaulle/Macmillan meeting of 15–16 December 1962] it became fashionable here [Paris] to allege that the real trouble about Rambouillet was that the Prime Minister [Macmillan] did not make any proposals of this kind and arguments of this kind are advanced by quite serious and well-disposed people. For example, the former French Ambassador in London, Monsieur Chauvel, told a member of my staff early in January [1963] that he was convinced that General de Gaulle had decided very early on that he would be able to make an arrangement with us whereby we cooperated fully with France in the production of nuclear weapons and delivery systems (including, naturally, supplying the French with all our own and American secrets) in return for which General de Gaulle would consent to allow us to join the E.E.C. ....

Personally, I cannot believe that it would have been possible to come to a tolerable agreement with him [de Gaulle]. To do so we should have had to choose him rather than the United States. We should have had to go far further than offering to co-operate in nuclear warheads (if we could ever have obtained American permission even for that). We should have had to agree to hand over all our own and the American secrets without getting in return any commitment of French forces to NATO or any control over the French force. This would have meant in the last resort being prepared to break with the United States and to join him in pursuing third force policies. Presumably it would never have entered our minds to jettison the American connexion and help General de Gaulle to break up the Atlantic Alliance in the hope that this would enable us to join the Common Market. Furthermore even if it was true that he was expecting us to make proposals for Anglo-French co-operation in the construction of a nuclear deterrent and thought that he would be able to draw some advantage from this, it does not necessarily follow that he was planning to negotiate with us in good faith. He might only have hoped to involve us in a quarrel with the Americans or perhaps that we should enter into a negotiation with him, find that we could not meet his terms, and withdraw. No one can say. I certainly cannot assert categorically that he would not under any circumstances have made an arrangement with us under which we gave him nuclear secrets and he allowed us to join the Common Market.

58.   However in my despatch No. 177 of the 30th of November, 1962 I argued that the arrangement for the nuclear organisation of the West which would fit in both with General de Gaulle's aims and attitudes and those of the United States were unattainable. I continue to hold that this was so. On the whole, re-reading the record of Rambouillet December, 1962, I do not believe that General de Gaulle himself believed otherwise or that he expected a process to be begun at Rambouillet which would lead to our 'choosing Europe rather than the United States' in defence matters.

Source: PRO, FO 371/171449

4   Kith and kin: the Commonwealth and Europe, 1945–1961

The extracts in this section explore the interrelationship between British policy towards Europe and Britain's Commonwealth links between 1945 and 1961. During this period British governments portrayed Commonwealth commitments and interests as the major external barrier to closer British involvement in European integration. British policymakers' perception of this obstacle, however, underwent marked changes in this period. The degree of change was often clouded by the popular appeal and mystique of the Commonwealth that had intensified as a result of wartime experience. Furthermore, policymakers frequently insisted that it was difficult to gauge the importance of Commonwealth ties that were so imponderable and 'not a matter of a pure economic calculus' (4.1).

One of the most pronounced shifts in official thinking during this period concerned the value of the Commonwealth in buttressing Britain's global power and influence and in serving British commercial and financial interests. In 1945 these emphases were widely acknowledged and invariably meant that British involvement in any form of European cooperation could not be pursued at the expense of Commonwealth ties. By 1961, Britain's Commonwealth trading ties still remained a formidable obstacle to British membership of the EEC. Yet the Commonwealth had lost much of its allure as a base for British power in the world, and the government's rationale for seeking EEC membership focused on the enhancement of the Commonwealth's strength as a result of British membership of the EEC. In effect, the Commonwealth was no longer a source of power sufficient in itself to curtail British involvement in Europe or to stand in the way of a new definition of the British national interest.

During the early post-war years, the British Empire and Commonwealth (or the Commonwealth as it was formally designated in 1949) was widely viewed by British policymakers and public alike as the centrepiece of Britain's claim to great power status. As a source of power and prestige, it compensated for and also masked Britain's weaknesses. London was the hub of a Commonwealth network of political, economic, commercial and financial ties that incorporated the white self-governing Dominions of Australia, Canada, New Zealand, South Africa and the Irish Free State (until 1948), the newly independent countries of India and Pakistan (1947) and Ceylon (1948) and a host of colonies in Africa, Asia, the Caribbean and the Mediterranean still under direct control.

It was in the field of economic, commercial and financial relations that Commonwealth ties assumed their most tangible form, most notably in the workings of the imperial preference system and the sterling area. These commercial and monetary arrangements had emerged during the period of economic depression and world trade contraction in the early 1930s. The imperial preference system, originating in the Ottawa Agreements of 1932, provided for preferentially lower tariff rates on trade within the Empire and Commonwealth. This arrangement encouraged the growing concentration of British trade in the Empire and Commonwealth during the period 1931–50, when British imports from the rest of the Empire and Commonwealth (as a percentage of total British imports) increased from 24.5 per cent to 41.1 per cent while British exports to the rest of the Empire and Commonwealth (as a percentage of total British exports) rose from 32.6 per cent to 47.7 per cent. In the early post-war years of food and raw materials shortages and dollar deficits, this system offered such an assured market to British exports and also access to cheap food and raw materials that British policymakers were determined to resist any American attempts to dismantle it in return for dollar aid (4.1).

The sterling area covered much of the Empire and Commonwealth (Canada being the most significant exception) and also included non-Commonwealth countries especially in the Middle East. It operated as a monetary union within which sterling was the major reserve currency and Britain acted as the central banker supervising the common pool of the area's exchange reserves. In addition, the Commonwealth had preferential access to investment capital in London. Throughout this period, British policymakers were particularly concerned to maintain confidence in sterling within the sterling area. This was especially the case as sterling area controls were removed in the 1950s and as recurring sterling crises highlighted the weakness of Britain's external financial position, with gold reserves amounting to less than one-third of the sterling liabilities to other countries. (4.2B, 4.5 and 4.9).

The possibility of a close association between Britain's Commonwealth ties and colonies and the west European imperial powers as the basis for a third world power found fleeting expression in Bevin's Western Union plan of 1948 (4.2A). At this time Bevin was particularly concerned to develop the resources of Africa in order to reduce the need for American financial aid, believing that if Britain 'only pushed on and developed Africa, we could have the US dependent on us and eating out of our hand in four or five years'. The implications of this plan, however, and especially the idea of British membership of two 'clubs' – the imperial preference system and a European customs and monetary union – were considered in Whitehall, only to be ruled out as neither desirable nor feasible. The shortcomings of Bevin's grandiose scheme were increasingly recognised by British policymakers in the face of Cold War rivalries and European dependence on American aid. A Foreign Office paper of April 1950 reflected Bevin's revised views in its assessment of the factors that weighed heavily against the prospect of a British-led Commonwealth bloc and also in its dismissal of the idea of a Commonwealth–Western Europe bloc in global politics (4.2B).

In the heightened Cold War atmosphere following the outbreak of the Korean War (June 1950), British politicians claimed to discover a new-found sense of purpose for the Commonwealth as a bulwark against Soviet expansionism. While acknowledging the Commonwealth's value in this context, however, the Americans were far less impressed by Whitehall's view that Commonwealth ties necessarily limited the degree of British involvement in Europe. In Washington as in other circles, this British position was viewed as an excuse for a European policy that Britain would have undertaken regardless of Commonwealth considerations (4.3). Against that, however, British political leaders shared and fairly represented deeply rooted domestic support for the Commonwealth over and against any European ties. This order of priorities was evident, for example, in the Labour Party's idealised vision of and commitment to the Commonwealth (4.4).

The British view of the Commonwealth as emblematic of the country's world power status remained intact until 1955. The adverse impact of British membership of a European common market on links with the rest of the Commonwealth was a powerful consideration in the decision of the Eden government (November 1955) to withdraw from the post-Messina talks of the Six (4.5). At this time British trade with the rest of the Commonwealth and the sterling area still far exceeded trade with any other region or country (4.6 Table A). It was becoming apparent, however, that British exports to the buoyant North American and European markets were growing at a faster rate than exports to more sluggish Commonwealth markets (4.6 Table B). It was also increasingly evident that the imperial preference system was eroding away as a result of a combination of factors, notably the global trend towards trade liberalisation and dissatisfaction with the system among some of the Commonwealth states (4.7).

In the period 1956–61 British commercial policy underwent changes in response to the increasing importance of the European market and the emergence of the EEC. There was also a growing recognition that the Commonwealth market was no longer sufficient for British exports and that the British market could not absorb the rising tide of Commonwealth food imports. In this problematical process of adjustment the preferences on British exports to the rest of the Commonwealth and the largely duty-free entry of Commonwealth food and raw materials into Britain loomed large as critical issues. The average margin of preference on British exports to the Commonwealth that qualified for preferences was approximately 15 per cent in 1948, but thereafter declined, especially as Australia (1957) and New Zealand (1958) negotiated reductions in the margins. Nevertheless, a Whitehall report in 1960 concluded that the margins of preference had still to fall much further before reaching the minimum significant level of 5 per cent and that even preferences of this order over 20 per cent of total British exports would remain of 'real psychological value'. There was no less keen interest in maintaining the system of cheap

Commonwealth food imports into Britain. The large suppliers like Canada, Australia and New Zealand accounted for some 60 per cent of Britain's total wheat and meat imports in 1955 (4.6 Table C).

It was in seeking to reduce the threat posed by the embryonic common market of the Six in 1956 that ministers began to contemplate changes to Britain's Commonwealth trading links. Harold Macmillan, Chancellor of the Exchequer, and Peter Thorneycroft, President of the Board of Trade, were the principal movers in this direction as authors of 'Plan G' for a European free trade area. The case for 'Plan G' was that British commercial policy could no longer be based on the Commonwealth connection (4.8). Reservations were expressed by the Commonwealth Secretary, but these carried less weight than at the time of the decision to withdraw from the post-Messina talks in the previous year. In any case the exclusion of agricultural trade from 'Plan G' preserved the system of British food imports from the rest of the Commonwealth. One of the most significant aspects of the plan was the government's willingness to abandon preferences on Commonwealth manufactured exports to Britain. While these goods amounted to only 7 per cent (1956) of total Commonwealth exports to Britain, the proposed equal treatment of Commonwealth and European manufactured exports to Britain conceded an important principle at the heart of the imperial preference system.

The course and outcome of the free trade area negotiations (see section 5) and the successful inauguration of the EEC in the period 1956–58 highlighted the increasingly acute dilemma confronting the Macmillan government in its management of trade relations with the Commonwealth and Europe. This dilemma arose out of the incompatibility between continued adherence to the imperial preference system and association with or membership of the EEC. In talks with Macmillan, de Gaulle was not slow to point out this predicament. He implicitly used long-standing British views about the irreconcilable requirements of the imperial preference system and a European common market to thwart the possibility of any major move by the Macmillan government towards EEC membership (4.9). Attempts to safeguard Britain's growing trading interests with the EEC could be pursued only at the expense of Britain's Commonwealth trading ties. In particular, this raised the unpalatable prospect of 'reverse preferences' whereby British trade with the EEC received more favourable tariff treatment than trade with the Commonwealth. How far the Macmillan government was prepared to go in this direction became a matter of crucial importance, both in the making of the 1961 decision to apply for EEC membership and in the subsequent negotiations between Britain and the EEC states.

A combination of conflicting considerations concerning the Commonwealth complicated the making of this decision. Some idea of the balance of the arguments in official circles about the value of the Commonwealth to Britain is evident from the wide-ranging 'Future Policy Study, 1960–1970' (4.10). This review was commissioned by Macmillan and its conclusions predictably coincided with his own thinking. In some respects it merely reiterated established views about the importance of the Commonwealth as a mechanism for exercising British influence, for cultivating relations between developed and undeveloped countries and for strengthening the West's position in the context of East–West relations. In other respects, however, it registered the post-Suez changes in Britain's standing within the Commonwealth and in the world at large. Britain was no longer a world power but a 'Power with worldwide interests', and was no longer at the centre of a huge trading empire but managing the 'wasting asset' of Commonwealth preference. Furthermore, the opportunity for British leadership of the Commonwealth was rapidly diminishing, to leave an organisation that was politically sometimes 'more of an embarrassment than an asset' and that was fast losing the image of a white man's club under the impact of the second wave of decolonisation (1957–63). The expulsion of South Africa from the Commonwealth in 1961 on account of its apartheid system marked the emergence of a new constellation of forces within the Commonwealth. This episode clearly upset the long-standing dominance of Britain and of the white Dominions in the management of Commonwealth affairs (4.11).

In seeking to reconcile Britain's Commonwealth interests with an application for EEC membership, Macmillan had no intention of playing 'the role of Lord North', as he put it in 1960 at the height of the row over South Africa's continued membership of the Commonwealth. He was very sensitive to cross-party support for the Commonwealth. The trading interests of the white Dominions were the focal point of concern. Australia and even more so New Zealand were heavily dependent on exporting duty-free temperate foodstuffs to Britain; one-third of Australia's total exports and over 50 per cent of New Zealand's went to Britain. Much of this trade was likely to suffer discriminatory tariff treatment in the event of British membership of the EEC. The British government's concern to maintain the existing level of this trade was evident in the Cabinet's formulation of an opening negotiating position on the application for EEC membership (4.12). In September 1961, on the eve of the opening of these negotiations, Macmillan advised Heath, the leader of the British negotiating team, that it was 'very important' to retain Commonwealth preferences and that 'it is in a sense on the Commonwealth system of free entry and preferences that the whole of the negotiation turns'. The government's vulnerability on the issue was immediately exploited by a Labour Opposition determined to mobilise popular support for the Commonwealth (4.13).

Document 4.1

The imperial preference system was an important symbol of Britain's trading relations with the rest of the Empire–Commonwealth in the early post-war years. During the UK/US loan negotiations in the autumn of 1945, for example, American moves to make financial assistance conditional on the elimination of imperial preferences were strongly resisted by the British as illustrated by the following notes: (A) Dalton (Chancellor of the Exchequer) to Keynes (head of the British negotiating team), 8 October 1945; (B) Keynes to Dalton, 9 October 1945.

A

It is not entirely clear . . . whether Americans really have the intention to make elimination of Imperial Preference a condition of financial assistance.

We have repeatedly expressed our willingness to consider preferences as part of a satisfactory tariff settlement, but not to treat them separately. Certainly there will be very violent reaction here if preference issue is formally linked, not with commercial talks, but with financial deal. Indeed, a financial settlement otherwise acceptable might be wrecked on this issue.

Therefore, if you have real apprehension that American tactics are going to make this mistake will you consider . . . whether you . . . should not see Vinson [Secretary of the Treasury] personally as from me and speak to him in the sense of this telegram? You can explain that it is not too easy for me to find a basis of financial settlement acceptable to my colleagues and Parliament, and that my task would be made hopeless if anyone can represent that a financial pistol has been held at our head on the subject of Imperial Preference.

This is a matter in which all parties in Parliament feel the same. Moreover, Australian and New Zealand Governments are attached to preference system and our present Government has political affiliations with them. Therefore Dominions aspect of American attempt to trade horses at the wrong fair would add to difficulties.

B

Stated in its most simple form our problem lies in the fact that the Americans are demanding firm assurance from us regarding the reduction and elimination of preferences before they will promise further financial aid. We have told them that their demand in its present form is unacceptable . . .

There is doubtless some force in their [American] insistence that the economic price is not great. But this is not a matter of a pure economic calculus. We do not doubt that Ministers would feel the strongest repugnance to the idea of our being forced, by reason of financial weakness, to abandon even the residual tokens of habits which for many, symbolise membership of a common community. We have therefore emphasised to the Americans, both in plenary session and in private conversation, that if they file their demand in this way, they are likely to produce a breakdown of the negotiations.

In saying this, we do not wish to overstate the difficulties of the position though they are as yet unresolved. Many of the Americans with whom we are dealing are as convinced as we are that further financial aid is essential to us and to their own welfare too. They know that they have much to gain from a restoration of our economic strength and much to lose from a rupture in circumstances in which the rest of the world would tend to regard us as the injured party. The State Department contemplate with real apprehension the prospect of our turning aside to bilateralism. They know too that if the negotiation broke down on this point, we should tend to secure much support from the Dominions who, however lukewarm some of them may be regarding present preferential arrangements, would certainly rally to our support if we were threatened in this particular way.

Source: *DBPO* (1986), series I, vol. III, pp. 200–2

Document 4.2

In the early post-war years the Commonwealth figured in British plans for constructing a third world power in association with the west European imperial powers. Bevin subscribed to this idea in his Western Union speech of January 1948 (Extract A). The shortcomings of this grandiose scheme, however, were increasingly recognised by British policymakers in the face of Cold War rivalries and European dependence on American aid. A Foreign Office paper of May 1949 (Extract B), which was entitled 'A Third World Power or Western Consolidation' and was later circulated to the Cabinet by Bevin, commented on the weaknesses of the third world power concept in relation to the Commonwealth.

A

Perhaps I may now return to the subject of the organisation in respect of a Western Union. That is its right description. I would emphasise that I am not concerned only with Europe as a geographical conception. Europe has extended its influence throughout the world, and we have to look further afield. In the first place, we turn our eyes to Africa, where great responsibilities are shared by us with South Africa, France, Belgium and Portugal, and equally to all overseas territories, especially of South-East Asia, with which the Dutch are closely concerned. The organisation of Western Europe must be economically supported. That involves the closest possible collaboration with the Commonwealth and with overseas territories, not only British but French, Dutch, Belgian and Portuguese.

These overseas territories are large primary producers, and their standard of living is evolving rapidly and is capable of great development. They have raw materials, food and resources which can be turned to very great common advantage, both to the people of the territories themselves, to Europe, and to the world as a whole. The other two great world Powers, the United States and Soviet Russia, have tremendous resources. There is no need of conflict with them in this matter at all. If Western Europe is to achieve its balance of payments and to get a world equilibrium, it is essential that those resources should be developed and made available, and the exchange between them carried out in a correct and proper manner. There is no conflict between the social and economic development of those overseas territories to the advantage of their people, and their development as a source of supplies for Western Europe, as a contributor, as I have indicated, so essential to the balance of payments . . .

Therefore, if we get the plan, we intend to develop the economic co-operation between Western European countries step by step, to develop the resources of the territories with which we are associated, to build them up a system of priorities which will produce the quickest, most effective and most lasting results for the whole world. We hope that other countries with dependent territories will do the same in association with us.

We shall thus, bring together resources, manpower, organisation and opportunity for millions of people. I would like to depict what it really involves in terms of population whose standard of life can be lifted. We are bringing together these tremendous resources, which stretch through Europe, the Middle East and Africa, to the Far East. In no case would it be an exclusive effort. It would be done with the object of making the whole world richer and safer. We believe there is an opportunity, and that when it is studied there will be a willingness on the part of our friends in the Commonwealth to co-operate with us in this great effort.

Source: *H.C. Deb.*, vol. 446, cols. 400–1, 22 January 1948

B

POSSIBLE COMPOSITION OF A THIRD WORLD POWER

7.   The first question that requires consideration is what the composition of a Third World Power might be. The only serious suggestions that have been made are that it should consist of the Commonwealth, or of Western Europe (including the United Kingdom) with its overseas territories, or of these groups combined. These suggested groupings may be examined under three headings, political, economic and military.

Commonwealth

(a) Political

There are no political tendencies in the Commonwealth to-day which suggest that it could successfully be consolidated as a single unit. The Commonwealth is not a unit in the same sense as the United States or the Soviet Union. It has no central authority and is unlikely to create one, and its members are increasingly framing their policies on grounds of regional or local interests. The only member of the Commonwealth which might assume a position of leadership within it is the United Kingdom, and it seems unlikely that any proposals originating in London for a closer co-ordination of Commonwealth policy would be welcomed at present. It should not be assumed that centrifugal forces are certain to increase and it remains true that concerted action may well be achieved in a crisis. The substantial identity of view among Commonwealth countries is undoubtedly an important influence for world peace. Nevertheless, there is no guarantee that a common policy will be followed.

(b) Economic

9.   Since the creation of the O.E.E.C. [Organisation for European Economic Cooperation] machinery the economic planning of the United Kingdom is

tending to become more closely tied in with Western Europe than with the Commonwealth . . . There is little sign that the Dominions would accept collective planning arrangements for the Commonwealth similar to the O.E.E.C., but we may well hope to persuade them increasingly to discuss their long-term problems individually with the United Kingdom. Even so, Commonwealth countries are likely to take the view that their needs for investment capital for industrial development cannot be met by co-operation with the United Kingdom and Western Europe alone, but that dollar assistance will be needed . . .

(c) Military

10.   The miltary picture is similar. As a result of the Brussels Treaty the United Kingdom has gone much further in military planning with Western Europe than it has with the Commonwealth. Moreover, the Commonwealth is not a strategic unit, and here again it must be clear to the Dominions that their defence cannot be assured without United States support . . .

(d) Conclusion

11.   Despite the possibility of improved economic consultation, there seems little prospect of the United Kingdom being able to unite the Commonwealth as a single world power. The attraction exerted by the pound sterling and the Royal Navy is now less strong than that of the dollar and the atom bomb. An attempt to turn the Commonwealth into a Third World Power would only confront its members with a direct choice between London and Washington, and though sentiment might point one way interest would certainly lead the other . . .

The Commonwealth and Western Europe Combined

20.   Unfortunately, the objections to either group in isolation are not removed by their combination, and this alternative is therefore not examined in detail. Political cohesion of the Commonwealth countries with Western Europe is even less likely than with the United Kingdom, and the dangerous choice between London and Washington is not eliminated. Moreover, the economic and military weaknesses of Western Europe are not significantly diminished by the addition of the Commonwealth countries other than the United Kingdom, and the need for American support remains.

Source: PRO, FO 371/76384

Document 4.3

The following extracts from a US State Department paper of 19 April 1950 reflect an American view of Britain's Commonwealth links. While recognising the value of the Commonwealth in the Cold War conditions of 1950, the paper disputes the widely held view in Britain that Commonwealth ties ruled out a closer British association with Western Europe. On the contrary, close British involvement in Western Europe was most likely to contribute to the long-term vitality of the Commonwealth. British political leaders did not advance this view until the second half of the 1950s when they began to contemplate major changes in British commercial policy towards Europe.

Economically, the British attach great importance to their extra-European economic ties. This springs in part from the fact that the UK is so dependent upon raw material imports from overseas, and hence must carry on a large compensating trade with non-European countries. In addition, they believe that a major part of their position as a world power depends upon their overseas connections, particularly with the whole sterling system which is essentially managed from London . . .

While there is a tendency for the British to say that their Commonwealth responsibilities make it impossible for them to associate themselves too closely with the Continent, this is probably often an excuse rather than a position taken as a result of objective analysis. While it is certainly true that Empire and Commonwealth defense relationships must continue to play an important role in British defense thinking as well as in U.S. planning, and while it is also true that a real political merger with the Continent would undoubtedly lead to the dissolution of the Commonwealth relationship, the welfare of the Commonwealth is in the long run dependent upon a strong Western Europe with which the UK is closely associated and close relationships between the US and the UK. The form and very nature of the Commonwealth relationship has undergone great changes in recent years, and we cannot foresee its future. It still seems to retain, however, a considerable degree of cohesion and does represent an institutional arrangement which can be of great value to us so long as it remains strong. It should be an objective of our policy to strengthen the Commonwealth, always bearing in mind that its validity as an organization depends upon the maintenance of the security and prosperity of the whole Western world and particularly upon a continuing close relationship between the US and the UK . . .

It should be our line with the British to assure them that we recognize the special relationship between our two countries and that we recognize their special position with regard to the Commonwealth. We should insist, however, that these relationships are not incompatible with close association in a European framework. In fact, the close U.S.–U.K. relation and the Commonwealth today find their significance in their ability to contribute to the attaining of other ends, including the strengthening of Western Europe and resistance to Soviet expansion everywhere.

Source: *FRUS*, 1950, vol. III, pp. 874–5

Document 4.4

This extract is taken from a statement issued by the National Executive Committee of the British Labour Party in June 1950.

THE COMMONWEALTH AND STERLING AREA

Finally the Labour Party cannot see European unity as an overriding end in itself. Britain is not just a small crowded island off the Western coast of Continental Europe. She is the nerve-centre of a world-wide Commonwealth which extends into every continent. In every respect except distance we in Britain are closer to our kinsmen in Australia and New Zealand on the far side of the world, than we are to Europe. We are closer in language and in origins, in social habits and institutions, in political outlook and economic interest. The economies of the Commonwealth countries are complementary to that of Britain to a degree which those of Western Europe could never equal. Furthermore Britain is also banker of the sterling area. This is the largest multilateral trading system in the world – within which exchange controls are not applied and all transactions are conducted in a single currency. We believe it is in the interest of the world at large that this system should be protected and maintained. In any case it is a vital British interest.

By transforming four hundred millions of Britain's Asian subjects into friends and equal partners the Labour Government has built a bridge between East and West, between the white and coloured peoples. The Commonwealth now represents the nucleus of a potential world society based on free co-operation. We believe that our overriding aim in the present age must be to unite all the non-Communist peoples into a single system which is both economically stable and politically secure. Such a system is needed to preserve both peace and prosperity . . .

Any changes in Britain's relations with Western Europe must not impair her position as nerve centre of the Commonwealth and banker of the Sterling Area. Close co-operation with Asia and America is vital to Europe's peace and prosperity.

> Source: National Executive Committee of the British Labour Party,
> *European Unity*, London, 1950

Document 4.5

The British decision in November 1955 to withdraw from the Brussels discussions of the six prospective EEC states was taken by ministers on the basis of a report by officials (Trend report). The report, from which this extract is taken, considered the political implications of British membership of a common market and the likely impact on UK relations with the rest of the Commonwealth.

A major political consequence of our joining a European common market would be that we should thereby be assuming new obligations and loyalties to the other members which would conflict with our obligations and loyalties to our Commonwealth partners . . . In particular, one of the results of our joining the market would be to increase the relative importance of our trade with Europe and reduce our economic links with the Commonwealth. All this, as a move away from the Commonwealth towards Europe, would have a profound effect on Commonwealth sentiment and on the continued readiness of other Commonwealth countries to co-operate with us in Sterling Area and general economic policy.

One of the most immediate examples of this conflict mentioned above would be the damage to the Imperial Preference system which would inevitably result from our joining a European Common Market. We could not join a Common Market without renegotiating our Ottawa agreements and this would inevitably result in a substantial loss of preference and other advantages . . . But to renegotiate them in the context of our joining a European common market would mean our asking the other Commonwealth countries to give up preferences of great importance to them (particularly if we assume that the common market arrangements might include agriculture, at least in the long term) for the purpose of securing preferences for ourselves in Europe. The effect of this would be to give the negotiations on which we should be embarking the character of a major move towards dismantling the Imperial Preference system. The shock to Commonwealth sentiment (particularly in the 'old' Commonwealth countries) would be severe, and would do much damage to our position in the Commonwealth.

In the longer term, it seems clear that, once we became members of a common market, we should be subject to strong political pressures to extend the 'harmonisation' of our policies with those of the other members beyond the field of tariffs into other fields both of internal and external policy. This process would, in general, restrict our freedom to take account of the interests of other Commonwealth countries in formulating our policies. (For example, we might not find it possible to maintain their present preferential access to the London capital market.) This would itself decrease the value to them of their Commonwealth relationship with us. Moreover, they might well see reason, on account of the European influences on the conduct of our economic policy, to question our continued ability to manage our economy in a prudent manner (which would affect their confidence in sterling) and our ability to concert acceptable policies with them in the international economic field.

In joining a common market, we should, in all these ways, be substantially weakening the Commonwealth relationship, which, although not based on contractual obligations, and, therefore, difficult to assess in real terms, is of immense importance to our position as a world power. It is very doubtful if we could place anything like the same reliance on the 'contractual' arrangements in Europe which we should be gaining in exchange.

Source: PRO, CAB 134/1030, M.A.C. (55) 200, 24 October 1955

Document 4.6

Table 4.6a indicates the relative values of UK trade with the Commonwealth, the sterling area and Western Europe: 1952–54. Table 4.6b shows the area distribution of UK exports for the period 1952–56. Exports to sterling area countries grew at a slower rate than exports to non-sterling area countries. Table 4.6c indicates the principal sources of British wheat and meat imports in 1955.

Table 4.6a Annual average expressed as a percentage

Area	Total external trade	Imports	Exports
Commonwealth			
Sterling	41	39	42
Non-sterling (Canada)	7	9	5
Sterling			
Commonwealth	41	39	42
Non-Commonwealth (Burma, Iraq, Irish Republic, etc.)	5	4	5
Non-Sterling			
Commonwealth	7	9	5
ECSC countries	12	12	13
Scandinavia	8	8	9
Rest of non-sterling area	27	28	26

Source: PRO, T234/195.

Table 4.6b Area distribution of UK exports (£ million)

	1952	1953	1954	1955	1956
Non-sterling					
US and Canada	276	316	281	324	421
Other dollar area countries	633	70	79	73	100
Total dollar area	339	386	360	397	521
OEEC countries and dependencies	649	692	722	760	847
Other non-sterling countries	324	251	261	318	356
Total non-sterling countries	1313	1328	1344	1474	1724
Total sterling countries	1272	1254	1331	1431	1448
Total all countries	2585	2582	2674	2905	3172

Source: PRO, CAB 129/86 C. (57) 65.

Table 4.6c Wheat and meat imports 1955 ('000 tons)

Wheat		Meat	
Canada	2,259	New Zealand	326
France	644	Argentina	232
Australia	502	Australia	180
USA	474	Total UK imports	847
Argentina	302	Total UK production	1,325
Total UK imports	4,504		
Total UK production	2,783		

Source: PRO, FO 371/122030.

Document 4.7

The following extract from the Financial Times *(20 June 1956) deals with some of the main features of the imperial preference at a time when Australia was pressing for a review of the Ottawa Agreements of 1932.*

Of over £600m. British exports which benefited last year from Imperial Preference, over £500m. were accounted for by Australia, New Zealand and Canada. It looks as though New Zealand and Canada may remain neutral over Australia's request and it does not seem as if it will have much support from the newly independent Dominions.

Approximately half Britain's trade is with the Commonwealth, and Imperial Preference applies to just under half Commonwealth trade. As a rule British imports are subject to a 10 per cent. duty under the Import Duties Act of 1932 and other duties apply under the 1921 Key Industries Act. Staple commodities such as wheat and wool are among the chief exceptions, to which no duty applies. As a general rule, wherever a duty applies, Commonwealth imports are allowed in either free of all duty or at preferential specific rates.

The proportion of U.K. exports enjoying preferential entry varies immensely from one Dominion to another. At the head of the list come Australia and New Zealand, where the proportion is about 90 per cent. At the bottom of the list come India and South Africa where the proportion is about 30 per cent. Canada occupies an intermediate position. Similarly the average percentage *margin* of preference on all imports from the U.K. varies a great deal. Australia and New Zealand are foremost with about 16 per cent. and 13 per cent. respectively. Canadian margins probably average just under 10 per cent., while in the case of India and South Africa they are less than 5 per cent.

Less is known about Commonwealth exports to the U.K., but in many cases the proportion of exports enjoying preference is much less, as so many Commonwealth exports consist of food and raw materials. In the case of India, for example, although textiles and tobacco are among the exports enjoying preference, the bulk of exports are unaffected.

The basis of the Australian contention is that Britain gains far more than Australia from the present arrangements. British exports to Australia, which are mostly manufactured goods, benefit from preferential tariffs, while Australian exports to Britain consist to a large extent of staple commodities such as wool and wheat, which are sold in Britain at world prices . . .

Behind these detailed Anglo-Australian dissensions lies the general consideration that Imperial Preference is much less important for Commonwealth trade than it used to be. In rough terms Britain gives and receives preferential margins amounting to an average of 6 per cent. on all goods entering Commonwealth trade . . . There are two main reasons why the Ottawa Agreements have lost some of their former importance. One is the deliberate reductions in rates of duty made under G.A.T.T. [General Agreement on Tariffs and Trade] and other trade agreements. Most of the important G.A.T.T. reductions date from the post-war years, although even the recently negotiated reductions should result in some further whittling away of preferences. The second and more important reason for the decline in the value of Imperial Preference since the end of the war is that rising world prices have drastically reduced the *ad valorem* incidence of specific margins.

Source: *Financial Times*, 20 June 1956

Document 4.8

At a Cabinet meeting (14 September 1956) ministers considered the implications of 'Plan G' (for a European free trade area) for future ties between Britain and the rest of the Commonwealth. The following extract reflects some of the considerations that were taken into account and also the different emphases of the President of the Board of Trade (Peter Thorneycroft), who played a leading role in devising the plan, and the Commonwealth Secretary (the Earl of Home).

The President of the Board of Trade said that it had been the aim of our commercial policy to secure the advantages of liberal trade practices in the world at large while retaining the benefit of the preferences system within the Commonwealth. This policy was now under pressure and we could no longer expect to continue to enjoy the best of both worlds. Australia had taken the initiative in seeking a review of the preferences system and New Zealand would follow her lead . . . We might soon be confronted in Europe by a powerful discriminatory economic *bloc*, dominated by Germany and developing into a formidable base for German competition in our markets overseas. There was no prospect of our being able to pursue our traditional policies undisturbed and the proposals in Plan G had been devised to turn the developments in Europe to the advantage of the United Kingdom and of the Commonwealth as a whole.

Discussion showed that the Cabinet were impressed by the arguments in support of a new economic initiative on these lines [Plan G], and conscious of the limited scope for an alternative policy which would offer the prospect of economic security in the longer term. Although a commercial policy based on the Commonwealth connection would be much to be preferred, the conditions for such a policy no longer existed. The preferences system was already crumbling away, and there was no hope of re-invigorating it, as the United Kingdom market could not absorb much more of the primary products of the Commonwealth . . . The capacity to invest was even more important in the modern world than the ability to trade. Commonwealth countries were already being attracted to the United States as a source of investment capital. The economic unification of much of Western Europe would create a new source of investment capital for overseas development which might be expected to flow out to Commonwealth countries through London under our management . . .

The danger must be foreseen, however, of a free trade area being dominated by the Germans and if we entered into such an association we should do so with a determination to assume the leadership of it. This, indeed, was now our best means of ensuring our continuing status as a Great Power. The strengthening of the United Kingdom in this way would enhance the security and strength of the Commonwealth and the proposed free trade area would provide not only an additional market for those Commonwealth products which we could not absorb but a source of new funds for Commonwealth development . . .

The Commonwealth Secretary said that, as the United Kingdom turned to Europe, Canada, Australia and New Zealand – with whom we had the firmest bonds – must be expected to turn increasingly towards the United States. Indeed, the United States, disquieted by the formation of a regional group in Europe, would possibly make efforts to attract them. If, therefore, it was decided that these proposals were in our economic interest, every effort must be made to convince Commonwealth countries that the plan, by strengthening the United Kingdom, would strengthen them. But Commonwealth countries would not be convinced by this argument alone, for they would see how vulnerable under the plan our balance of payments would be in the short term. The status of the United Kingdom depended on her position as head of the Commonwealth. In adopting an expansionist policy towards Europe we must therefore be prepared and able to pursue a corresponding policy towards Commonwealth trade. This would entail a positive and far-reaching plan for trade in Commonwealth agricultural products without which the support of the Commonwealth could not be expected. Until such proposals were formulated he must reserve his position.

Source: PRO, CAB 128/30 C.M. (56), 65th Conclusions, 14 September 1956

Document 4.9

The following extract is taken from a British record of talks between de Gaulle and Macmillan at Rambouillet (28–29 January 1961). De Gaulle aimed to demonstrate that a UK/EEC agreement could be had only at the expense of existing Commonwealth or EEC practices.

President de Gaulle said that he would like very much to hear the Prime Minister's ideas about an arrangement between the Six and the Seven. He did not see how this could be made. **The Prime Minister** said that at the time of the negotiations for a Free Trade Area the United Kingdom had accepted the idea of a common internal tariff but had not accepted a common external tariff. Now the United Kingdom felt that there might be a method by which in fact they could associate themselves with the Six and accept the common external tariff subject to certain exceptions to allow for the import of Commonwealth raw materials and temperate foodstuffs. They realised that it would be necessary to exclude Commonwealth industrial goods from the free area. This was only an idea at the moment and it needed to be worked out by experts. They should consider whether a common external tariff could be combined with a protocol of exceptions. This would admittedly be difficult for some Commonwealth countries, particularly Canada, to accept. Also some horticultural arrangement would have to be made to help people like the Italians. There were strong pressures from agricultural and Commonwealth interests in the United Kingdom and such an arrangement would not be easy to carry there. It could only be carried as part of a large concept of the re-organisation of the West.

President de Gaulle said that he did not see how an arrangement between the Six and the United Kingdom and some of the Seven was possible without a change in the system of imperial preferences; if there was a change this would harm the Commonwealth and if there was no change the system would not work. **The Prime Minister** said that the United Kingdom recognised that if an accommodation was reached preferences might in time disappear but this might happen in any case in a changing world. That was one reason why he could only carry the United Kingdom into such an arrangement if it was part of a bigger project and not just a trade bargain . . .

President de Gaulle suggested that the United Kingdom did not do a great deal of trade with Europe since most was done with the Commonwealth. **The Prime Minister** said that a great deal of trade was in fact done with Europe and the proportion was increasing. In any case the Commonwealth itself was changing as the countries in it became more industrialised and developed wider interests.

President de Gaulle said he still did not see how it was possible for the Commonwealth and the Six to make an economic community without destroying one or the other.

Source: PRO, PREM 11/3322

Document 4.10

The following extracts assess the likely evolution and value of the Commonwealth in the 1960s. They form part of an interdepartmental review in Whitehall – 'Future Policy Study, 1960–1970' – which was undertaken in 1959 and completed in early 1960.

While the Commonwealth would not survive if its ties were made definite and tangible, their lack of definition makes their value largely imponderable. But the likely course of events over the next 10 years may illuminate the nature of the Commonwealth in the following respects:-

(a) It is not and with its present and prospective membership will certainly not become a *political* or *military* unit. Indeed, as more colonial territories gain independence or internal autonomy, the formal ties both political and military will tend to become looser. Nor is there any likelihood of a united policy in the struggle between the Sino-Soviet *bloc* and the free world. Some new members of the Commonwealth as well, naturally, as the old, are likely to remain closely aligned with the United Kingdom; for instance Malaya and Nigeria. But in Pakistan there is a risk that the present régime might collapse and a period of instability ensue. If, however, Russia and China adopt conspicuously aggressive policies a greater degree of Commonwealth political and even military co-operation will be a possibility.

(b) The Commonwealth is likely to become less of an *economic* unit. We shall
probably maintain a high and increasing level of trade with members
(although imperial preferences are likely to continue to dwindle), and continued preferential access to the London money market, the tie of healthy
sterling and sizeable United Kingdom contributions to economic development would help to keep the Commonwealth together. But a Britain which
is slipping backwards in relative economic power cannot expect to increase
her proportion of the trade of other Commonwealth countries, and the next
10 years may see a decrease in this proportion . . .

14.   The Commonwealth is neither a military entity nor a source of military
power comparable to America or Western Europe. But some members make small
but valuable contributions to the Free World's defence alliances and it furnishes
bases of the highest strategic importance. Economically, though Commonwealth
Preference will be a wasting asset, Commonwealth countries will be important to
us because of the high proportion of our trade for which they account and the
network of trading and financial interests based on past associations and on
sterling.

15.   The Commonwealth association is a very important source of political
influence which buttresses our standing as a Power with world-wide interests. It
can make a valuable contribution to the problems arising out of the relationships
between advanced and backward countries and between different racial societies.
But the fact that it is a conglomeration of often disparate and occasionally
incompatible elements, each with its own interests and points of view, means that
this influence can rarely be applied directly with any precision. Indeed, politically
it can sometimes be more of an embarrassment than an asset. Nevertheless, this
unique association of independent nations undoubtedly contributes to world
stability. We should lose much, both in terms of direct economic interest and of
wider political influence, if the Commonwealth association were to disintegrate.
Our exclusion from Europe would probably lead to such disintegration or, at any
rate, to a weakening of our leadership.

Source: PRO, CAB 134/1929, F.P. (60) 1, 24 February 1960

Document 4.11

*The following extracts from correspondence between Macmillan and Robert Menzies, the
Australian Prime Minister, in January–February 1962 focus on the changing character of
the Commonwealth in the aftermath of South Africa's expulsion from the Commonwealth in
1961. Menzies was disenchanted with the newly independent Commonwealth countries, while
Macmillan appeared to view diplomatic management of these countries as the latest version of
the white man's burden.*

A

As you know, I [Menzies] think that the action in relation to South Africa was
disastrous since it broke down the vital principle that in Commonwealth

meetings we do not discuss the internal policies of individual members . . . We already have a mass of new members of the Commonwealth, some of whom have no real independence except political, and quite a few of whom are strangers to our notions of self-government and civilised administration. Many of us have great anxiety about the Commonwealth and the disappearance of so many of its old characteristics . . . The plain English of it is that the new Commonwealth has nothing like the appeal for us that the old one had. It appears to have no instinct for either seeking or obtaining unity. The votes in the United Nations indicate that there are completely different approaches to world problems. The divisions have only to be carried to the Prime Ministers' Conference room in London, with the new lining up against the old, to bring the whole structure down. I know that we have prided ourselves on having a genius for compromise and on pursuing pragmatic policies. But we can of course follow these lines too far, and by extending the form of the Commonwealth ultimately deprive it of substance. When I ask myself what benefit we of the Crown Commonwealth derive from having a somewhat tenuous association with a cluster of Republics some of which like Ghana are more spiritually akin to Moscow than to London, I begin to despair.

Source: PRO, PREM 11/3644

B

If the analysis that I have tried to give of the shift of power in the world, a change in fifty years greater than has happened in many past periods in two or three hundred years, then what are we to do about the Commonwealth? [*sic*]. Of course it is not the same. How can it be? They who all felt that they belonged to the same intimate family might quarrel, as families do, but they *were* the family. They had the King or the Queen as the object of their personal loyalty, and the conferences were agreeable as well as valuable. There was no dispute; there was interesting discussion, an opportunity of meeting old friends, the charm of the Royal presence, and all on a scale that was like a small and pleasant house party. Now it is becoming a sort of miniature United Nations, with various groups; the Afro-Asian strength strongly organised, and the older members not quite knowing how to handle it . . .

But if we have to stay in the United Nations it is all the more necessary to keep the New Commonwealth together with all its frustrations and difficulties. I am bound to confess that I now shrink from any Commonwealth meeting because I know how troublesome it will be, whatever the subjects immediately under discussion . . . But I think the real reason for keeping the Commonwealth together is that I believe we *can* influence it, slowly and gradually, but effectively. Ghana is very dictatorial and almost crazy today; that makes Nigeria a little more moderate. And as the years pass I think it is possible with patience and putting up with a lot of trouble and insults from them that it will be worth doing. I think it is certainly worth doing while the Communist/Free World division really holds the front of the stage. Indeed in this situation we are forced to try.

Source: PRO, PREM 11/3644

Document 4.12

Shortly before the formal decision to apply for EEC membership, Macmillan and a number of senior ministers met on 18 June 1961 to settle British objectives in negotiations with the EEC. The following extract is taken from a record of this meeting dealing with the issue of Commonwealth trade.

Discussion showed general agreement that provisions which safeguarded Commonwealth interests during the transitional period only would not be acceptable to Commonwealth countries or to public opinion in the United Kingdom. It would be necessary to ensure permanent provision for at least some Commonwealth imports into the United Kingdom at broadly the present level of trade. There were many arguments we could adduce in support of this. Some Commonwealth countries, e.g. New Zealand, were largely dependent on the United Kingdom market. It would not be in the political or the economic interests of the free world to deprive New Zealand of that market and allow them to collapse. The Six themselves had recognised that their common agricultural policy must take account of the Community's external trade interests, and it would be in the interests of the industrialists of the Six that the earnings of their overseas customers were not unnecessarily depressed . . .

The crucial question would be the arrangements made for the Common Market period. What Commonwealth countries would secure as a result of the proposed review could not be left completely open. Our objective should be to secure transitional arrangements which maintained substantially the Commonwealth's present position, and an understanding that those arrangements would continue except to the extent that it could be shown that changes were essential if the common agricultural and other policies of the Community were not to be frustrated. Even so, any changes would have to be of a kind that did not cause serious damage to the essential interests of the Commonwealth countries.

Discussion then turned to the range of products for which we should seek to continue free entry into the United Kingdom. Although we would no doubt wish to start a negotiation on the basis of free entry in full on all commodities, we could not hope to secure this and would have to decide in the course of the negotiations which were the essential interests for which we were prepared to make a stand. In the case of manufactured goods for Canada, Australia and New Zealand, there seemed no chance of continuing unrestricted free entry. We should, however, try to safeguard the position of the under-developed Commonwealth in the United Kingdom market, and to obtain the best access we could for their exports to the rest of the Common Market. In the case of foodstuffs, our acceptance of the common agricultural policy would necessarily mean the end of unrestricted duty free entry for the Commonwealth. We would have to try to secure that Commonwealth countries had opportunities for exports (either to the United Kingdom market or to the Common Market as a whole) broadly comparable with those they enjoyed at present. The method would be changed, but the aim would be to see that producers' incomes in Commonwealth countries did not diminish . . .

The Meeting –

(1) Agreed that, in any negotiation to accede to the Treaty of Rome, the United
Kingdom should seek arrangements which –
  (i)   in the transitional period, would permit exports to the United Kingdom
        of Commonwealth goods of major significance (with the possible
        exception of manufactured goods from the developed countries of the
        Commonwealth) to be maintained at substantially the same level as at
        present;
  (ii) in the Common Market period, would continue unchanged except to
        the extent that it could be shown that changes (a) were necessary in
        order not to frustrate the purposes of the Community, and (b) would
        not damage the essential interests of Commonwealth countries.

Source: PRO, CAB 134/1821, E.Q. (61) 21

Document 4.13

*In the House of Commons debate following Macmillan's announcement of the decision to seek
terms of entry to the EEC, Harold Wilson, Shadow Chancellor of the Exchequer, emphasised
the importance of safeguarding Commonwealth interests in the forthcoming negotiations. His
populist regard for the Commonwealth was carried over into government in 1964 and also
figured in his renegotiation of the terms of entry in 1974–75.*

We are told that the Commonwealth will not suffer. Last night, the President of
the Board of Trade [Reginald Maudling] sought to console us – and, I suspect, to
console himself – with the rather meaningless piece of fluff which he held out
to us –

> 'We must not get into the frame of mind of choosing between the
> Commonwealth and Europe. It would be tragic if this country were forced
> to make that choice.'

Official Report, 2 August, 1961; H.C.Deb., vol. 645, col. 1604

I would like to be certain that we are not to have to make that choice. I would
like to be certain that the Government have not already made that choice in their
own minds.

Let us strip the problem of all these fair words and get down to realities. I want
to put this question, because the Government ought to put it in the negotiations.
In, say, seven years from now, on the assumption of going in, do we expect to see
as much Australian and Canadian wheat coming to Britain as today, or will it be
wholly or substantially replaced by French wheat? The French make no secret of
their aim to be the granary of Europe.

This question should be put, for it is the acid test of the words about the
Commonwealth. Shall we have as much of those commodities coming into
Britain seven years from now – as at present? Will there be the same amount of

New Zealand meat, or will it be replaced by French production? New Zealand butter? This question must be put and answered, because it is the only criterion by which these fair words about the Commonwealth can be judged . . .

The public Press has inevitably been filled with countless articles and letters for months past about all these problems, but for me – and, I think, for many others – the most pointed and moving of all of them was the letter written to the *Guardian* by my right hon. Friend the Member for Middlesborough, East (Mr. Marquand), about three weeks ago. My right hon. Friend was Secretary for Overseas Trade immediately after the war. I followed him in that capacity, and I know the kind of problems with which he was dealing. In the letter he referred to the difficult negotiations this country had in the immediate post-war years when we sought to get the food and raw materials that we needed with very little to offer in terms of the steel, chemicals and engineering goods that other countries so desperate [*sic*] needed and that we could ill-afford.

My right hon. Friend wrote:

> Then one day I sat down with the New Zealand delegation. I expected a bargaining session as difficult as any other. Instead the leader of the New Zealand delegation opened the proceedings in words I shall never forget 'We have not come to ask you "What can you give?" but simply "What do you need?" When you stood alone you preserved our freedom for us. Now tell us what butter, what meat, what grains you need, and – whatever the sacrifice may be for the New Zealand people – we will supply it.'

I [Wilson] submit to the House that we cannot consistently with the honour of this country take any action now that would betray friends such as those. All this and Europe, too – if you can get it. The President of the Board of Trade last night seemed to think that we can. I hope that he is right, but if there has to be a choice we are not entitled to sell our friends and kinsmen down the river for a problematical and marginal advantage in selling washing machines in Dusseldorf.

Source: *H.C.Deb.,* vol. 645, no. 162, cols. 1662, 1664–5, 3 August 1961

5 Knocking at the door: 1959–1963

The documents in this section relate to the first British application for membership of the EEC, the ensuing negotiations and the veto exercised by de Gaulle, the French President. In July 1961 the Macmillan government decided to begin exploratory talks with the Six about possible terms of entry. This decision followed an exhaustive policy debate. As the documentary extracts make clear, it was taken with great reluctance and only after the failure of all attempts to reach an accommodation with the EEC short of full membership.

During 1957–8 British policymakers were increasingly preoccupied with the potential threat to UK economic and political interests posed by the Community's early success. Efforts to counter this threat centred on gaining acceptance of the British proposal, based on Plan G, for the creation of a free trade area (FTA) in manufactured goods only which embraced the Six and all other members of the OEEC. From October 1957 this proposal was considered by a committee set up by the OEEC under the chairmanship of Maudling. Not unexpectedly, the sticking point was the UK's continuing insistence on the exclusion of agricultural products. Maudling himself was from the outset deeply pessimistic about the outcome. Although hopeful of obtaining some support from West Germany, Belgium and the Netherlands, he anticipated strenuous opposition from France, where protectionist-minded industrialists feared the impact of British competition. In this he proved to be correct. Moreover, initial French hostility to the British proposal intensified following the collapse of the Fourth Republic in May 1958 and de Gaulle's return to power after 12 years in the political wilderness. De Gaulle rightly took the view that the proposed FTA offered little to France since it would not apply to agriculture. He was therefore determined to block its implementation.

Prospects for acceptance of the British scheme were not improved by the rebuff suffered by de Gaulle in his attempt to reduce American and British influence within NATO at the same time as the deliberations of the Maudling committee were taking place. In September 1958 the French leader sent a memorandum to Eisenhower and Macmillan proposing replacement of the organisation's existing political and military command structure by a triple directorate consisting of the US, Britain and France (5.1). Their reaction was discouraging, and it has been suggested by some historians that Macmillan's negative attitude on this question made de Gaulle even less cooperative over Britain's FTA plan than he would otherwise have been.

As the FTA negotiations dragged on throughout 1958, the British became increasingly frustrated at their lack of progress. For a time Macmillan contemplated the adoption of a number of extreme measures in order to exert pressure on the French and Germans in particular. These included threats to withdraw from NATO and pull British troops out of West Germany (5.2). In the event, however, no such drastic steps were taken and the British government confined itself to somewhat crude diplomatic manoeuvring aimed at isolating the French. This tactic was completely ineffective: the French were in fact in a much stronger bargaining position than was generally appreciated in British official circles, especially after de Gaulle had won backing from Adenauer. In September 1958 ministers of the Six meeting in Venice agreed that any decisions on the FTA must be unanimous. This gave de Gaulle what amounted to a veto and he proceeded to use it. The *coup de grâce* was delivered by the French Minister of Information, Jacques Soustelle, at a press conference on 14 November 1958.

Following this major setback, the British government continued to negotiate with those members of the OEEC which had reacted favourably to its proposal. This led to the signature of the Stockholm Convention in July 1959, its ratification in November of the same year and the establishment of the European Free Trade Association (EFTA). The new organisation was made up of seven countries – Austria, Denmark, Norway, Portugal, Sweden, Switzerland and the UK – and its objective was strictly limited to the creation by 1970 of a free market in manufactured goods amongst its members.

For British policymakers, EFTA was never more than a second-rate option. A key motive for bringing it into existence was to strengthen London's hand in dealing with the EEC, the hope being that it might thereby be possible to negotiate a satisfactory agreement between the Six and the Seven. The central problem with this strategy was that the UK lacked any strong cards. Bonn continued to align itself with the French, while the Eisenhower administration was hostile to EFTA and wholly unreceptive to the idea of a 13-strong European economic bloc (5.3 and section 3). In the meantime, the infant EEC was making great strides both economically and politically and showing no interest whatever in a deal with EFTA. It is hardly surprising that Maudling, by now President of the Board of Trade, approached the task of negotiating with the Six in late 1959 without any expectation of success (5.3).

By early 1960 Europe was divided into two rival economic groupings, the EEC and EFTA. The UK found itself in the unfortunate position of belonging to the smaller, weaker and less dynamic of the two. Furthermore, because of a decision by the Six to accelerate tariff reductions between themselves from July onwards, British exporters would soon be at a major disadvantage in rapidly expanding markets which were of growing importance to them. The damaging economic and political implications of the situation were spelt out clearly in an influential report produced in May 1960 by an interdepartmental committee of senior civil servants which had been instructed to review Britain's stance towards the EEC (5.4). The committee – chaired by Sir Frank Lee, the Joint Permanent Secretary at the Treasury – advanced a strong case for British membership, not least as a way of promoting the political cohesion of the West and preventing Britain being superseded by the EEC as the main partner of the US.

Despite the Lee committee's call for an end to drift, the government continued to equivocate. Members of the Cabinet were equally impressed by the benefits and costs of joining the EEC (5.5). On the one hand, it was suggested that membership would provide the opportunity to avoid tariff discrimination by the Six, access to a large, prosperous market and an enhancement of British political influence throughout the world. On the other, it was recognised that there was bound to be an adverse effect on commercial and other ties with the Commonwealth, as well as the need to adjust to a radically different agricultural system which brought higher food prices. The competing arguments were seen to be finely balanced. The result was a paralysis of political will and a tendency to take refuge in the belief that it might somehow be possible to obtain terms of entry entailing minimal sacrifice for the UK.

Macmillan himself was not immune from this form of wishful thinking. By the end of 1960, however, he had finally decided that British membership of the EEC was essential in the longer-term interests both of the UK and of the West as a whole. His thinking – set out at length in a memorandum called 'The Grand Design' (29 December 1960 – 3 January 1961) – was influenced by a combination of economic and political considerations (5.6). Macmillan believed that exclusion from such a strong economic bloc as the EEC would be extremely damaging for the UK. Entry would offer British industry not only a much bigger market, but also the benefit of exposure to invigorating competition. Politically, membership of the EEC was seen as a way of bolstering Britain's declining international position. In addition, Macmillan was anxious to end the economic division between the Six and Seven which he saw as a source of grave weakness in an embattled Western alliance facing intense Soviet pressure over Berlin.

On 31 July 1961 Macmillan announced in the Commons that preliminary talks were to be held with the Six on British entry to the EEC. His statement was cautious and unenthusiastic, and it is generally agreed that this was deliberate so as to avoid alarming a public which was predominantly lukewarm or hostile to membership. Macmillan's contribution to the parliamentary debate that followed was similarly low key. He was concerned among other things to calm fears about loss of sovereignty. This was a potentially explosive issue and in November 1960 Edward Heath, the Foreign Office minister with special responsibility for European affairs, had sought the opinion of the Lord Chancellor, Lord Kilmuir, on the extent to which signature of the EEC's founding treaties might mean a loss of sovereignty (5.7A). Kilmuir's view was that there would be a substantial surrender of sovereignty (5.7B). He advised strongly against any attempt to gloss over the fact. Yet that was precisely what Macmillan did (5.8).

Negotiations with the Six – conducted in Brussels – were complex and protracted. They began with a formal opening statement by the principal British negotiator, Heath, on 10 October 1961 and lasted until the French veto in January 1963. Macmillan always expected formidable difficulties with de Gaulle, but overestimated the assistance that might be obtained from the 'friendly five' in overcoming his obstructionism. Adenauer proved particularly disappointing. What Macmillan failed to grasp was the paramount importance that the West German Chancellor attached to the Bonn–Paris axis. From 1958 there was a steady improvement in relations between France and West Germany, culminating in the signing of the Treaty of Friendship and Cooperation in Paris in January 1963. It was inconceivable that Adenauer would jeopardise this process of reconciliation by putting pressure on de Gaulle on the UK's behalf, particularly since he shared the other's scepticism about the British commitment to joining the EEC (5.9).

From the British standpoint, the negotiations were complicated by undertakings given to EFTA partners and by the fact that the EEC was evolving during the bargaining. Further complications arose from a policy shift by the Labour Opposition. Hugh Gaitskell, Labour's leader, was initially non-committal: his attitude was that everything depended on the terms. This stance was dictated largely by a desire to maintain unity in a party badly split on the EEC issue and still recovering from bitter rows over nationalisation and unilateral nuclear disarmament. But it also reflected Gaitskell's essential agnosticism on the question of entry (5.10). During 1962 Gaitskell became increasingly critical of the way the negotiations were going and in a warmly applauded speech to Labour's annual conference at Brighton on 3 October he laid down five conditions for British membership which were manifestly unattainable. One immediate consequence of this was to undermine Macmillan's claim that he spoke for the whole nation in seeking admission to the EEC.

Of the various issues addressed during the Brussels negotiations those that proved most intractable were British commercial relations with the Commonwealth and domestic agriculture. Macmillan was convinced that the only serious obstacle to resolving these and all other problems was the unyielding attitude of de Gaulle. He therefore gave considerable thought as to how that might be changed. One approach that he tried was to capitalise on the French President's intense disappointment over the failure in the spring of 1962 of his efforts (through the Fouchet Plan) to foster closer political union – on a strictly intergovernmental basis – between the Six. Macmillan sought to persuade de Gaulle that the admission of Britain to the EEC would serve to lessen the smaller states' concerns about domination by France and Germany and thus facilitate progress in the political field (5.12). De Gaulle was unimpressed.

Other ideas were equally unproductive. Long before the beginning of negotiations with the EEC, Macmillan had examined the possibility of a bargain with de Gaulle by which the UK would gain entry to the EEC in return for concessions over nuclear weapons and reform of NATO's command structure (5.6 and section 3). In the event, however, such an approach proved impracticable. Shortly before his crucial meeting with de Gaulle at Rambouillet (15–16 December 1962), Macmillan canvassed the views of senior advisers on the feasibility of Anglo-French cooperation in the nuclear field. Their unanimous conclusion was that they were 'unable to see any fruitful possibilities', mainly because of the French determination to have a completely independent nuclear deterrent (5.13). Any deal with the French was, in any case, wholly dependent on prior approval from the Americans, something which was completely out of the question. Opposition from Washington, and especially from the Pentagon, was equally fatal to any concessions over the organisation of NATO.

There has been much speculation over what was said at Rambouillet, with claims being made that de Gaulle was misled into thinking he had received an offer on nuclear cooperation (see section 3). The available evidence does not permit a definite conclusion. The related debate over the connection between the Nassau agreement on Polaris and de Gaulle's veto of Britain's application for admission to the EEC has likewise remained inconclusive. Thus it is still a matter of conjecture whether Nassau exerted a decisive influence on de Gaulle by convincing him that Britain would act as a 'Trojan horse' within the EEC or whether it merely provided a pretext for a decision already taken on other grounds. At his celebrated press conference of 14 January 1963, de Gaulle specifically mentioned Nassau. But he also offered a lengthy list of other reasons for his opposition to British entry (5.15). What these boiled down to was the assertion that Britain was not yet ready to join the EEC because its distinctive history, character and economic structure made it profoundly different from all existing members. Adjustment – especially to the common agricultural policy (CAP) agreed by the Six in January 1962 – would impose unacceptable sacrifices on the British themselves. Besides, if Britain did become a member it would be followed by many other states and the result would be wholesale undesirable changes in the nature of the EEC.

De Gaulle's veto came as a severe shock to Britain and to France's partners. Echoing his reproach at Rambouillet (5.14), Macmillan complained that de Gaulle had failed to make clear until the very end that he had fundamental objections to British membership. Yet there was no shortage of warnings: as early as May 1962 Heath provided Macmillan with an accurate appraisal of the deep-seated nature of de Gaulle's objections (5.11). What is striking, indeed, is the sheer consistency of de Gaulle's position. The views which he expounded on 14 January 1963 were essentially those that he had repeatedly set out in his various meetings with Macmillan during 1961–62. At Rambouillet, Macmillan was dismayed by de Gaulle's analysis of the basic difficulties over agriculture and other matters which were preventing agreement at Brussels (5.14). De Gaulle was saying nothing new. Perhaps for the first time, however, Macmillan realised that he was not engaged in a game of diplomatic bluff, but was in earnest.

Document 5.1

One of de Gaulle's grievances against the 'Anglo-Saxons' was that they exerted too much control over NATO. In September 1958 he sent a memorandum to Eisenhower and Macmillan proposing a reform of NATO's command and political structure which would give more influence to France.

Recent events in the Middle East and in the Straits of Formosa have gone to show that the present organization of the Western Alliance no longer answers the essential security requirements of the free world as a whole. Risks are shared in common without there being any corresponding indispensable cooperation over decisions taken and responsibilities incurred . . .

1. The Atlantic Alliance was conceived and functions in the context of a hypothetical area of operations which no longer corresponds to political and strategic realities . . .
2. France cannot then consider that N.A.T.O. in its present form meets the security requirements of the free world, and more particularly, French requirements. It seems necessary to France that, at the world-wide level, a political and strategic organization should be instituted comprising: the United States, Great Britain and France. The functions of this organization would be on the one hand to take common decisions in political questions affecting world security and on the other to establish and, where need arises, to apply strategic plans for action, with particular reference to the use of nuclear weapons. It would then be possible to consider and to organize whatever theatres of operations might be necessary . . .
3. The French Government regards such an organization for security as indispensable. Henceforth the whole development of their present participation in N.A.T.O. is predicated on this . . .
4. The French Government suggest that the questions raised in this Note should form the subject of the earliest possible consultations between the United States, Great Britain and France . . .

Source: PRO, PREM 11/3002, memorandum, 17 September 1958

Document 5.2

Frustration at the lack of progress over negotiations for an FTA in industrial goods during 1958 prompted Macmillan to contemplate the adoption of a tougher approach towards the Six. In the following extract he seeks the views of the Foreign Secretary, Selwyn Lloyd, on a number of possible measures designed to exert pressure on the French and Germans in particular.

I think sometimes our difficulties with our friends abroad result from our natural good manners and reticence. We are apt not to press our points too strongly in the early stages of a negotiation, and then when a crisis arises and we have to take a definite position we are accused of perfidy. I feel we ought to make it quite clear to our European friends that if Little Europe is formed without a parallel development of a Free Trade Area we shall have to reconsider the whole of our political and economic attitude towards Europe. I doubt if we could remain in NATO. We should certainly put on highly protective tariffs and quotas to counteract what Little Europe was doing to us. In other words, we should not allow ourselves to be destroyed little by little. We would fight with every weapon in our armoury. We would take our troops out of Europe. We would withdraw from NATO. We would adopt a policy of isolationism. We would surround ourselves with rockets and we would say to the Germans and the French and all the rest of them: 'Look after yourselves with your own forces. Look after yourselves when the Russians overrun your countries.'

I would be inclined to make this position quite clear both to de Gaulle and to Adenauer, so that they may be under no illusion. What do you say?

Source: PRO, PREM 11/2315,
Macmillan to the Foreign Secretary, 24 June 1958

Document 5.3

After the failure of the FTA negotiations in November 1958 Britain took the lead in forming the European Free Trade Association (EFTA) the following year. One of the main objectives here was to improve the chances of an accommodation with the Six. From the outset, however, Maudling, by now President of the Board of Trade, thought there was little hope of success, principally because of the hostile attitude of the French.

11.   What is the position now? We have said that the E.F.T.A. is to be the foundation of our end of the bridge to the Six. We are pressed by the Swiss, Austrians and Danes to ask for urgent negotiations with the Six. Clearly, in the absence of negotiations, we shall have increasing difficulty in keeping our flock together.

12.   It would be folly to commence another negotiation unless we can be reasonably confident of success. Yet our experience has shown that any attempt to negotiate an economic agreement in the absence of unanimous political intention is bound to fail . . .

15.   The only countries that matter in this are France and America . . .

17.   Throughout the original negotiations the Americans were quite unhelpful. They do not understand the problems of European economic relations and they listen to few of their representatives in Europe. The formation of the Six meant discrimination against them, but they were prepared to swallow it because of the vision of the United States of Europe built in their own image. The E.F.T.A. they dislike because it has not got these federalist overtones. They have, however, accepted it, but what they will dislike will be the union of the Seven and the Six. This means a much wider European bloc discriminating against them, and the possibility is now arising just at a time when American opinion is suffering from panic about the balance of payments and an almost pathological belief that every country is against them . . .

18.   It appears therefore, that we have neither strong allies nor compelling arguments. The Germans have been a broken reed, and, though the Seven, as it develops, will put increasing pressure on German industry, I do not think we can rely on this being reflected in German government policy. The Americans, in so far as they take any line, are likely to be against us. The Commonwealth is bewildered and suspicious. The French are sitting pretty and they know it.

19.   This is, I know, a gloomy picture, but I believe it to be a true one. I am convinced our major objective remains a system of trade in Europe where all tariffs and other forms of discrimination are removed, but it is not easy to see how we will achieve it. We must

(i)   concentrate on ratifying the E.F.T.A. and strengthening our allies;
(ii) try to persuade the United States that, whatever the economic arguments, a permanent division of Europe and the disruption of the O.E.E.C. must be a political disaster for them too;
(iii) deal direct with the French because they hold all the cards.

Source: PRO, PREM 11/2678, Maudling to Prime Minister,
27 November 1959

Document 5.4

The findings of the Lee Report were influential in persuading Macmillan and his colleagues that the practical alternatives to joining the EEC were unacccceptable.

I

THE IMMEDIATE OUTLOOK

2.   It is possible that the failure of the [Paris] Summit [of May 1960] may bring about a radical change of attitude in the months ahead. But at the moment it is not possible to say with confidence that this will happen.

3.   It therefore still seems likely that after the 1st July next the Six and Seven will go their separate ways at least for the time being. Each will discriminate against each other and against the rest of the world . . .

4.   This division in Europe . . . may well continue for a considerable time – say eighteen months or two years at least.

II

IMPLICATIONS FOR THE UNITED KINGDOM

5.   The economic divisions of Europe will confront the United Kingdom with a most serious situation. There are significant political dangers which Ministers have emphasised in recent months . . . economic divisions may weaken the political cohesion of the West at a time when a common Western front is

more than ever necessary. If, as seems to be the intention, the policy of the Six is to press forward with economic integration, impetus will be given to political integration. The Community may well emerge as a Power comparable in size and influence to the United States and the U.S.S.R. The pull of this new power bloc would be bound to dilute our influence with the rest of the world, including the Commonwealth. We should find ourselves replaced as the second member of the North Atlantic Alliance and our relative influence with the United States in all fields would diminish . . .

6.   From the economic standpoint the immediate and overt effects will not be disastrous . . . But even in the short term the fact that our exports will be increasingly at a disadvantage in the markets of the Six (where the rate of economic growth has been high and is likely to continue so) will be a serious matter at a time when our balance of payments position once more gives cause for concern.

7.   In the longer term . . . the situation will be still more serious, for the following reasons:-

(a) So far as direct trade is concerned, much may depend on the levels of the common external tariffs of the Six. If these are relatively low, the United Kingdom should be able to continue to export freely to the Six . . . not-withstanding the tariff barrier. But, a great part of the success of the Six will derive from the dynamic of the new large common market and the scale on which their industries can think and plan. To share in that dynamic requires us to be 'in'. To be 'out', even with a low tariff, is to be cut off from it. In addition, given the strength which will come from their large internal market, the industries of the Six may well develop into most formidable competitors in third markets . . .

(b) The Seven is not a despicable grouping in economic terms . . . But it is doubtful whether a heterogeneous and scattered grouping – brought together by ties of common funk, rather than by any deeper purpose or by geographical contiguity – can develop a real cohesion or even continuity. In any event, the basic factors of population and economic resources must mean that the Seven is bound to be a weaker economic group than the Six. This is likely to have a profound psychological effect on United Kingdom industry. We have already been warned privately that . . . there is great uneasiness, amounting almost to dismay, amongst leading industrialists at the prospect of finding ourselves yoked indefinitely with the Seven and 'cut off' by a tariff barrier from the markets of the Six. The prospect is seen of three powerful economic groupings – the U.S.A., the U.S.S.R., the Six – able to develop internal markets of scale and therefore strong and competitive industries based on such markets – whereas the United Kingdom will have a preferential position only in the Seven and in the Commonwealth markets (where we face tariff barriers in any event and where our position is likely to weaken rather than grow stronger).

(c) 'Nothing succeeds like success'. There is already a belief that the Six are going to come out on top in Europe. This will almost certainly lead to a diversion of United States investment . . . to the Six, and to a move by United Kingdom industrialists themselves to invest in the countries of the Six. And the psychological feeling that the United Kingdom is bound to 'lose out' in the countries of the Six can have a serious effect on the efforts of our exporters to hold their position in these markets . . .

(d) In these circumstances, it is doubtful if we could hold E.F.T.A. together. Some members – notably Austria and Switzerland – depend so heavily on their trade with the Six that it is doubtful whether, if they could no longer see the prospect of a Single Market, they could avoid making an accommodation with the Six on the best terms they could negotiate unilaterally.

8.   The conclusion is inescapable – that it cannot be compatible with either our political or our economic interests to let the situation drift on indefinitely on the basis of a divided Europe, with the United Kingdom linked to the weaker group. We must therefore seek a wider economic grouping which should at least comprise a single European market . . . and we must be prepared to examine what this is likely to mean in the way of positive 'contributions' on the part of the United Kingdom itself.

Source: PRO, CAB 134/1852, E.Q. (60) 27,
The Six and the Seven: Long Term Arrangements, 25 May 1960

Document 5.5

Despite the recommendations of the Lee committee, the Cabinet remained uncertain about what course to take. This was reflected in its confused and inconclusive discussion of the committee's report on 13 July 1960.

The Chancellor of the Exchequer [Heathcoat Amory] recalled that the Prime Minister had previously said that the Government would eventually have to choose between (i) initiating a dramatic change of direction in our domestic, commercial and international policies and (ii) maintaining our traditional policy of remaining aloof from Europe politically, while doing all we could to mitigate the economic dangers of a divided Europe. The report before the Cabinet clarified the issues which would arise in making that choice. A decision to join the Community would be a political act with economic consequences, rather than an economic act with political consequences. The arguments for joining the Community were strong. If we remained outside it, our political influence in Europe and the rest of the world was likely to decline. By joining it we should not only avoid tariff discrimination by its members against our exports, but should be able to participate in a large and rapidly expanding market. However, the arguments against United Kingdom membership were also very strong. We should be surrendering independent control of our commercial policies to a European *bloc*, when our trading interests were world-wide. We should also have to abandon our special relationship with the Commonwealth, including free entry for

Commonwealth goods and the preferential system, and should instead be obliged to discriminate actively against the Commonwealth. We should have to devise agriculture and horticulture [*sic*] new policies under which the burden of support for the farmers would be transferred from the Exchequer to the consumer, thus increasing the cost of living. Finally, we should sacrifice our loyalties and obligations to the members of the European Free Trade Association (E.F.T.A.), some of which would find it impossible to join the E.E.C. as full members . . .

The Chancellor said that his personal opinion was that we should be ready to join the Community if we could do so without substantially impairing our relations with the Commonwealth . . .

The President of the Board of Trade [Maudling] said that . . . We should find it difficult to renounce our national control of policy, especially in respect of agricultural and commercial policies and our special relationship with the Commonwealth. On the other hand, the development of the Community was a serious economic threat to the United Kingdom, as regards both our trade to Europe and our competitive position in the world. As our economic influence declined in comparison with that of the Community, we should find that the United States and other countries would increasingly attach more weight to the views and interests of the Community . . .

The Government should not allow themselves to be pushed into hasty decisions by the campaign in some parts of the Press. There was need of an authoritative statement in which the Government would make it clear that this was not a suitable moment for negotiations with the Community and, while expressing readiness to work towards a single trading system in Europe, would emphasise the fundamental objections to United Kingdom membership of the Community.

The Foreign Secretary [Selwyn Lloyd] said that from the point of view of our future political influence in the Atlantic Community there were strong arguments for joining the E.E.C. We might hope eventually to achieve leadership of it and we could use our influence in it to keep West Germany independent of the Soviet *bloc*. On the other hand our wider interests and influence throughout the world depended to a considerable extent on our links with the Commonwealth; and if, by joining the E.E.C., we did fatal damage to these we should lose our power to exert our influence on a world scale. An association short of membership would not secure for us enough influence in the Community to make the price worth paying. We should therefore consider full membership, but seek special terms to meet our fundamental interests and those of the Commonwealth . . .

Discussion showed that the Cabinet fully agreed that the United Kingdom could not accept full membership of the Community on the terms of the Treaty of Rome . . .

In further discussion it was suggested that the advantages of joining the Community and the dangers of staying outside had been exaggerated. Many other parts of the world besides Europe were expanding rapidly; and as a country with world-wide trading connexions we were in a good position to exploit these wider opportunities. To become a member of the E.E.C. could be positively harmful to our position in the world, since some of the political and economic policies of the E.E.C. countries did not inspire respect. France and Belgium had colonial difficulties, Germany was following an ungenerous credit policy, and the E.E.C. countries generally were seeking to expand their production of primary commodities at the expense of the less-developed countries. In trying to negotiate a settlement with the Community we might run grave risks of impairing the unity of the Commonwealth and undermining the confidence of its other members in the United Kingdom, with serious financial and economic consequences to ourselves.

On the other hand, over a period of years our relationship with the Commonwealth would in any case change, as would other factors in this problem, including the agricultural difficulties. It would therefore be necessary to adapt our policies to new situations.

Source: PRO, CAB 128/34, CC 41 (60), 36th Conclusions, 14 July 1960

Document 5.6

Macmillan himself came to a decision on the advisability of seeking terms of entry during the Christmas/New Year holiday period in 1960–61. In a memorandum prepared at that time he set out the difficulties the UK would face if it remained outside the EEC. He also examined the possibility of winning French consent to British membership.

(d)   E.E.C. and E.F.T.A. (Sixes and Sevens)

13.   It is now pretty clear that an accommodation *could* be reached – which would at any rate reduce, and perhaps altogether eliminate the economic split in Western Europe.

It is equally pretty clear that it *will not* be reached, as things are going now . . .

The Germans, Italians, etc. would agree to one of the schemes now under tentative discussion. The French will not. The French means de Gaulle.

Yet, by a strange paradox, if de Gaulle were to disappear, an accommodation might be still more difficult. Whatever happened in France, there would be great confusion, perhaps even disintegration. French Federalist opinion would be strengthened (Monnet and all that) and timid Frenchmen would seek refuge in a European Federalist State. Difficult as de Gaulle is, his view of the proper *political* structure (Confederation not Federation) is really nearer to ours. If he wished us to join the political institutions it would be easier for us if they took the form which he favours.

If a settlement is not reached in the near future, the split will get worse and will become (again, from the point of view of our overriding aim – the joint struggle against Communism) dangerous and perhaps fatal. The economic consequences for Britain may be grave. However bold a face it may suit us to put on the situation, exclusion from the strongest economic group in the civilised world *must* injure us.

It must also injure the world, because economic exclusion must in the long run force us into military isolationism and political neutralism.

The triumph of extreme Federalists in Europe means, sooner or later, the triumph of the unilateralists and neutralists here.

We ought therefore to make a supreme effort to reach a settlement while de Gaulle is in power in France ...

25.　What do we want?

What does de Gaulle want?

How far can we agree to help him if he will help us?

(a) We want Sixes and Sevens settled

We must make it clear to the French that we mean what we say – that if it is not settled, Europe will be divided politically and militarily.

We should have to denounce our liabilities under W.E.U. ...

It is obvious that the conditions which led to W.E.U. have disappeared, and the basis on which we undertook those obligations has radically changed. *Then* France did *not* discriminate against British trade. *Then* France wanted British support against the danger of a renascent Germany. The first condition has gone. We assume the French are happy about the second. Or *are* they? The French must judge.

(b) De Gaulle wants the recognition of France as a Great Power, at least equal to Britain.

He suspects the Anglo-Saxons.

So long as the 'Anglo-Saxon domination' continues, he will not treat Britain as European, but as American – a junior partner of America, but a partner ...

De Gaulle feels that ... the vital decisions [in NATO] are made – or not made – between the American and British Governments in Washington. De Gaulle feels that he is *excluded* from this club or partnership. Hence –

(a)　his persistent efforts towards 'Tripartitism' – which the Americans and the British have accepted 'en principe' to a limited extent, but have never really operated;

(b)　his determination – whatever the cost – that France should become a *nuclear* power. For it is France's *exclusion* from the nuclear club that is the measure of France's inferior status. It is particularly galling for him that Britain should have an independent nuclear capacity; he accepts that the United States is in a different category.

26.　Can what *we* want and what *de Gaulle* wants be brought into harmony? Is there a basis for a deal?

Britain wants to join the European concern; France wants to join the Anglo-American concern. Can terms be arranged? Would de Gaulle be ready to withdraw the French veto which alone prevents a settlement of Europe's economic problem in return for politico-military arrangements which he would accept as a recognition of France as a first-class world power? What he would want is something on Tripartism and something on the nuclear. Are there offers which we could afford to make? And could we persuade the Americans to agree?

Source: PRO, PREM 11/3325, memorandum by the Prime Minister, 29 December 1960 to 3 January 1961 ('The Grand Design')

Document 5.7

The possible loss of sovereignty from British accession to the EEC was a highly sensitive issue for the Macmillan government. Edward Heath, the Foreign Office minister with special responsibility for European affairs, sought an opinion on the matter from the Lord Chancellor, Lord Kilmuir (A). In his reply, Kilmuir indicated that there would inevitably be a considerable surrender of sovereignty (B).

A

One of the aspects of our relations with Europe which continues to trouble all of us a good deal is that of sovereignty and the extent to which our ability to act independently would be compromised by our entry into some new organisation. In the past the arguments against our participation in supranational institutions have been perhaps the most potent in causing us to decide against joining the European Coal and Steel Community and in withdrawing from the conversations which led eventually to the drafting of the Treaty of Rome. As things now stand it seems probable that a solution of our relations with Europe cannot be achieved without some political act which continental opinion can take as an earnest of our determination to play a full part in and with Europe . . .

I am myself inclined to feel that we have allowed ourselves to be over-impressed by supranationality, and that in the modern world, if from other points of view, political and economic, it should prove desirable to accept such further limitations of sovereignty as would follow from the Treaty of Rome, we could do so without danger to the essential character of our independence and without prejudice to our vital interests. This is, however, a question of the broadest constitutional importance and I am now seeking your opinion as to the compatibility of the Treaty of Rome and the institutions set up under it with the supremacy of parliament and the essential independence of our own institutions and system of law . . .

I think . . . that the strict legal interpretation of the provisions of the Treaty of Rome can be off-set to some extent by the consequences of our accession to the Treaty. If we participated fully in the organs of the European Economic Community, we could exert a strong influence on the formulation of policy and on the decisions taken. Under the system of qualified majority voting, we would not alone be able to prevent unpalatable decisions being taken against our wishes . . . But it is reasonable to assume that, if we joined the European Economic

Community, Norway and Denmark would do the same and that, if the number of votes allocated to us and the number required for a qualified majority vote remained proportionately the same, we would jointly (and assuming that our interests remain identical) be able to exercise a veto.

I am not suggesting that this is a factor which should weigh heavily with us in deciding whether to accede to the Treaty of Rome. We would clearly have to accept the basic philosophy of the Six and to use any veto at our disposal only in very exceptional circumstances. Nevertheless, in cases where provision is made for a qualified majority vote, it could serve to extricate us from a position which might otherwise have serious constitutional or juridical consequences in the United Kingdom.

Similarly, we must work on the assumption that denunciation of the Treaty in its totality would be politically disastrous and that our accession would be an irrevocable step towards closer integration with Western Europe.

Source: PRO, FO 371/150369, Heath to Kilmuir, 30 November 1960

B

Adherence to the Treaty of Rome would, in my opinion, affect our sovereignty in three ways:-

(a) Parliament would be required to surrender some of its functions to the organs of the Community;
(b) The Crown would be called on to transfer part of its treaty-making power to those organs;
(c) Our courts of law would sacrifice some degree of independence by becoming subordinate in certain respects to the European Court of Justice ...

Of these three objections, the first two are by far the more important. I must emphasise that in my view the surrenders of sovereignty involved are serious ones and I think that, as a matter of practical politics, it will not be easy to persuade Parliament or the public to accept them. I am sure that it would be a great mistake to under-estimate the force of the objections to them. But these objections ought to be brought out into the open now because, if we attempt to gloss them over at this stage, those who are opposed to the whole idea of our joining the Community will certainly seize on them with more damaging effect later on. Having said this, I would emphasise once again that, although these constitutional considerations must be given their full weight when we come to balance the arguments on either side, I do not for one second wish to convey the impression that they must necessarily tip the scale. In the long run we shall have to decide whether economic factors require us to make some sacrifice of sovereignty: my concern is that we should see exactly what it is that we are being called upon to sacrifice, and how serious our loss would be.

Source: PRO, FO 371/150369, Kilmuir to Heath, 14 December 1960

Document 5.8

It is a truism that Macmillan played the Commons announcement of his intention to seek terms of entry (31 July 1961) as a low-key affair. In the ensuing debate he was at pains to ease fears of a loss of sovereignty. The line which he took was not in keeping with that recommended by Kilmuir.

I must remind the House that the E.E.C. is an economic community, not a defensive alliance, or a foreign policy community, or a cultural community. It is an economic community, and the region where collective decisions are taken is related to the spheres covered by the Treaty, economic tariffs, markets and all the rest. Of course, every treaty limits a nation's freedom of action to some extent . . .

A number of years have passed since the movement began which culminated in the Treaty of Rome and I am bound to say that I do not see any signs of the members of the Community losing their national identity because they have delegated a measure of their sovereignty. This problem of sovereignty, to which we must, of course, attach the highest importance is, in the end, perhaps a matter of degree. I fully accept that there are some forces in Europe which would like a genuine federalist system. There are many of my colleagues on both sides of the House who have seen this at Strasbourg and other gatherings. They would like Europe to turn itself into a sort of United States, but I believe this to be a completely false analogy.

The United States of America was originally born out of colonists with only a few generations of history behind them. They were broadly the same national origins and spoke the same language. Europe is too old, too diverse in tradition, language and history to find itself united by such means. Although the federalist movement exists in Europe it is not one favoured by the leading figures and certainly not by the leading Governments of Europe today. Certainly not by the French Government.

The alternative concept, the only practical concept, would be a confederation, a commonwealth if hon. Members would like to call it that – what I think General de Gaulle has called *Europe des Patries* – which would retain the great traditions and the pride of individual nations while working together in clearly defined spheres for their common interest. This seems to me a concept more in tune with the national traditions of European countries and, in particular, of our own. It is one with which we could associate willingly and wholeheartedly. At any rate, there is nothing in the Treaty of Rome which commits the members of E.E.C. . . . to any kind of federalist solution, nor could such a system be imposed on member countries.

Here again, unless we are in the negotiations, unless we can bring our influence to bear, we shall not be able to play our part in deciding the future structure of Europe. It may be . . . that we shall find that our essential needs cannot be met, but if they can I do not feel that there is anything on the constitutional side of which we need be in fear and which cannot be resolved to our satisfaction.

Source: H.C.Deb., vol. 644, cols. 1490–1, 2 August 1961

Document 5.9

Indications that the British intended to apply for membership of the EEC were received with deep scepticism by some leaders of the Six, including the West German Chancellor, Konrad Adenauer. Adenauer's lack of faith in British intentions comes out clearly in the following report of a conversation between him and George Ball, the US Under-Secretary of State for Economic Affairs.

I [Ball] mentioned that we were watching with keen interest evolution [of] Brit opinion towards possible adherence European Common Market. I said I had seen Heath in London and gained impression from him and others that Brit Govt was in process of making decision. Chancellor [Adenauer] then asked when did I expect Brit Govt to make up its mind. I replied that presumably they would have to educate Brit opinion first and that Heath had said in reference to his speech in the House of Commons, 'This is the beginning of the great debate'. I further said that Heath had indicated that this represented a major decision for Britain since it meant reversal of several hundred years of policy towards the continent.

The Chancellor responded vigorously, pointing his finger at me and saying, 'Mr Ball, don't you know that this is just what Churchill and Eden both told me. They also said that they were reversing hundreds of years of policy towards Europe. Then they set up the Western European Union which has been in a state of rigor mortis ever since'. The Chancellor continued, 'No, Macmillan will never join in any serious move towards European unity. Heath might wish to and several of the other Ministers. Selwyn Lloyd I believe has been converted. But the Macmillan govt will never make the necessary decision'. He said he had just discussed the matter with de Gaulle and that he and de Gaulle fully agreed on this view. That was why they had decided to move quickly to extend the political character of [the] Community. They had decided to have political consultation by heads of State of the Six four times a year and were going to move towards political unity as fast as possible.

Chancellor said that he and de Gaulle were convinced that some day Britain would join Europe but not while the Macmillan govt was in power. Macmillan would never make the necessary decision and he and de Gaulle had decided that they could not wait for the British . . .

The vehemence with which the Chancellor indicated his and de Gaulle's extreme skepticism regarding Macmillan's intentions clearly suggests that de Gaulle is not likely to view a British proposal to join the Common Market with hospitality.

Source: *FRUS*, 1964–8, Vol. XIII, no. 10, Telegram from the Mission at Geneva to the Department of State, 24 May 1961

Document 5.10

The initial reaction of the Labour Opposition leader Hugh Gaitskell towards the decision to seek terms of entry to the EEC was non-committal. This stance was dictated in part by the need to avoid deep splits in his party.

There are those who see the problem of whether or not we should enter the Common Market as a clear-cut and simple one. They have no doubts. Some are passionately in favour of our entry and others are equally passionately against, unconditionally in both instances . . .

Those who are for are convinced that economically to enter the Common Market will provide our salvation, that we shall be miraculously caught up in the dynamic economy of Europe, that there will be perhaps some transitional difficulties, but that these will not be on a great scale and that when they are over we shall by this means be on the high road to permanent prosperity.

As for our political relationships, they take the view that either we shall retain our political independence in full and our markets with the Commonwealth or – if they happen to be European federalists – they would say that while federal Europe is inevitable we must be part of it and even lead it. Equally, of course, they paint in the gloomiest terms the prospects for us if we do not enter the Common Market, that we are faced then with continued economic decline, that we shall become politically less and less influential in the world. They imply that the Commonwealth, if we really think about it, has no real future and that our very impotence *vis-à-vis* Europe will contribute to the decline and decay of the Commonwealth.

At the other extreme there are those who hold with equal passion the opposite view. They reserve their gloom for the picture when we enter the Common Market. The economic growth, they say, is a mirage and, anyhow, if there is dynamism in that economy we shall not be able to compete with it. Our foreign policy, they say, will be dictated by others, our ancient Parliament deprived of its authority and our Commonwealth destroyed by a foolish and fatal decision. For them, equally, the picture, if we stay out, is totally different. It is bright with promise, Commonwealth markets can and will expand while Europe languishes and squabbles. We shall go ahead economically and politically while our influence, spanning five Continents, will continue to be strong and beneficent.

These are the two extreme points of view and both of them, I know, are held by some hon. Members in the House, but I think that a large majority of us in both parties . . . suspect that both extremes are wrong, that the issue is not as clear-cut and that a more careful analysis will show that it is much more a matter of balance.

For example, the economic case for going in is said to be very powerful because of the great expansion that has taken place in the Common Market in recent years . . . but for my part I do not hold the view that this is overwhelmingly due to the Common Market. I think that there are, to any objective observer, other influences at work. For instance, in the case of France – let us face it – the devaluation of the franc was a powerful aid to the expansion of its exports and industry. In the case of Germany . . . emigration from the east has helped West Germany to move faster.

Certainly, not every country in the Common Market has been so prosperous and dynamic. Belgium is mostly at the bottom of these league tables, even below us in production . . .

On the other side, I do not think that the political consequences which some fear from our entry into the Common Market are as dangerous or profound as they are sometimes made out to be. I agree with the Prime Minister in that I do not think that we are necessarily bound for federalism in Europe. Equally, I think that one can exaggerate all too easily the picture of the Commonwealth prospect as apart from Europe in economic terms. Above all, those of us who take this intermediate position, and who cannot accept either extreme, say that before we make our minds up we must know the conditions.

Source: *H.C.Deb.*, vol. 644, cols. 1494–6, 2 August 1961

Document 5.11

On 19 May 1962 Heath, Macmillan and Home discussed the current state of negotiations with the Six. Attention focused on de Gaulle's unhelpful attitude and Heath expressed the view that the French leader's objections to UK membership of the EEC were of a fundamental nature.

3. The nature of President de Gaulle's objections to British entry into the Community

The Lord Privy Seal suggested that the following were the main points in President de Gaulle's mind:-

(a) In public and indeed in private conversations with British Ministers President de Gaulle had laid a lot of stress on the danger that British membership would weaken the Commonwealth. In fact this was probably disingenuousness . . . More serious reasons for this equivocal attitude must exist.

(b) The present Community was an organic whole and the countries were complementary to each other. There was therefore a natural unity, particularly in economic matters. The U.K.'s economy was not naturally complementary to those of the Community and would therefore have to adapt itself to some degree to British membership.

(c) Politically the Six had a greater chance of achieving a close political unity than with an enlarged body including not only the U.K. but Scandinavian countries as well. The implications of bringing E.F.T.A. in with the U.K. are becoming more and more evident . . .

(d) Basically President de Gaulle hated the United States and disliked the U.K. He believed that the U.K. was subservient to the United States and he therefore feared the role which Britain might play in the Six. We seemed like a Trojan horse . . .

(e) While the Community was small President de Gaulle could hope to dominate it.

Source: PRO, PREM 11/3775

Document 5.12

In his conversation with de Gaulle at Rambouillet on 16 December 1962 Macmillan tried to persuade him that Britain's accession to the EEC would increase the likelihood of achieving the kind of political cooperation proposed in the Fouchet Plan.

President de Gaulle said that he had not abandoned hopes of Europe being united one day, but so far nothing had been possible. He was against any supranational body. In the Fouchet Plan his idea had been regular meetings of Governments plus a Secretariat, a sort of conference of Ambassadors, and he had hoped that this would operate particularly in the military field . . . The European countries were not yet ready for a European policy and the economic arrangements had changed nothing in that respect. **The Prime Minister** replied that he believed that there would be progress in the political field six months after the British entry into the Common Market. For several centuries Britain had tried to maintain a European equilibrium. This would not be present in an organisation containing France and Germany but not Britain and the smaller countries felt this. After British entry the smaller countries would be more ready to co-operate and they already recognised that no United States of Europe was yet possible. The Fouchet Plan had coincided very much with the British ideas, because it ensured that the Governments would govern and that everything would not be run by civil servants. The Fouchet Plan was in principle acceptable to the United Kingdom. If the Brussels negotiations could be brought to a successful conclusion, the prospect of unity would be much greater. It would be possible to begin again the movement towards a political arrangement. It was the lack of balance in the present Community which was preventing progress. Of course any arrangement ought not to be a federal one; equally it would be a mistake to feel that in the modern world one could completely separate politics, economics and defence; they were all linked together.

Source: PRO, PREM 11/4230

Document 5.13

The following minute by Sir Philip de Zulueta, Macmillan's private secretary, records the conclusions of a group of senior advisers on the possibility of Anglo-French cooperation in the field of nuclear weapons.

RAMBOUILLET AND ANGLO-FRENCH RELATIONS IN THE NUCLEAR FIELD

As you wished, Sir Burke Trend has now discussed this question with Sir Harold Caccia, Sir Robert Scott and Sir Roger Makins and this minute has been agreed by all of them.

You will recall that you made two basic assumptions which would be essential before any Anglo-French co-operation in this field could be contemplated. These were:-

(1) That British entry into the European Economic Community had been secured, and:
(2) That American agreement had been secured.

Assuming for the sake of argument that these conditions had been fulfilled you wished for three aspects of this question to be considered. These were:-

(a) Possible Anglo-French co-operation in the production and manufacture of nuclear material.
(b) A joint Anglo-French targeting programme for the deterrent forces.
(c) Anglo-French co-operation in the building of delivery vehicles in the post-bomber era.

The committee were unable to see any fruitful possibilities of Anglo-French co-operation in any of these fields. The main general reason for this is the expressed French determination to be completely independent of any other country as regards their own nuclear deterrent. Specific reasons on each of the three points above are:-

(a) The French have now made their own long-term contracts with their indigenous uranium producers and will not want uranium from outside. They are so far committed to their diffusion plant that they will probably not want enriched material from us.
(b) It is not realistic to think in terms of an Anglo-French joint targeting plan. That the British V-Bomber Force is committed, in one of its roles, to an Anglo-American plan might not necessarily rule out an alternative Anglo-French plan. Neither would the fact that the credibility of a purely Anglo-French deterrent would be small. But the operational staff who would be involved on our side employ, for the purpose of the existing targeting plans, a joint system of Anglo-American intelligence which cannot be communicated to the French. To set them to work on a new Anglo-French targeting plan would appear to the Americans to involve a risk of compromising the system of intelligence, a risk which the Americans would certainly not accept.
(c) The French are not yet convinced that it will be too expensive for them to produce their own independent delivery system in the post-bomber period. Moreover, it does not at the moment seem that, even if the French were willing to co-operate in an Anglo-French launcher, the extra expense involved for the United Kingdom would be justified by the theoretically greater degree of independence which we would secure for the British deterrent.

If you accept these arguments it follows that there is no future in pursuing this line of thought any further still less in mentioning it to de Gaulle. You may, however, think it worth while to try to discover what role the President envisages for the French nuclear deterrent when it exists. Does he contemplate the possibility of associating it, or part of it, with some form of joint European deterrent? Within the NATO framework? On a tripartite basis outside NATO? On a purely European basis, whether Anglo-French or wider, which excluded the Americans? (For our part, we should deprecate any suggestion of American exclusion). Has he thought at all about this? Or is he looking no further for the present than to the acquisition of a wholly independent nuclear deterrent for France? If you were able to sound de Gaulle on this, it might be very useful for your subsequent talks with President Kennedy.

Source: PRO, PREM 11/3712, P. de Zulueta to Macmillan,
7 December 1962

Document 5.14

During the final session of their meeting at Rambouillet on 16 December 1962 de Gaulle, to Macmillan's dismay, reiterated his view that there were fundamental obstacles to British membership of the EEC. Prominent among these was the difficulty of reconciling the British agricultural system with the CAP.

President de Gaulle . . . If the United Kingdom joined she would be followed by Norway, Denmark, Ireland, Portugal and perhaps even Spain. It was not a desperate situation and perhaps something could be worked out gradually. The United Kingdom had certainly taken the right road and was moving towards a European organisation. The Brussels negotiations were not finished and Mr Macmillan had given the impression that the reasons were not, in themselves, very important and could be overcome if the will to do so existed. The difficulties for France, however, particularly in the agricultural sector, were real ones. The existing arrangements on agriculture had been worked out with the utmost difficulty by France and her partners and there were still further regulations to be made. For France it was important that the Common Market should remain 'as it is'. The real point for France was that her agricultural products 'doivent être mangés' [must be eaten]. The Prime Minister had put this whole problem in a grand perspective but, the General implied, in Brussels the delegates were talking about hard realities . . .

The Prime Minister . . . As regards Europe he had felt obliged to reproach President de Gaulle with his pessimism. He was surprised at what the President had said about his disillusionment with Europe but he quite understood it. In the Brussels negotiations the problems consisted first of a certain number of rather minor questions of tariffs, secondly of the agricultural problem and the different approaches to it and thirdly, of certain particular difficulties such as that presented by New Zealand. At the moment Europe imported some £2,500 million worth of foodstuffs every year but it was not in Europe's interests to cut these off. First of all there would be a loss of European exports in return and no doubt considerable political upheavals in the supplying countries, whose support was often most important in the cold war. Furthermore, it would really be immoral for Europe to adopt such a selfish attitude. Europe should be prepared, not only to accept a reasonable quantity of agricultural products, but also to accept some of the simpler industrial products. The question was how to resolve Europe's agricultural problem. The key to this was the adoption of a reasonable price level which would in turn permit reasonable access to the European market by traditional suppliers. This policy should not be incompatible with an increase in European production; this was proved by the British experience where in ten years although home agricultural production had increased by about 25 per cent, imports had remained at the same level. In addition there was a particular problem concerning the method of agricultural support. Hitherto, the United Kingdom had supported agriculture through the general tax system but Britain had now accepted the principle of the levy or tariff on imports. This had the theoretical disadvantage that the poorer sections of the community would be most affected, but in modern societies food was relatively less important in the family budget. The question here, therefore, was the rate, pace and method of the change. In addition there was, of course, the question of New Zealand, which was really a farm in the Pacific and which needed special treatment.

As regards the general question of the negotiations the Prime Minister did not feel that these could be allowed to drag on much longer. The whole future of Europe was at stake . . . For Britain there were two solutions; she could either abandon her traditional role and become a mere client state of the United States, or she could help to build up a strong Europe in close alliance with the United States. The Prime Minister himself was attracted by the second solution which he believed to be practicable and desirable. Europe had the capacity, the population and the resources to equal the United States and Russia. For this possibility to come into being, it was necessary for the European countries to be both independent and interdependent . . . This argument had, with great effort, been deployed in Britain so that the United Kingdom was now ready for the move towards Europe. This moment must, however, be seized or it would pass for good . . . If the Brussels negotiations could be finished, then a great step forward would have been taken and the base of Europe constructed . . . But if this process did not begin soon, probably before the spring of 1963, then the moment would be lost in Britain and in Europe. This would not be a disaster and life would no doubt continue, but it would be a tragic failure to match the level of events . . .

President de Gaulle said that . . . he still foresaw difficulties at Brussels. In the Six as they existed France had some weight and could say no even against the Germans. France could stop policies with which she disagreed because in the Six she had a very strong position. Once the United Kingdom and the Scandinavians and the rest had entered the organisation things would be different. In addition the rest of the world would no doubt demand special arrangements; at that point who in the Common Market would be strong enough to resist such pressures? The result would be a sort of world free trade area which might be desirable in itself, but would not be European. After a pause, **the Prime Minister** said that this was a most serious statement. The view which President de Gaulle had just put forward was, in fact, a fundamental objection of principle to the British application. If this was really the French Government's view, it should have been put forward at the very start. It was a fundamental objection to the whole idea of Britain's entry into the Common Market.

Source: PRO, PREM 11/4230, Record of a Conversation
at Rambouillet, 16 December 1962

Document 5.15

On 14 January 1963 de Gaulle gave a press conference at the Elysée Palace, in the course of which he justified his decision to reject Britain's application to join the Community.

The Treaty of Rome was concluded between six continental States – States which are, economically speaking, one may say, of the same nature. Indeed, whether it be a matter of their industrial or agricultural production, their external exchanges, their habits or their commercial clientele, their living or working conditions, there is between them much more resemblance than difference . . .

Thus, it was psychologically and materially possible to make an economic community of the Six, though not without difficulties. When the Treaty of Rome was signed in 1957, it was after long discussions; and when it was concluded, it was necessary in order to achieve something that we French put in order our economic, financial and monetary affairs . . . and that was done in 1959.

From that moment the community was in principle viable, but then the treaty had to be applied. However, this treaty, which was precise and complete enough concerning industry, was not at all so on the subject of agriculture. However, for our country this had to be settled.

Indeed, it is obvious that agriculture is an essential element in the whole of our national activity. We cannot conceive, and will not conceive, of a Common Market in which French agriculture would not find outlets in keeping with its production . . .

This is why when, last January, thought was given to the setting in motion of the second phase of the treaty – in other words a practical start in application – we were led to pose the entry of agriculture into the Common Market as a formal condition.

This was finally accepted by our partners but very difficult and very complex arrangements were needed – and some rulings are still outstanding . . .

Thereupon Great Britain posed her candidature to the Common Market. She did it after having earlier refused to participate in the communities we are now building, as well as after creating a free trade area with six other states, and, finally, after having . . . put some pressure on the Six to prevent a real beginning being made in the application of the Common Market. If England asks in turn to enter, but on her own conditions, this poses without doubt to each of the six States, and poses to England, problems of a very great dimension.

England in effect is insular, she is maritime, she is linked through her exchanges, her markets, her supply lines to the most diverse and often the most distant countries; she pursues essentially industrial and commercial activities, and only slight agricultural ones. She has in all her doings very marked and very original habits and traditions . . .

What is to be done in order that England, as she lives, produces and trades, can be incorporated into the Common Market, as it has been conceived and as it functions?

For example, the means by which the people of Great Britain are fed and which are in fact the importation of foodstuffs bought cheaply in the two Americas and in the former dominions, at the same time giving, granting considerable subsidies to English farmers? These means are obviously incompatible with the system which the Six have established quite naturally for themselves . . .

Once again, what is to be done to bring England, as she is, into this system?

One might sometimes have believed that our English friends, in posing their candidature to the Common Market, were agreeing to transform themselves to the point of applying all the conditions which are accepted and practised by the Six. But the question, to know whether Great Britain can now place herself like the Continent and with it inside a tariff which is genuinely common, to renounce all Commonwealth preferences, to cease any pretence that her agriculture be privileged, and, more than that, to treat her engagements with other countries of the free trade area as null and void, that queston is the whole question.

It cannot be said that it is yet resolved. Will it be so one day? Obviously only England can answer.

The question is even further posed since after England other States which are, I repeat, linked to her through the free trade area, for the same reasons as Britain, would like to enter the Common Market.

It must be agreed that first the entry of Great Britain, and then these States, will completely change the whole of the actions, the agreements, the compensations, the rules which have already been established between the Six, because all these States, like Britain, have very important peculiarities. Then it will be another Common Market . . . but one which would be taken to 11 and then 13 and then perhaps 18 would no longer resemble, without any doubt, the one which the Six built . . .

It is to be foreseen that the cohesion of its members, who would be very numerous and diverse, would not endure for long, and that ultimately it would appear as a colossal Atlantic community under American dependence and direction, and which would quickly have absorbed the community of Europe.

It is a hypothesis which in the eyes of some can be perfectly justified, but it is not at all what France is doing or wanted to do – and which is a properly European construction.

Source: *The Times*, 15 January 1963

6   Another veto: 1964–1969

In the summer of 1967 the UK applied again for membership of the EEC. As in 1963, this second bid was frustrated by a French veto. The documents in this section relate to these events. They shed light on the reasons why Harold Wilson's Labour government decided to seek admission, the issues that dominated discussions with the Six and the difficulties presented by de Gaulle. In addition, they deal with the emergence of differences within the Labour Party over entry to 'the Common Market'.

Labour's growing enthusiasm for Europe in 1967 formed a strong contrast with its predominantly hostile stance while in Opposition. During the Brussels negotiations of 1961–63 Gaitskell's rejection of entry to the EEC on the terms available had shocked some of his closest political allies, including George Brown and Roy Jenkins, both of whom were staunchly pro-European. It struck a chord with the Labour movement as a whole, however, and among those who responded favourably was Wilson, then Shadow Foreign Secretary. In January 1963 Wilson was elected to succeed Gaitskell following the latter's sudden death. When Labour assumed power in October 1964, therefore, it was led by a man who was basically sceptical about British membership of the EEC. Within less than three years, however, Wilson's attitude had undergone a transformation.

Wilson presided over two administrations in the 1960s (October 1964 – March 1966 and March 1966 – June 1970). During the first of these the question of Britain's accession to the EEC was not a high priority. Since the government had only a slender parliamentary majority, a major foreign policy initiative was out of the question, especially on an issue that was likely to prove extremely divisive. The government's overriding objective was to hang on to power until it could call a general election and win a comfortable working majority. In the meantime, Wilson and his colleagues faced a desperate battle to maintain the parity of the pound – a battle which they finally lost in November 1967 when there was an enforced devaluation. Their energies were also absorbed by the implementation of a massive programme of social and economic reform, a central feature of which was the so-called National Plan. Launched in September 1965, this was intended to reverse the UK's long-term economic decline. It was to be overseen by a new super-ministry, the Department of

Economic Affairs (DEA), headed by George Brown, the deputy leader of the Labour Party.

The general election of March 1966 brought the EEC issue to the fore. Heath, who had recently replaced Sir Alec Douglas-Home as leader of the Conservative Party, had a pro-European record stretching back to 1950 when he had criticised the Attlee government's cool reaction to the Schuman Plan. He had conducted the Brussels negotiations with great enthusiasm and went into the 1966 election campaign firmly committed to making a second attempt to secure entry to the EEC. As a result, Wilson was obliged to set out his own position. His principal concern, as so often, was to avoid damaging splits in Labour's ranks. He therefore adopted a stance which was deliberately ambiguous. While claiming to favour entry in principle, he insisted on conditions which were essentially those laid down by Gaitskell at Brighton in October 1962: safeguards for the interests of the Commonwealth and domestic agriculture and for the British government's right to use national economic planning and pursue an independent foreign policy (6.1). This calculated ambivalence was designed to satisfy both pro- and anti-marketeers within the Labour Party. It also enabled Wilson to present the electorate with an alleged contrast between his own determination to defend national interests and Heath's subservience to the Six and to the French in particular (6.1).

After obtaining a substantial parliamentary majority in the 1966 general election the Wilson government set up a Cabinet committee to deal with the question of Britain's application for admission to the EEC and George Thomson, the Chancellor of the Duchy of Lancaster, was given responsibility for conducting negotiations. In August 1966 George Brown left the DEA to replace Michael Stewart as Foreign Secretary, a move rightly seen as an indication of the government's seriousness about membership of the EEC. From this time onwards the drive towards seeking entry gathered momentum.

Various explanations have been advanced for Labour's decision to apply for membership of the EEC. There is broad agreement among historians that Wilson was impelled by the same underlying economic and political realities that had persuaded Macmillan that there was no alternative. He was also subject to the influence of a Whitehall establishment which by now generally accepted the case for joining the EEC. A recent study by Hugo Young has emphasised the key role of the Foreign Office. The newly created DEA has likewise been identified as a major force pushing for entry. Another suggestion is that the government was reacting to the failure of its economic strategy, and more specifically the collapse of the National Plan during the sterling crisis of July 1966. At the time, remaining outside the EEC was increasingly viewed as an unattractive prospect. This perception owed much to growing reservations about the Commonwealth, the 'special relationship' and Britain's global commitments. Wilson had a long-standing emotional attachment to the Commonwealth. He was also convinced of its economic value to the UK. From the early 1960s he consistently called for an expansion of Commonwealth trade and in the 1964 general election campaign blamed Conservative neglect for allowing the Commonwealth's share of British trade to fall from 44 per cent to only 30 per cent (6.2A). His pledge to reverse this trend was not fulfilled, however, and within a few years he was to be found criticising the Australian, New Zealand and other governments for their supposedly uncooperative attitude (6.2B). At the political level, too, disenchantment soon set in, mainly because of the crisis over Rhodesia. When the Rhodesian Prime Minister, Ian Smith, made a unilateral declaration of independence in November 1965, Wilson tried to topple the illegal white regime by means of an economic embargo. The policy proved wholly ineffective and exposed Wilson to fierce criticism, especially from African leaders. Adding to Wilson's disillusionment with the Commonwealth was the fact that India and Pakistan made use of Soviet rather than British mediation to settle their conflict over Kashmir in 1965 (6.7).

Mounting doubts about the Commonwealth in the second half of the 1960s were accompanied by a fundamental questioning of Britain's role as joint world policeman with the US. The Wilson government's support for American policy in Vietnam caused serious tensions in the Cabinet and in the Labour Party at large. At the same time, the maintenance of armed forces 'east of Suez' – in the Indian Ocean, the Persian Gulf and Malaysia – imposed a severe financial, economic and military burden on the UK: the 1966 Defence White Paper warned of badly overstretched resources (6.3B). Some leading figures in the government, notably Denis Healey, the Defence Secretary, and Wilson himself, were reluctant to abandon the 'East of Suez' role (6.3A). It came under fire, however, not only from the left, but also from many of Labour's right-wing pro-Europeans who saw it as both an expensive luxury and an obstacle to British entry to the EEC. This was the line taken by ministers like Roy Jenkins (Home Secretary) and George Brown who wanted a shift of emphasis away from the 'special relationship' and a military presence 'east of Suez' towards a greater concentration on Europe. By 1966 Brown was thoroughly convinced that Britain's future influence depended on its assumption of a leadership role in the EEC. It was generally accepted that sterling would need to be devalued before entry could take place, but this presented no difficulty for Brown since he was in favour of devaluation in any case (6.3C).

On 22 October 1966 the possibility of a British application was discussed by senior ministers and officials at Chequers. Ministerial opinion was sharply divided, with a small majority in favour (6.4). Wilson suggested that he and Brown should conduct an exploratory tour of the capitals of the Six. Despite resistance – particularly from Brown – Wilson was determined to go ahead, and on 10 November announced in the Commons that it was the government's intention to join the EEC, provided safeguards could be secured for essential national and Commonwealth interests.

The exploratory probe by Prime Minister and Foreign Secretary took place between 15 January and early March 1967. Even before it began it was thought unlikely that the 'friendly five' would be prepared to exert pressure on France if it proved obstructive (6.5A). Discussions in the capitals concerned, and especially in Bonn, confirmed that little could be expected in that direction (6.5B). As Wilson and Brown fully appreciated, the key to entry was French consent. Their talks with de Gaulle and his Prime Minister, Georges Pompidou, on 24–25 January were therefore critical. De Gaulle was characteristically delphic (6.6A). Although acknowledging that the UK had made progress in detaching itself from the 'special relationship' and becoming more European, he emphasised the formidable problems still to be overcome before it could join the EEC. He anticipated great difficulties over British adjustment to the CAP. In addition, he believed that the continuing weakness of sterling – highlighted by the July 1966 crisis – and its status as a reserve currency constituted a fundamental obstacle to UK membership. Wilson, for his part, conceded that acceptance of the CAP would entail heavy financial costs for the the the UK: he insisted, indeed, that there would have to be changes in the existing arrangements (which were due for renegotiation in 1969). His line on sterling was that the pound was now much stronger as a result of the deflationary measures taken in July 1966 and that it would be possible to reach a satisfactory agreement on the sterling balances. Rejecting a suggestion that the UK might consider associate membership of the EEC, Wilson stressed that it had much to offer the Community, especially in the development of closer relations with the Soviet Union and of a European technology freed from dependence on the US (6.6B).

After completing their exploratory tour, Brown and Wilson presented a report to the Cabinet which provided the basis for regular discussions during April 1967 (6.7). There was still considerable ministerial opposition to joining the EEC – notably from Douglas Jay (President of the Board of Trade), Barbara Castle (Transport) and Fred Peart (Minister of Agriculture) – but it was disunited and ineffective. Jay was on the right of the party and consequently unable to rally those on the left who shared his views on the EEC but little else. Other opponents of entry, including Healey and Richard Crossman (Lord President and leader of the House of Commons), were inclined to place their trust in a French veto. Outside the Cabinet, a substantial section of the Parliamentary Labour Party (PLP) – predominantly on the left – wanted nothing to do with a Community which they regarded as a product of the Cold War, an enemy of socialist planning, an impediment to improved relations with Eastern Europe and a threat to the sovereignty of Parliament (6.8).

On 30 April 1967 the Cabinet took a vote on the matter – a sure sign of irreconcilable differences – and decided by 13 votes to 8 to seek admission to the EEC (6.7). After announcing his intentions to Parliament on 2 May, Wilson then submitted a formal application on the 10th. Less than a week later, however, de Gaulle applied the so-called 'velvet veto' at a press conference held on 16 May. Although couched in polite language, de Gaulle's speech had a clear message: Britain was still so different from existing Community members that its entry would necessarily entail drastic changes. An important section of the speech was devoted to the position of sterling which de Gaulle portrayed as a fundamental problem (6.9).

Wilson refused to accept de Gaulle's intervention as his final word on the UK's application and on 21 June he had another interview with the French President (6.10). As in their meeting of the previous January, the prospect of extensive technological cooperation figured prominently in Wilson's pitch. De Gaulle showed little interest though, his principal concern being British involvement with the US, especially in relation to Vietnam. Wilson believed that there was still a chance. British hopes were dealt a final blow on 27 November, however, when de Gaulle formally vetoed the UK's application. A furious Brown sought to mobilise the 'friendly five' and the Americans against France, but without success (6.11). For the second time in four years, then, Britain's attempt to enter the EEC had been blocked by de Gaulle, and there seemed little prospect of a more favourable outcome as long as he remained in power.

Document 6.1

During the 1966 general election campaign Wilson expressed a generally positive attitude towards UK entry into the EEC, but only if the conditions were right. His circumspect approach was reflected in the keynote speech which he made at Bristol on 18 March 1966.

The Government regards recent statements in France, and in the Ministerial Conference of Western European Union held in London this week, as removing one major impediment to Britain joining the European Economic Community, if suitable terms and conditions can be agreed. For over three years the question of Britain's joining, on any terms, has been academic, because of the French refusal to agree . . .

Although there is deep imprecision in what the French leaders are saying, the present French attitude is markedly different from the situation three years ago . . .

Much more remarkable is the change of attitude on the part of the leader of the Conservative Party. Three years ago he reacted to the French decision in a mood of surly petulance. No words were harsh enough. Anglo-French relations were almost blocked – even a royal charity visit to Paris was cancelled.

Now one encouraging gesture from the French Government, which I welcome, and the Conservative leader [Edward Heath] rolls on his back like a spaniel . . . Some of my best friends are spaniels, but I would not put them in charge of negotiations into the Common Market.

Labour welcomes the growing improvement in Common Market attitudes.

The Government's position, as we have stated again and again, is that we are ready to join if suitable safeguards for Britain's interests, and our Common-wealth interests can be negotiated. But, unlike the Conservative leader, we shall not proceed on the basis of an unconditional acceptance of whatever terms are offered to us . . .

Given a fair wind, we will negotiate our way into the Common Market, head held high, not crawl in. And we shall go in if the conditions are right.

And those conditions require that we must be free to go on buying food and raw materials, as we have for 100 years, in the cheapest markets – in Canada, Australia, New Zealand, and other Commonwealth countries – and not have this trade wrecked by the levies which the Tories are so keen to impose on agricultural products . . .

We are not unilateral economic disarmers. So: Negotiations? Yes. Unconditional aceptance of whatever terms we are offered? No . . .

Two final points I would make: The Conservative leaders have been totally evasive on the one central question which they refused to answer during the last set of negotiations. Do they regard any move towards Europe as principally economic, or – as many good Europeans and some Tory frontbenchers insist – as a step towards political, and ultimately, military integration? We believe that given the right conditions, it would be possible and right to join EEC as an economic community. But we reject any idea of supranational control over Britain's foreign and defence policies. We are in Europe, but our power and influence are not, and must never be, confined to Europe . . .

My second point is this. The Common Market is no cure-all for Britain's economic problems. There are strong industrial arguments for being in Europe, particularly the extension of the market for sophisticated science-based products, and the resulting economies of scale. But we should not accept too easily that the cold wind of competitive imports will, of itself, make British industry more efficient . . .

Unless we modernise, streamline our industries, base our attitude on a full day's work for a full day's pay at all levels within industry, unless we continue, as we have in the past 18 months, to strengthen sterling and the balance of payments – then the Common Market choice is simply between being a backwater inside Europe and a backwater outside Europe.

Source: U. Kitzinger, *The Second Try: Labour and the EEC*,
London, Pergammon Press, 1968, pp. 108–12 *passim*

Document 6.2

During the early 1960s Wilson was convinced that UK trade with the Commonwealth could be revived and expanded. Labour's manifesto for the 1964 general election blamed the Conservatives for not making sufficient efforts to arrest its recent decline and held out the prospect of a substantial improvement (A). Within three years of taking power, however, Wilson was complaining to the Cabinet of a disappointing response from Britain's Commonwealth trading partners (B).

A

Under the Tories the Commonwealth share of our trade has been allowed to fall from 44 per cent to 30 per cent and the defeatist view that it will decline still further has gained ground.

Worse still, the Commonwealth itself came near to disintegration at the time of the Common Market negotiations. The recent Commonwealth conference showed its sturdy resilience, but what is lacking is any coherent policy at the centre.

We shall:

(i)   Promote more effective and frequent consultation between Commonwealth leaders, for example by the establishment of a Commonwealth Consultative Assembly.

(ii)   Make a new drive for exports through a Commonwealth Exports Council.

(iii) Build a firmer base for expanding trade by entering into long-term contracts and commodity agreements providing guaranteed markets for Commonwealth primary producers at stable prices.

(iv)   Ensure that development and capital investment programmes are geared to Commonwealth needs . . .

(vi)   Encourage joint Commonwealth activity on developments required throughout the Commonwealth, such as a communications satellite and passenger aircraft designed for Commonweath routes.

> Source: *Let's Go with Labour for the New Britain*,
> Labour Party general election manifesto, 1964

B

Relations with the Commonwealth in recent years in economic matters had been disapppointing. There had been little attempt on the part of the other Commonwealth countries to look other than to their narrow national interests. In spite of the initiatives we had taken at the Meeting of Commonwealth Prime Ministers in 1965 there had been a complete failure to take concerted Commonwealth action, even in respect of Government purchases. New Zealand and Australia preferred to purchase American aircraft of types not superior to our own. Canada had done nothing to redress our adverse trade balance with her and although she was giving economic aid, especially in the Caribbean, she was doing less in proportion to her GNP than we were. In the Far East the policies of Australia and New Zealand were increasingly diverging from our own, with a very strong emphasis on their own narrow area of interest in South-East Asia.

> Source: PRO, CAB 128/42, CC (67) 26th Conclusions, 30 April 1967

Document 6.3

The Labour governments of 1964–70 faced growing pressures over defence expenditure. Wilson was reluctant to abandon Britain's 'East of Suez' role (A), but the problems involved in the maintenance of such a role were emphasised by the 1966 Defence White Paper (B). To pro-European ministers like George Brown the strains imposed by global commitments reinforced the case for a reorientation of foreign policy, with greater emphasis being placed on the UK's place in Europe. Brown's views are conveyed in an account of a conversation which he had with Barbara Castle, a strong opponent of British membership of the EEC, and Tony Benn, who at the time of the conversation was a supporter (C).

A

Taking first our own expenditure in money and resources on defence programmes, whether of manpower or equipment, the plain fact is that we have been
trying to do too much. The result has been gravely to weaken our economic
strength and independence without producing viable defences. Planned defence
expenditure in the present year represents 7.1 per cent of the gross national
product. This is a higher figure than in any other major Western country, with
the exception of the United States . . .

The problem we are facing derives from the fact that alone in the world – apart
from the United States and the U.S.S.R. – we are trying to maintain three roles.
There is the strategic nuclear role. There is our conventional role within
N.A.T.O., our commitment to the defence of Europe, to which we are committed
by interest and by treaty. And there is our world role, one which no one
in this House or indeed in the country, will wish us to give up or call in
question . . .

The Government's conclusion from the first long, cool look at this whole
problem is that . . . we cannot do all that has so far been thought ideally desirable
without fatally weakening our economy and, correspondingly, weakening our
real defences.

I want to make it quite clear that whatever we may do in the field of cost
effectiveness, value for money and a stringent review of expenditure, we cannot
afford to relinquish our world role – our role which, for shorthand purposes, is
sometimes called our 'East of Suez' role . . .

Source: *H.C.Deb.*, vol. 704, cols. 419–24,
16 December 1964

B

I

THE PURPOSE OF THE REVIEW

1.   On taking office in October 1964, the Government decided to carry out a
far-reaching examination of the nation's defence needs in the next decade, with
two objectives: to relax the strain imposed on the British economy by the defence
programme which it had inherited, and to shape a new defence posture for the
1970s.

2.   . . . The defence plans of the previous Government would have imposed
an excessive burden both in resources and in foreign exchange. As we emphasised in the National Plan (Command 2764), to continue spending over 7 per cent
of the Gross National Product on defence would be seriously damaging to the
British economy . . . We plan, therefore, to bring our defence expenditure
down to a stable level of about 6 per cent of Gross National Product by 1969–70,
thereby improving our ability to compete successfully with other exporting
countries . . .

MANPOWER STRETCH

5.   Although our political commitments have become fewer in recent years, larger military tasks have been imposed by those that remain . . . As a result, the bulk of our fighting forces outside Europe have been permanently tied down in operational tasks all over the world . . .

8.   Such over-stretch has the most damaging consequences in our defence policy as a whole . . .

II

BRITAIN'S MILITARY ROLE OUTSIDE EUROPE

16.   At first sight, a direct threat to our survival seems less likely outside Europe. Although we have important economic interests in the Middle East, Asia and elsewhere, military force is not the most suitable means of protecting them, and they would not alone justify heavy British defence expenditure. We have, however, a number of obligations, which we cannot relinquish unilaterally or at short notice; some of these obligations will still exist in the 1970s . . .

19.   Nevertheless, to maintain all our current military tasks and capabilities outside Europe would impose an unacceptable strain on our overstretched forces, and bear too heavily both on our domestic economy and on our reserves of foreign exchange. For all these reasons we have decided that, while Britain should retain a major military capability outside Europe, she should in future be subject to certain general limitations.

Source: Cmd 2901 (February 1966), *Statement On The Defence Estimates 1966 Part I The Defence Review*

C

Just then Wedgie [Anthony Wedgwood Benn] put his head round the door and George [Brown] waved him in. 'We've got to break with America, devalue and go into Europe.' 'Devalue, if you like,' I [Castle] said, 'but Europe, no. I'll fight you on that.' 'But I believe it passionately. We've got to go somewhere. We can't manage alone. That is what Pompidou said to us: "Devalue as we did and you're in"'. Wedgie and I tried to persuade him that if he brought Europe into the argument, he'd lose the battle that really mattered. We could argue the Europe issue out later. He was very het up about it but we finally persuaded him. Wedgie: 'Are you doing this for Europe?' 'No, of course not. I'm doing it for Britain. Even if there was no Europe in it, I'd still do it.'

Source: Barbara Castle, *The Castle Diaries 1964–1976*, London, Papermac, 1990, diary entry for Monday 18 July 1966, p. 75

Document 6.4

On 22 October 1966 an all-day meeting was held at Chequers to discuss the question of British entry to the EEC. It was attended by members of the Ministerial Committee on Europe and other ministers whose departmental interests were particularly affected: some senior officials were also present at the morning session. In the following extract, Burke Trend, the Cabinet Secretary, summarises the arguments that were deployed.

There are various possible courses of action. The first is, in effect, to go on as we are – i.e. neither trying to approach more nearly to the EEC nor appearing to retreat from it. A few of the Ministers at Chequers thought that, on balance, this would be the least disadvantageous course. The majority, however, rejected it. Their reasons for doing so were not very explicit; but they were probably a combination of the following arguments:-

(i) Objectively, i.e. on the merits of the case, the growing tendency for individual countries to group themselves in larger aggregates of economic power implies that merely to go on as we are would mean adopting a 'Little England' policy which would reduce this country, in political terms, to an international ranking which not many people would willingly accept.

(ii) Presentationally, i.e. in terms of political tactics, Mr George Thomson's recent 'probings' in the European capitals have created a general expectation about our intentions which we must now either carry forward and develop or allow to fall away once more. The latter course would be so counter-productive, in terms of the effect on both our international standing and business confidence in the United Kingdom itself, that it must be dismissed. We are therefore driven to consider how we can best carry the 'probings' a further stage forward. Moreover, the United States seem to think that we should 'get into Europe'; and the Community itself – with the probable exception of France – is clearly anxious that we should accede to it. We should not lightly ignore these indications. Finally, the general climate of domestic public opinion appears to be favourable to a renewed attempt to see whether we can 'get into Europe' not least because people seem to feel instinctively that the sort of Europe which we should now try to enter is perhaps rather different from the sort of Europe which we tried, but failed, to enter nearly four years ago.

Source: PRO, PREM 13/909

Document 6.5

In a report to Wilson of 25 November 1966, following a meeting of the OECD, the Chancellor of the Exchequer, James Callaghan, warned that it would be unwise to rely on pressure from the 'friendly five'. What counted was the attitude of France (A). Wilson reached the same conclusion as a result of his and George Brown's 'exploratory probe' of the EEC capitals during January–March 1967 (B).

A

I thought you might like to have a note of the comments I picked up at the O.E.C.D. meeting in relation to the Common Market . . . There was general agreement both among the E.F.T.A. countries and the Five that we cannot be expected to risk another veto, and everyone was conscious that a veto would probably mean the final division of Europe and that this was not to be tolerated. On the other hand I agree with Winters, the Canadian Minister of Commerce, who expressed the view after he had held a number of conversations that we cannot rely on the Five standing up to the French, and further it would be unwise to try to line them up.

In a talk I had with a group of French journalists they all emphasised that one of Heath's mistakes was that he appeared to be lining up with the Five and in the end he was left alone with them. The French journalists were, perhaps understandably, strongly of the view that indirect approaches via other countries were of very little meaning and that everything hinged upon a direct confrontation between General de Gaulle and yourself. France is the only one that matters was naturally the opinion of the French journalists and I am bound to say from my conversations with others that I agree with them. In the end I do not think that the remaining members of the Six will count for very much.

Source: PRO, PREM 13/910

B

The Five for their part all wished the United Kingdom to join the EEC and some, particularly the Benelux countries, were extremely anxious that we should do so. For the most part they had in their discussions with the Foreign Secretary [Brown] and himself [Wilson] sought not so much to raise difficulties on their own account as to get from us explanations of our position which they in turn could use to dispel French opposition. In the last resort, however, the Five would not be prepared to disrupt the EEC in order to force the French Government to agree to our admittance if the latter were determined to oppose it. In particular, the new Federal German Government would not be prepared to take action which would threaten the resumption of cordial Franco-German relations, although this relationship would be unlikely to persist for long in the face of the real attitude of General de Gaulle towards Germany.

Source: PRO, CAB 128/42, CC (67), 14th Conclusions,
Cabinet minutes of 21 March 1967

Document 6.6

During their 'exploratory probe' of the EEC capitals (January–March 1967) Wilson and Brown had a vital meeting with de Gaulle. The message from the French leader was a mixed one which was difficult to interpret (A). Wilson denied the suggestion that either the CAP or sterling's role as a reserve currency represented a fundamental barrier to UK membership of the EEC and stressed the benefits that would accrue to the Community if Britain did join (B).

A

He [de Gaulle] had the impression of an England which now really wished to moor itself alongside the continent and was prepared in principle to pledge itself to rules in the formulation of which it had had no part, and which would involve it in definite links with the system which had grown up on the continent. He had the impression of an England which seemed disposed to detach itself to some extent from the relationship which it had, or had had, with the U.S.A., thus enabling it to be a European country . . .

But what practical conclusions should be drawn?

The Common Market existed. It was a practical reality. It had been constructed with the utmost difficulty. Its six members . . . were countries whose industry, commerce, finance, currency arrangements, agriculture and technology were, not indeed identical, but very similar. It was this similarity which had made the construction of the Community possible . . .

But the participation of Britain in the Community presented great problems, given the differences of its economic interests, its monetary arrangements, its contacts with the outside world. To solve all these would be a political as well as an economic problem. Would the presence of the United Kingdom in the Community enable it to remain what it was now? This was the question he asked himself.

B

But the Treaty of Rome itself need not be a decisive obstacle to our entry . . . nor need the Common Agricultural Policy as such . . . As regards the price levels prescribed by the Common Agricultural Policy, some were certainly higher than either economic sense warranted or the French authorities themselves desired. But even here there might be reasons for cautious optimism. The general tendency of world prices of cereals was to rise, as the United States surpluses ran down and the import requirements of countries such as India and China continued to escalate. On the other hand, there was no doubt that the adjustments which we should be compelled to make in our own agricultural policies if we entered the EEC would be very considerable. The most serious burden which we should have to face would be the payment to the Guidance and Guarantee Fund under the financial regulations – a payment which would involve both budgetary and balance of payments problems for us. On the other hand, it was surely beyond dispute that the entry of a new member into the Community would make certain changes in this respect inevitable, if only because a British subscription to the Fund calculated on the basis of the existing formula would raise the Fund's income so far above its legitimate requirements as to make it clear that some adjustment would be necessary.

The other basic issue which confronted us was the international character of sterling and the related problem of the sterling balances – though not the sterling parity. He understood that the President [de Gaulle] had had the opportunity to study the record of his discussion with M. Pompidou on the previous afternoon; and the President would therefore be able to appreciate the reasons why we were convinced that, if we entered the Community, the sterling balances would not be a drag on it.

The accession of a new member – perhaps several new members – to the

Community would admittedly involve change . . . But how would it [the Community] stand in the 1970s if Britain had been unable to enter fully into membership? Clearly, there would be less scope for the kind of intensified technological collaboration between Britain and the member countries which he had outlined the previous day; and we should all be weakened in this respect by being compelled to be more dependent on the technological resources of third countries. The effects would be felt not only in terms of the relative standards of living of our individual countries but also in terms of the independence of Europe as a whole and the part which she could play in world affairs. In fact, the strength of Europe's voice in international councils would depend on her technological vigour and independence more than any other single factor. Moreover . . . the continued exclusion of Britain from the Community would be bound to have far-reaching consequences. Because Europe would be divided economically, her political unity would be proportionately diminished; and the world role which she could play would be far less effective than if Britain and France pursued a common policy, as he believed they could.

Source: PRO, PREM 13/1476, record of a meeting
at the Elysée Palace, 25 January 1967

Document 6.7

At a critical Cabinet meeting of 30 April 1967 strong differences emerged over whether Britain should join the EEC. In the following extract Wilson sums up the debate and puts the case for entry. The case against is urged almost entirely on economic grounds.

a) The case for entry

Even if . . . the economic consequences of joining the Community proved to be no more than evenly balanced, the political advantages of joining were decisive. If we continued in our present position we must recognise that in international politics our influence had markedly declined. For example, we had been obliged to adopt United States policies in a number of fields and even in relation to a former dependency, Guyana; the Soviet Union had been the effective mediator between India and Pakistan during the recent conflict in Kashmir; and we had been unable to discharge fully our obligations in respect of Rhodesia. In other spheres we had to a substantial extent felt bound to follow the policies of the United States; and it would be contrary to the views of a large number of the Government's supporters to be forced to continue in that position. We must not in any event allow ourselves to become totally dependent on the United States nor on the other hand could we contemplate aligning ourselves with the Soviet *bloc*: joining the Community was essential if we were to avoid finding ourselves increasingly isolated and powerless in world affairs. We must also have regard to the dangers that would arise in Europe if we were not to become a member of the Community. In that event, and particularly after the death of President de Gaulle, the Community would become increasingly dominated by Western

Germany and there were ample indications of the fears of other countries of the consequences of such domination, whether or not it was accompanied (to our further disadvantage) by a closer relationship between Western Germany and the United States. In fact if we failed to enter the EEC there was a serious danger that the Community would become increasingly estranged from the United States. Since the United States was the only major Power which was committed to the maintenance of the democratic freedoms in which we believed, it was fundamental to our interests to prevent such a development. The EEC had, despite its diversity, become a group with substantial power and influence. This had recently been exemplified in the discussions on international monetary reform and in the Kennedy Round [on tariffs]. If we were to join the Community we could expect to be influential in persuading the other members to adopt more liberal and less inward-looking policies. We could hope to gain a new role of political leadership which would provide the political stimulus formerly given by our imperial role . . .

Major difficulties and perhaps a period of disorder might occur in France after the death of President de Gaulle and disquieting tendencies were discernible in Germany. If we were inside the EEC we would be able to exert our influence in the formative stages of policy, whereas outside it we should not be able to do so and might be forced into a closer association with United States policy in the Far East. Similarly, if we were a member of the EEC we could influence developments of Community policy on world's liquidity.

b) The case against entry

. . . It was suggested that the additional strain which accession would impose on our balance of payments could be as much as 10 times the net cost of our overseas defence expenditure. After intensive effort by the present Administration over a period of two years since coming to office, there had still been in 1966 a deficit on the balance of payments of £200 million and the prospect of only a small surplus in 1967. This had been achieved at the cost of reducing the rate of growth of the gross national product (GNP) to only 1 per cent. To achieve a large enough surplus to offset the disadvantages of entry in terms of balance of payments we should require an annual rate of growth of GNP of 3 per cent and it was by no means certain that we could achieve that rate, despite the present estimate for the ensuing year. Even if we did so, the Government would still not be able to offer the country any hope of relief from this policy of austerity by the early 1970s. Entry into the Community would on the contrary entail the need to bring about a shift of resources and to reduce personal consumption in order to offset the adverse effects on the balance of payments. This continuing policy of austerity would not be acceptable to the country. Nor should we assume that even in the longer term our balance of payments would be secured by membership of the Community. It was noteworthy that France and Germany were now in difficulties over their balance of payments.

Source: PRO, CAB 128/42, CC (67), 26th Conclusions, 30 April 1967

Document 6.8

Shortly before Wilson lodged Britain's application for membership of the EEC on 10 May 1967, a large body of Labour MPs signed a public statement setting out the case against entry.

An application to join the Common Market would open out the most vital questions for our future . . . We are international Socialists, not British nationalists. This is the spirit in which we have approached this complex problem. After a thorough review of the facts and arguments, we are convinced that the Common Market is not a step towards a wider Europe or world government; and that the economic and political case against entry is decisive, unless satisfactory arrangements can be made, not merely to safeguard essential British and Commonwealth interests, but also to transform the European Economic Community into an outward-looking body, unhampered by a doctrinal adherence to private competition.

POLITICAL CASE AGAINST ENTRY

1.   The Treaty of Rome is dedicated to the principle of free competition, within the Community, behind a high external tariff . . . Despite elaborate administrative machinery for planning, the Community is basically against *Socialist* planning . . . Planning is *not* being used, nor is it likely to be used, to reallocate resources or redistribute income. There is no realistic prospect of progressive social or economic policies. Moving towards a Socialist society is out of the question, within this framework.

2.   The Treaty of Rome was drawn up in the years immediately before 1957 and was strongly influenced by Western fears of a Soviet threat to the West. It is for many the economic reflection of NATO. No Communist Government will sign such a Treaty, and the prospect of a link with Eastern Europe is thus destroyed. Indeed, the EEC is tending to intensify the division of Europe.

3.   Moreover, it has shown itself to be a barrier to economic co-operation with Eastern Europe, with the Middle East and with Africa. Some countries which have associated with the Community are becoming increasingly critical of the heavy disadvantages of the arrangements . . . And Kenya, Uganda and Tanzania have been offered even worse terms. This has the flavour of economic colonialism.

4.   British membership of the EEC would create severe difficulties for the Commonwealth countries with which we have had a special relationship . . . Politically the consequences of moving away from these countries, especially the poorer countries, are incalculable.

5.   Internally, the Community is managed by a Permanent Commission in Brussels, serviced by a staff of 3,000. The power of initiative rests with the Commission which is not accountable to Parliament. If Britain enters, we will surrender important powers to this undemocratic bureaucracy.

6.   The Common Market is also a political community 'requiring a modicum of common foreign policy', as Dr. Kiesinger [West German Chancellor] explained recently. This has been blocked for the time being by President de Gaulle, but a political union with a Supranational Government for the Community is the aim of many leading adherents of the Treaty of Rome. This could lead to a West European nuclear deterrent with active West German participation, thus ending all hope of a nuclear-free zone in Central Europe.

Source: Statement signed by 74 Labour MPs, *Tribune*, 5 May 1967

Document 6.9

On 16 May 1967 de Gaulle held a press conference in Paris at which he delivered the 'velvet veto'. While making the usual points about the UK's extra-European interests, he also dwelt on the difficulties created by sterling's weakness and its role as a reserve currency.

Also, how can it not be seen that the very situation of the pound sterling prevents the Common Market from incorporating Britain. The very fact that the organisation of the Six is entirely freeing their mutual trade necessarily implies that the currency of the member countries has a constant relative value and that, if it happened that one of them were disturbed, the Community would ensure its recovery. But this is possible only due to the well-established soundness of the mark, the lira, the florin, the Belgian franc and the French franc. Now, without despairing of seeing the pound hold its own, for a long time we would not be assured that it will succeed. We would be even less so in that it presents, in relation to the currencies of the Six, a very particular character of being, as we say, a reserve currency, which means that a large number of countries in the world, those of the Commonwealth, hold enormous claims in pounds. Some can certainly try to distinguish the fate of the pound as a national currency from that of the pound as an international currency. Also, some can certainly hold that once England has entered the organisation, the latter could shirk all responsibility for what would happen to the pound sterling. But all this is only intellectual games. In other words, monetary parity and solidarity are the essential conditions of the Common Market and assuredly could not be extended to our neighbours across the Channel, unless the pound appears, one day, in a new situation and such that its future value appears assured; unless it also frees itself of the character of reserve currency; unless Great Britain's deficit within the sterling area disappears. When and how will this happen?

Source: Translation issued by the
Présidence de la Republique on 18 May 1967

Document 6.10

The following extract is from a telegram sent by Wilson to Brown describing his interview with de Gaulle at the Trianon Palace on 21 June 1967. In the light of de Gaulle's subsequent veto, Wilson's assessment of his attitude appears hopelessly optimistic.

De Gaulle's gloomy apocalyptic mood characterized much of our discussion. He is visibly ageing, not only physically, but also in the sense of being unwilling to contemplate any new thinking: but he is still realistic enough to see that his own foreign policy, based on his past experiences, prejudices and humiliations, has left France with woefully little world influence . . . He spoke with some bitterness about [President Lyndon B.] Johnson's failure ever to consult or talk to France; but he admitted that France made no effort herself at such consultation and was now 'separated' from the United States – as he now seemed to recognise that she was also from the Soviet Union. The general theme that ran through the whole discussion was that, as he put it at one point, the United States, which was now the greatest power in the world, behaved (as France and Britain had done in their hay-day [*sic*]) exclusively in her own interests. The only way for a medium sized power like France (or in his view Britain) to conduct their affairs in such a situation was to disengage and 'to make it clear that America's quarrels are not our quarrels and their wars will not be our wars'. All this was of course related primarily to Vietnam and the Far Eastern situation and to the danger of world war arising from it. This, he said, was the main reason for France's withdrawal from NATO, so that she could keep her hands free. Britain's involvement with the United States made it inevitable that we should be dragged into their wars. It also affected us damagingly in such areas as the Middle East where we were now suffering because we were regarded by the Arabs as indistinguishable from the pro-Jewish Americans. I rubbed it into him that in the thermo-nuclear age, it was unrealistic to think that France could keep out of wars in this way and that, far from being 'disengaged', he and we should try to be jointly 'engaged' in a positive exertion of influence designed to avoid the 'eyeball to eyeball' situations.

This led on naturally to our European discussion. We had a useful run over the ground on technological and industrial cooperation and on the lesson that political influence is related to economic strength. Here again his constant theme was our involvement with the Americans and the danger that if we came in all the weaker brethren in the Six ('the poor Italians', the 'poor Belgians', the Germans exposed to constant temptation and the Dutch, already on our side anyway) would follow our lead and the whole thing would become an American dominated Atlantic arrangement. It was to prevent this that France was in the Community.

Painted in this way, the picture looks pretty sombre for our prospects. And so, on the basis of what he actually said, I suppose it is. But in practice I and those with me believe this to have been a useful visit and I think that I shook him a little out of his complacent gloom. In the broader context I think he was generally attracted at the possibility of Britain and France playing a more effective role together in world issues – and particularly over the Middle East: while in the European context he showed unmistakable interest in what I told him about our willingness to cooperate (if we got in) in the advanced technologies and particularly in the civil nuclear field. The fact that we were not buying Poseidon was also a bull point. He accepted that in these major economic and industrial areas we were now becoming increasingly independent of the Americans.

To sum up (and even if it sounds a shade far-fetched) I found myself watching this lonely old man play an almost regal 'mine host' at the Trianon, slightly saddened by the obvious sense of failure and, to use his own word, impotence that I believe he now feels. His concept of France's role, as he describes it, is oddly reminiscent of the days of the Maginot Line. There is nothing he can do but sit behind his force de frappe and watch the world move towards Armageddon. Against this background I feel paradoxically encouraged. He does not want us in and he will use all the delaying tactics he can (though incidentally the word association was not once mentioned or anything like it). But if we keep beating firmly at the door and do not falter in our purpose or our resolve I am not sure he has the strength finally to keep us out – a dangerous prophecy, as prophecy always is with the General.

Source: PRO, PREM 13/1521

Document 6.11

After de Gaulle's veto of 27 November 1967 the Labour government was still intent on pressing forward with its application for UK admission to the EEC. Brown contemplated using the 'friendly five' and the Americans to exert pressure on the French. This approach met with deep scepticism and discouragement from the US.

Subject: British entry to EEC. The question of British entry into the European Communities was the principal point of discussion between Secretary [Dean] Rusk and Foreign Secretary Brown at lunch December 12 . . .

Principal thrust of British presentation was that British wanted the Five in the EEC to push at December 18–19 Council [EEC Council of Ministers] meeting for a definitive position on the question of undertaking negotiations (as contrasted with definitive decision on membership).

Brown said that the UK position was eroding. Further inconclusiveness would cause only further erosion and a turning away of Britain from Europe. He stressed that he was devoted to the goal of British entry into the Communities for both economic and political reasons but felt that as a politician he was 'out' if he could not produce some forward momentum.

Therefore he wanted a definitive decision at the December 18–19 meeting. If it was negative, Britain would proceed to show its continued interest in Europe by working with willing countries in the economic, political, defense, and technological fields. He said that this could be with the Five, or three, or two or even one. (He was not specific on the details of these alternatives but at one point alluded to suggestions for strengthening EFTA and for cooperation work in field of armaments.)

If the answer from the EC Council meeting was positive, they would proceed to negotiations.

He also made it clear that he believed France was susceptible to pressure from the Five and felt that, if pressed, the French will agree to negotiations. He said, however, that some of his staff (O'Neill) [Sir Con O'Neill of the Foreign Office] did not share his view.

He stated flatly that anything short of straight negotiations was not acceptable. Talks by the UK with the Commission looking to resolving problems prior to outright negotiations, were not an acceptable substitute because they were not with the principals in the Community and could further erode the UK negotiating position by leading to a premature sacrificing of some issues important to UK.

In the course of the discussions he indicated that the need for a decision whether pro or con was being broached by him in his talks with the Five. Luns [the Dutch Foreign Minister] was particularly strong in commending Brown's tactic. Fanfani [the Italian Foreign Minister] was very firm in support of negotiations but Harmel [the Belgian Foreign Minister] was toying with unacceptable compromise solutions.

He urged Secretary Rusk to adopt a similarly firm line in his bilateral discussions with the Five here in Brussels.

The US side seriously questioned the Brown approach, noting that it was forcing the Five into a confrontation with the French with possible repercussions on the Communities, moreover, grave doubts were cast on Brown's belief that the Five could, in his words, force Couve [de Murville, the French Foreign Minister] to 'turn up his card'. The US side expressed the view that time was on the UK side and it was best to let the matter proceed for the time in a manner the Five deemed best. To force a likely negative decision could not produce the same positive results as following a perhaps slow but determined route towards entry. In this context, it was mentioned that talks with the [EEC] Commission could have value and maintain momentum, and should be looked at carefully. A historical note was sounded by citing past UK errors in dealing with the Common Market and the hope was expressed that such errors would not be repeated again.

Brown declined to accept the vigorous US presentation, noting that the lack of a decision on negotiations would only result in further deterioration of support for entry in the UK and the UK turning its back on Europe. Whether a 'yea' or 'nay' [the] answer would mean progress; the former meaning negotiation and the latter the pursuit of alternatives with interested Europeans. He urged the Secretary again to support him.

The Secretary indicated doubts as to the wisdom of Brown's proposed course, saying it was doubtful if the Five could be brought to such a decision. However, he said he would talk with his colleagues in the Five to see what their views were on the negotiating problem.

Source: *FRUS*, 1967, no. 280, Telegram from Secretary of State Rusk
to the Department of State, Brussels, 13 December 1967

7 Entry and renegotiation: 1970–1975

The documents in this section are mainly concerned with the UK's third, and successful, attempt to join the EEC. Among the topics covered are the Heath government's approach to the negotiations, the terms on which UK accession was agreed, the subsequent process of renegotiation initiated by Wilson and the referendum of June 1975 on the question of whether Britain should stay in the Community.

The success of the 1970 application was facilitated by a combination of developments within the EEC, notably the resignation of de Gaulle from the French presidency in April 1969. De Gaulle's replacement by Georges Pompidou, who had previously served as Prime Minister from 1962 to 1968, brought an immediate improvement in Anglo-French relations and removed the principal obstacle to a renewal of negotiations between the UK and the Six. Another factor assisting the British bid to join the EEC was that it coincided with a relaunch of the European idea comparable to that of 1955 – a development again made possible by the resignation of de Gaulle, who had frustrated any moves towards closer integration throughout the 1960s. The new upsurge of interest in consolidating and strengthening the Community manifested itself at the EEC summit held at The Hague in December 1969. At The Hague, Pompidou, Brandt, the West German Chancellor, and the other leaders of the Six took three major decisions: to complete the first stage of economic integration; to proceed towards full economic and monetary union (EMU) by 1980; and to open negotiations with Britain and the other applicants for EEC membership – Denmark, Ireland and Norway.

Before this last decision could be put into effect Wilson was defeated in the general election of June 1970 and the victorious Conservative leader, Heath, formed a new administration. Heath was the first post-war British Prime Minister to give relations with the European states a higher priority than those with either the US or the Commonwealth. His passionate and highly publicised commitment to securing British entry to the EEC provided him with a fund of political goodwill among the Six, but also rendered him vulnerable to the accusation that he was willing to pay any price to achieve it. In an attempt to preempt such a charge, the Conservative Party's 1970 election manifesto emphasised that there was a limit to the concessions that it was prepared to make (7.1).

Heath lost little time in submitting an application for Britain's entry to the EEC. On 30 June 1970 Anthony Barber, the minister heading the British negotiating team, delivered a formal opening statement in Luxembourg and serious negotiations began in Brussels in October – by which time Barber had been replaced by Geoffrey Rippon. First-hand experience of the 1961–63 negotiations had taught Heath some valuable lessons. One was the necessity of working with rather than against the French. Another was the futility of trying for fundamental changes in the Community's founding treaties or any of its central features such as the CAP. As Heath now recognised, the only strategy that could possibly succeed was the one urged by Monnet in 1961 – to accept the institutions and practices of the EEC as they stood and attempt to alter them only after Britain had become a member.

While adopting this basic approach, however, the Heath government nevertheless sought special arrangements in certain key areas. Thus it argued that the existing budgetary system was unfair to the UK and would need to be modified (7.2A). At the insistence of Pompidou, the formula for providing the EEC with its 'own resources' had been settled before the start of negotiations for British entry. As a result, the agreement reached by the Six (April 1970) took no account of what suited Britain (7.2B). Funds were to be raised from levies and tariffs on all imports from non-member countries, plus up to 1 per cent of value added tax (VAT). This would mean a disproportionately large financial burden for the UK because of its heavy dependence on imports from outside the EEC. The fact that some 80 per cent of the budget was spent on the CAP would also be disadvantageous to the UK since it had a relatively small agricultural sector. After much hard bargaining, it was eventually agreed that the British budgetary contribution would gradually rise over a five-year period from nearly 9 per cent to around 19 per cent of the total. Although the Heath government did not regard this as an entirely satisfactory outcome, it relied on an assurance from the Six that if an inequitable situation were to arise steps would be taken to correct it (7.2B).

Apart from the budgetary issue, the other matters which proved difficult to resolve related to the CAP, imports from the Commonwealth and sterling. It was inevitable that acceptance of the CAP would be painful for the UK: there was particular concern about the impact on food prices of changing from a system where producers received direct government subsidies to one based on indirect subsidies from the consumer. In the event, the best that the British negotiators could achieve was a transitional period of five years to help in cushioning the shock of adjustment. As regards the Commonwealth, the central problem facing the Heath government was to safeguard the preferential access to UK markets enjoyed by New Zealand meat and dairy products and Caribbean sugar. Here, too, a transitional arrangement was hammered out. The question of sterling was raised by the French Finance Minister, Valéry Giscard d'Estaing. As at the time of the Wilson application, the French were worried about sterling's vulnerability. They also felt that its role as a reserve currency might jeopardise plans for EMU by 1980. Although the British refused to allow sterling to be treated as part of the official negotiations for entry, a mutually satisfactory solution was reached as a result of talks between Heath and Pompidou in Paris on 20–21 May 1971.

The critical Heath–Pompidou summit originated in a British initiative to give fresh impetus to the faltering Brussels negotiations. It went extremely well (7.3). A broad understanding was reached on a gradual, orderly run down of the sterling balances. This formed the basis for a statement made by Rippon on 7 June and accepted by the Six as disposing of the issue – despite its lack of detail (7.4). More than that, Pompidou's closing comments to the press sent a clear signal of his commitment to the success of the negotiations (7.3). Within a matter of weeks the main outstanding issues had been settled and on 23 June 1971 the negotiations for British entry to the EEC were concluded in Luxembourg.

The terms were set out in a White Paper of 7 July. In this the government was at pains to deny that there would be any loss of sovereignty (7.5). It was greatly assisted in this respect by the existence of the Luxembourg Compromise (1966) which guaranteed the right of each member state to veto proposals it considered harmful to its vital interests. As part of its strategy for deflecting attention from the sensitive issue of sovereignty, the government also focused attention on the expected economic gains from UK membership of the EEC (7.6). Heath himself attached great importance to this consideration, having come to power determined to modernise the British economy through a combination of radical reform of industrial relations and exposure of domestic manufacturing to tough competition within the EEC. The economic case put forward in the White Paper leaned heavily on the experience of the Six and turned out to be unduly optimistic (7.6 and section 8).

Securing the passage of the necessary legislation for British entry to the EEC presented the government with serious problems. Although it had an overall majority of 25, there was a danger this would be cancelled out by the votes of Conservative dissidents like Enoch Powell. Much depended, therefore, on the attitude of the Labour Opposition. Following its defeat in the 1970 general election, Labour had swung sharply against the EEC – a development closely linked with its shift to the left – and by 1972 most sections of the movement were virulently opposed to UK membership. However, a substantial and influential minority within the PLP, including Roy Jenkins and Roy Hattersley, regarded entry to the EEC as essential to the national interest and a matter of principle on which they were not prepared to compromise (7.7). On 28 October 1971 the government won a parliamentary majority of 112 on a crucial motion approving in principle entry to the EEC on the terms negotiated. This outcome was only possible, though, because 69 Labour pro-marketeers defied a three-line whip to vote with the government, while another 20 abstained. In the ensuing legislative battle over the European Communities Bill the margin was often much narrower.

The Treaty of Accession was signed on 22 January 1972 and on 1 January 1973 Britain became a full member of the EEC. Yet the debate on membership continued unabated for various reasons. It was widely believed that Heath had not honoured his much-quoted undertaking that entry would only take place with the 'full-hearted consent of Parliament and the people'. Moreover, the UK's admission to the EEC coincided with a serious downturn in the international economy associated with the collapse of the Bretton Woods fixed exchange system in 1971 and a quadrupling of the price of oil during 1973–74. In the case of Britain, the position was aggravated by the impact of the national coalminers' strike in 1974. Between 1972 and 1975 inflation and unemployment rose sharply, industrial investment and production slumped, and a healthy balance of payments surplus was transformed into a massive deficit. Such a gloomy overall picture was far removed from the promising economic scenario outlined in the 1971 White Paper and gave some plausibility to anti-marketeers' claims that being in the EEC would adversely affect the UK economy. Finally, and most important, continuing controversy about EEC membership was closely bound up with developments in internal Labour Party politics.

Labour's increasingly bitter divisions over the EEC after 1970 – part of a wider ideological clash between left-wing and right-wing opinion – placed Wilson in an acute dilemma. What he wanted to avoid at all costs was an irreparable split between the pro- and anti-market tendencies, and his chosen tactic for achieving this was to concentrate on the terms of entry. Wilson's line was that he was not opposed to entry in principle, but would not have accepted the 'Tory terms' – an assertion that many even in his own party found incredible. In its manifestos for the general elections of February and October 1974, the Labour Party committed itself to a 'fundamental' renegotiation of the terms of entry before putting the issue of whether Britain should remain in the EEC to the electorate (7.8A and 7.8B). In neither manifesto, though, was it made clear whether voters would be consulted through a general election or referendum: it was not until 23 January 1975 that it was announced in the Commons that there would be a consultative referendum by June of that year at the latest.

Some of the original items on Labour's renegotiation agenda (7.8A) were soon revealed to be either irrelevant or relatively unimportant. It emerged, for example, that there was nothing to prevent the UK from retaining a zero VAT rate on basic necessities. In addition, the perceived dangers from EMU receded rapidly into the distance as turmoil on the international exchanges effectively ruled out the 1980 target date. Of the items remaining on the agenda, the most significant were reform of the CAP, a new deal on the UK's budgetary contribution, and improved arrangements for imports of Caribbean sugar and New Zealand meat and dairy produce. With assistance from Helmut Schmidt, the West German Chancellor, and Giscard d'Estaing, the French President, limited concessions were obtained in all these areas: the renegotiation exercise was completed at the Dublin European Council of March 1975. While conceding that he had failed to bring about major changes in certain respects, notably to the CAP, Wilson nevertheless claimed that the new terms were substantially better than the original ones and justified a government recommendation that Britain should remain in the EEC. Anti-marketeers disagreed profoundly, arguing that the changes were marginal and that the whole business had been nothing but a face-saving charade (7.9). About a third of Cabinet members, including Castle, Benn and Foot, were opposed to acceptance of the renegotiated terms and it was agreed that for the duration of the forthcoming referendum campaign ministers on both sides of the argument should be free to air their views.

After the Dublin European Council the date of the referendum was fixed for 5 June 1975. While some welcomed the idea of a referendum as an extension of the British people's democratic rights, it was attacked by critics as a dangerous experiment which posed a threat to parliamentary sovereignty. The government justified its use on the grounds that Heath had taken Britain into the EEC without a mandate and that the issue at stake was one of unique constitutional importance (7.10A). These arguments were rejected by both the Conservative Opposition and by most Labour pro-marketeers who claimed that the only reason a referendum was being held was to paper over Labour Party disunity (7.10B).

The referendum campaign began in earnest during May 1975. Having consistently advocated British membership of the EEC since the late 1950s, the Liberal Party campaigned vigorously for a 'yes' vote under the leadership of Jeremy Thorpe. The Conservative and Labour parties were divided, disastrously so in the case of the latter. The question was one that cut across normal party alignments, however, and the activities of the disparate elements on each side were coordinated by two umbrella organisations: Britain in Europe, which orchestrated the pro-marketeers' campaign, and its opposite number, the National Referendum Campaign.

The two issues that dominated the referendum debate were a possible loss of sovereignty and the economic advantages and disadvantages of being in the EEC. The 'no' campaigners alleged that the inevitable result of British membership would be a loss of political independence and absorption into a federal European superstate (7.11A). The retort from the other side was that there was not the slightest possibility of rule by Brussels bureaucrats. Besides, what counted was how best to protect UK interests, and in an increasingly interdependent world some pooling of sovereignty was not only unavoidable but positively beneficial (7.11B).

Although Powell and Foot in particular sought to highlight the sovereignty issue, opinion polls indicated that voters were chiefly interested in the effect of EEC membership on their living standards. The economic debate was complicated and made more so by the difficulty of disentangling the various factors responsible for the undoubted deterioration in the UK economy since 1972. Not unnaturally, the anti-marketeers sought to blame Britain's current economic difficulties wholly on entry to the EEC, pointing to a disproportionately large balance of payments deficit with the original Six and a massive increase in unemployment as direct consequences (7.12A). The counter-argument was that the international crisis and deep-seated structural problems in the domestic economy were much more important as contributory factors (7.12B). A report from the Confederation of British Industries (CBI), which gave powerful backing to the 'yes' campaign, reached the bleak conclusion that withdrawal from the EEC would be disastrous for British industry (7.13).

One of the most sensitive aspects of the economic debate was the question of food prices. Because of an enormous increase in world prices over the previous two years, the general level of food prices within the EEC in 1975 was no higher than outside. According to pro-marketeers, this was part of a long-term trend resulting from growth in demand and offered a timely warning that the days of cheap food were over (7.14A). This interpretation was challenged by Castle and other anti-marketeers who maintained that artificially high food prices were an inbuilt feature of the CAP (see 7.14B).

As these and other arguments were traded during the referendum campaign, public opinion began to move strongly towards a 'yes' vote and by 5 June it was clear that the result would be a decisive endorsement of the government's recommendation. On a high turn-out (nearly 65 per cent of the electorate) 67.2 per cent voted for Britain to remain in the EEC and 32.8 per cent voted against. On the surface, Wilson had achieved his twin objectives of ensuring British membership while holding the Labour Party together. In the longer term, however, the consequences of the referendum were to prove disastrous for Labour unity and played a major part in the formation of the breakaway Social Democratic Party in 1981.

Document 7.1

Heath's known enthusiasm for British membership of the EEC carried the risk that he would be accused of being willing to accept any terms to gain entry. In the 1970 general election campaign an attempt was made to forestall this danger by adopting a studiously hard-headed approach in the manifesto.

A STRONGER BRITAIN IN THE WORLD

If we can negotiate the right terms, we believe that it would be in the long-term interest of the British people for Britain to join the European Economic Community, and that it would make a major contribution to both the prosperity and the security of our country. The opportunities are immense. Economic growth and a higher standard of living would result from having a larger market.

But we must also recognise the obstacles. There would be short-term disadvantages in Britain going into the European Economic Community which must be weighed against the long-term benefits. Obviously, there is a price we would not be prepared to pay. Only when we negotiate will it be possible to determine whether the balance is a fair one, and in the interests of Britain.

Our sole commitment is to negotiate, no more, no less. As the negotiations proceed we will report regularly through Parliament to the country.

A Conservative Government would not be prepared to recommend to Parliament, nor would Members of Parliament approve, a settlement which was unequal or unfair. In making this judgement, Ministers and Members will listen to the views of their constituents and have in mind, as is natural and legitimate, primarily the effect of entry upon the standard of living of the individual citizens whom they represent.

Source: *A Better Tomorrow*, Conservative Party
general election manifesto, 1970

Document 7.2

One of the key issues in the negotiations for entry to the EEC was the question of Britain's budgetary contribution. In his formal opening statement in Luxembourg on 30 June 1970, Anthony Barber, the Chancellor of the Duchy of Lancaster and the head of the British negotiating team, stressed the need for a fair distribution of the burden (A). In the event, the financial arrangements which the UK was obliged to accept were unsatisfactory (B).

A

13.   The list of questions which we wish to see covered in negotiations remains the same as those put forward by the previous British Government in July 1967 . . . And it would be unrealistic not to face up to the fact, at the outset, that there are some very difficult problems to be solved . . .

14.   The position which the previous British Government took in July 1967 was, of course, subject to developments in the meantime . . . In the field of Community budgetary arrangements, recent developments have made the problems facing our membership more difficult. As you know, our predecessors had looked forward to Britain's taking part as a full member in the negotiation of the financial arrangements for the period after the end of 1969. Had we done so, the resulting agreement would no doubt have made fair provision for us as it has for each of the existing members of the Communities. But we were not party to your agreement. And the arrangements which must in any case be agreed to enable a new member to take part in the budgetary provisions of the European Communities will constitute one of the crucial elements in the negotiation on which we are embarking. When the European Commission gave its Opinion on our candidature in September 1967, it was recognised that the existing financial arrangements would, if applied to Britain, 'give rise to a problem of balance in sharing of financial burdens'. I think it will generally be agreed that the new decisions have for us made that problem of balance more severe. And we have to work together to find a solution to this basic problem which will be fair and sound for the enlarged Community and for all its members. If I appear to labour this point, it is only because, unless such a solution is found, the burden on the United Kingdom could not be sustained and no British Government could contemplate joining. Moreover, without such a solution, the whole basis of

stability and confidence, essential to the further development of the Communities, would be lacking.

Source: Cmd 4401, Miscellaneous no. 12 (1970), *The United Kingdom and the European Communities: A statement on behalf of Her Majesty's Government by the Rt. Honourable Anthony Barber, M.P., Chancellor of the Duchy of Lancaster at the meeting of the Conference in Luxembourg on 30th June, 1970*

B

CONTRIBUTION TO THE COMMUNITY BUDGET

91.   From the outset the Government recognised, as did their predecessors, that it would not be possible to make fundamental alterations in the system of providing funds for the Community. The existing members had finally agreed this system among themselves early in 1970 only after considerable difficulty and regarded it as an essential part of the process of 'completing' the Community envisaged in The Hague Communiqué . . .

92.   The solution which has been reached is as follows. A percentage or 'key' has been set, broadly corresponding to our present share of the total gross national product (GNP) of the 10 countries likely to form the enlarged Community. This will represent the proportion of the budget which we should *nominally* be expected to pay in the first year of membership. This key will then increase marginally in each of the four subsequent years, under similar arrangements to those agreed by the Six for themselves.

93.   However, we shall pay only a proportion of our *nominal* contribution over these first five years. The proportion will increase in annual steps. The effect of these arrangements is shown in the table below. Column 2 sets out the *nominal* key which has been agreed. Column 3 shows the proportion of this nominal key which we shall in practice be required to pay. Column 4 gives our resulting share of the Community budget in each year. Column 5 sets out the possible size of our gross contributions on the assumption that the budget amounts to £1,400 million in 1973 and rises to £1,600 million by 1977. Column 6 shows the estimated build-up of our receipts from the budget, and the resulting estimates of our net payments are shown in the final Column.

Table 7.2

1 Year	2 United Kingdom key (percentage of Community budget)	3 Percentage of key to be paid	4 United Kingdom contribution (percentage of Community budget)	5 Possible United Kingdom gross contribution (£m)	6 Possible United Kingdom receipts (£m)	7 Possible United Kingdom net contribution (£m)
1973	19.19	45.0	8.64	120	20	100
1974	19.38	56.0	10.85	155	40	115
1975	19.77	67.5	13.34	195	55	140
1976	20.16	79.5	16.03	245	75	170
1977	20.56	92.0	18.92	300	100	200

It will be seen that we should be required to pay 8.64 per cent of the budget of the enlarged Community in the first year, rising to 18.92 per cent in the fifth year – the latter being broadly comparable to our proportion of the gross national product of the enlarged Community.

94.   After the first five years, there will be a further period of two years during which the size of our contribution will continue to be limited . . .

95.   In 1980 and subsequent years we shall be required to contribute 90 per cent of our agricultural levy and customs duty receipts and such value added tax (VAT) (not exceeding the yield of a 1 per cent VAT) as is necessary from each member country to close any gap between Community expenditure and Community revenues from levies and duties. It is not possible to make any valid estimate of the size of our levy and duty receipts in the 1980s. The outcome depends on a large number of unpredictable factors . . .

96.   Thus, in the Government's view, neither our contribution to, nor our receipts from, the Community budget in the 1980s are susceptible of valid estimation at this stage. And it is for this reason that the Community declared to us during the course of the negotiations that if unacceptable situations should arise 'the very survival of the Community would demand that the institutions find equitable solutions'.

Source: Cmd 4715 (July 1971), *The United Kingdom and the European Communities*

Document 7.3

The Heath–Pompidou summit held in Paris on 20–21 May 1971 broke the stalemate that had developed in the negotiations for British entry to the EEC. The following extract is Pompidou's concluding statement to the press.

For two days you have been very patient. We have been working very hard. We have been talking for well-nigh 12 hours and all subjects have been broached and studied in depth.

Since the start of the negotiations the position of France has always been that it is for the Community that we are negotiating. That is why we have not solved all questions and were not qualified to settle them.

But of course you would not believe me if I said we had not discussed all things. We have. We have compared our views. We have considered the economies of each government in determining our position.

It would be unreasonable now to believe that an agreement is not possible during the conference in Brussels in June.

The spirit of our talks over the past two days enables me to think the negotiations will be successful . . .

On a certain number of major problems, we have concluded that our views were similar and even identical. On some others we have also been in a position to note that there were still different views but they do not present any obstacle to our cooperation in view of the full identity of our views as to the main aim . . .

There were many people who believed that Great Britain was not European and did not wish to become European, and that Britain wanted to enter into the Community only to destroy it. Many people also thought France was prepared to use all kinds of means and pretexts to propose a new veto to the entry of Great Britain into the Community. Well, ladies and gentlemen, you see tonight before you two men who are convinced to the contrary.

Source: *The Times*, 22 May 1971

Document 7.4

One of the issues effectively settled at the Heath–Pompidou summit was the question of sterling. On 7 June 1971 Rippon made a statement of the UK's intent to run down the sterling balances in a gradual and orderly fashion. This was accepted by the French and the rest of the Six. In the following extract Heath explains to the Commons the circumstances surrounding the resolution of the sterling question.

The Prime Minister (Mr. Edward Heath): . . . sterling is not an issue in the negotiations but is a matter to be discussed in the context of the negotiations. So when it was raised by the Six early in the year we readily agreed to discuss it.

At The Hague in December 1969 the Community declared its intention of moving towards economic and monetary union. That raises understandable and proper questions, put to us in good faith, about the adjustments that might be required for a currency in an enlarged Community which had an appreciable role as an international reserve currency.

We have said three things to the Community. We have said that as members of the Community we would play our full part in the progress towards economic and monetary union. That was confirmed in my talk with President Pompidou and in my statement to the House. We have said that we are prepared to envisage a gradual and orderly rundown of official sterling balances after our accession. We have said that after accession we would discuss measures by which a progressive alignment of the external characteristics of sterling with those of other Community currencies might be achieved.

Both of these developments would be viewed in the context of progress towards economic and monetary union. But let me make absolutely clear that we have given no undertakings as to how fast or by what means these developments could or should be brought about. These would be matters for discussion after our entry, when we should be a full member of the Community with all the rights of a member. As I emphasised at the Press conference following my meeting with President Pompidou and in my statement to the House, both President Pompidou and myself agreed that no country's vital interests would be overruled by other members. We have made clear the three conditions which any proposal for reducing the official sterling balances would have to satisfy: notably, of course, the protection of the interests of balance holders and the avoidance of unacceptable burdens on our balance of payments.

Progress towards economic and monetary union and the future of sterling in an enlarged Community do involve enormously complex problems. It has to be considered, for example, what alternative asset would be generally acceptable for sterling holders, what arrangements would be needed for holders to acquire such an asset, and what form and maturity of corresponding liability might be undertaken by us. These are not matters to which the Community has clear and agreed answers. They would need a great deal of discussion, both within the enlarged Community and with others concerned. It would be impossible to settle these problems in the context of these negotiations. It is an advantage to us, not a weakness, that they are now left for discussion after our accession, when we should contribute as members of the enlarged Community to the process of discussion and decision-making.

Two things have happened in our discussions with the Six . . . First, the Six have become clearer about the size and complexity of the problems to be dealt with in this area. Secondly, they have accepted that, if we become members of the Community, we shall be ready to discuss the whole subject in a fully Community spirit, without preconceptions or prejudices about how to deal with the problems. That is why we are not asked for and have not entered into any specific undertakings or commitments on methods or timetables, and that is why my right hon. and learned Friend's statement of our position has been accepted as disposing of the whole question in the context of the negotiations.

Source: *H.C.Deb.*, vol. 818, cols. 1235–7, 10 June 1971

Document 7.5

Heath later came in for a great deal of criticism on the grounds that he had been deliberately misleading over loss of sovereignty. At the time it was strongly denied that there would be any significant loss.

29.   We shall have full opportunity to make our views heard and our influence felt in the councils of the Community. The Community is no federation of provinces or counties. It constitutes a Community of great and established nations, each with its own personality and traditions. The practical working of the Community accordingly reflects the reality that sovereign governments are represented round the table. On a question where a Government considers that vital national interests are involved it is established that decisions should be unanimous. Like any other treaty, the Treaty of Rome commits its signatories to support agreed aims; but the commitment represents the voluntary undertaking of a sovereign state to observe policies which it has helped to form. There is no question of any erosion of essential national sovereignty; what is proposed is a sharing and an enlargement of individual national sovereignties in the general interest.

30.   All the countries concerned recognise that an attempt to impose a majority view in a case where one or more members considered their vital national interests to be at stake would imperil the very fabric of the Community. The Six have not lost any of their identities or their national institutions and points of view, nor shall we lose our national identity. They retain their own

ways of life: as any tourist knows, France and the French are no less French, Holland and the Dutch are no less Dutch, after 20 years of Community life. They retain their own Monarchs and Heads of State, their own Governments, their own Parliaments, Courts and local administrations. Where the members reach common agreement to pool resources and authority, it is done because they consider it in their interests to do so. At present the Communities' institutions are purely economic. But if the development of European policies in non-economic fields calls for new institutions, then as a member Britain will play a full and equal part in devising whatever additions to the institutional framework are required.

31.   The treaties establishing the European Economic Community and Euratom . . . contain no provision expressly permitting or prohibiting with-drawal. Nor do some other important treaties to which the United Kingdom is a party, for example the United Nations Charter. The Community system rests on the original consent, and ultimately on the continuing consent, of member states and hence of national Parliaments. The English and Scottish legal sytems will remain intact. Certain provisions of the treaties and the instruments made under them, concerned with economic, commercial and closely related matters, will be included in our law. The common law will remain the basis of our legal system, and our courts will continue to operate as they do at present. In certain cases however they would need to refer points of Community law to the European Court of Justice. All the essential features of our law will remain, including the safeguards for individual freedom such as trial by jury and *habeas corpus* and the principle that a man is innocent until proven guilty, as well as the law of contract and tort (and a Scottish equivalent), the law of landlord and tenant, family law, nationality law and land law.

Source: Cmd 4715 (July 1971),
The United Kingdom amd the European Communities

Document 7.6

The Heath government maintained that there were strong economic arguments for UK entry to the EEC, basing its case almost entirely on the experience of the Six from the late 1950s.

THE ECONOMIC CASE

40.   The central question here is how membership of the Community would affect the structure of our economy and so the prosperity of our people. For many years we have faced familiar problems: difficulties with the balance of payments, a disappointing record in industrial investment, and an inadequate rate of economic growth. The result is that we have begun to drop seriously behind other countries, and particularly the members of the Community, in attaining a higher standard of living.

41.   The Government believe that membership would provide the most favourable opportunity for achieving the progress which we all desire. Studies made by the Confederation of British Industries show that this belief is shared by

a substantial majority of British industry. Our entry would not, of course, of itself bring about some automatic improvement in our performance and it would involve us in costs as well as benefits . . .

EXPERIENCE OF THE SIX

50.   The members of the Community created a common market in industrial goods by steadily eliminating the tariffs on imports from one another over the years 1959–68. The abolition of tariffs provided a strong and growing stimulus to the mutual trade of Community countries. It is estimated that by 1969 the value of this 'intra-trade' in manufactured products was about 50 per cent higher than it would have been, had the Community not been formed; moreover it appears that the stimulus to intra-trade is continuing. The abolition of tariffs and this consequent increase in intra-trade were accompanied by important changes in the performance of manufacturing industries in the Six countries. Those industries which competed with imports faced an intensification of competitive pressure as tariffs fell, obliging them to seek ways of raising efficiency and reducing costs. By the same token, prospects for exporting dramatically improved. Import competition and export expansion were closely associated with a growth in investment. The outcome of these processes was a significant improvement in the rate of growth of manufacturing productivity, and, therefore, higher national incomes in the Community than the member countries believe they would have enjoyed otherwise . . .

52.   The rapid growth in manufacturing productivity in the Six was a key factor in their impressive economic record in the past decade. But other indicators also show clearly the extent of the advances made by comparison with the United Kingdom. For example, in 1958 average earnings in Britain were similar to those in France, Germany, Belgium and the Netherlands and well over half as high again as those in Italy. By 1969 average earnings in Italy had caught up with British earnings, and in the other Community countries, earnings were now between a quarter and a half higher on average than those in Britain. In real terms (*i.e.*, after allowing for price inflation), average British earnings had increased by less than 40 per cent between 1958 and 1969, while in the Community countries average real earnings had gone up over 75 per cent. Similarly, all the Community countries enjoyed rates of growth of gross national product (GNP) per head of population, or of private consumption per head, roughly twice as great as Britain's.

53.   Moreover, at the same time a high proportion of the Community's output continued to be channelled into investment, so providing the basis for further rapid growth. In the period 1959–69, the Six devoted 24 per cent of their GNP to investment, whereas the figure for Britain was 17 per cent.

54.   Finally, the Community as a whole have maintained a strong balance of payments position, earning a surplus on current account of more than $25,000 million over the period 1958 to 1969; by comparison the United Kingdom had a small cumulative deficit on current account over these years.

PROSPECTS FOR OUR ECONOMY

55.   This, then, has been the experience of the Community. It is the conviction of the Governments, of the industries, and of the trade unions in the Six countries that their economic progress has been promoted in large measure by the changes brought about by the creation of the Community . . .

56.   In the light of the experience of the Six themselves, and their conviction that the creation of the Community materially contributed to their growth, and of the essential similarity of our economies, the Government are confident that membership of the enlarged Community will lead to much improved efficiency and productivity in British industry, with a higher rate of investment and a faster growth of real wages . . . A more efficient United Kingdom industry will be more competitive not only with the enlarged Community but also in world markets generally.

57.   These improvements in efficiency and competitive power should enable the United Kingdom to meet the balance of payments costs of entry over the next decade as they gradually build up. The improvement in efficiency will also result in a higher rate of growth of the economy. This will make it possible to provide for a more rapid improvement in our national standard of living as well as to pay for the costs of entry. For example, if a standard rate of growth of national income a ½ per cent higher were to be achieved as a result of membership, by the end of the period of five years our national income would be some £1,100 million higher in the fifth year.

Source: Cmd 4715 (July 1971),
The United Kingdom and the European Communities

Document 7.7

In the crucial vote on the principle of entry on 28 October 1971 the Heath government obtained a majority of 112. Its success was dependent on the willingness of 69 pro-European Labour MPs to vote with the government, and a further 20 to abstain, in defiance of a three-line whip. In the following extract Roy Hattersley, one of the 69, explains his motives.

I have always regarded our membership of the Community as not only essential but inevitable. However, I have also always believed that the longer we waited to join the more difficult our joining would be. Every year that Europe has changed without our membership, the institutions of Europe have changed in a way which makes our eventual membership more difficult . . . The problems of harmonisation and adjustment are reflected in the bargain which has just been struck between the Six and the Government this year and last.

I wish to make my judgement on the Government's terms very plain. I do not regard them as ideal. I believe that had they been negotiated by a Labour Government they might have been marginally better because they would have reflected more the social and economic priorities which my right hon. and hon. Friends and I share. But the real comparison which the House must make before it decides how it votes tomorrow is not between the terms negotiated by the Government and the terms which might or might not have been negotiated by some regrettably hypothetical Labour Government but [between] today's package of terms and the sort of terms we might obtain were we to abandon our application now and make it again in future. That is the choice for those of us who believe in the principle of entry . . .

The implication of what I have said is . . . acceptance of the fact that a price must be paid for our entry. No sensible person denies that. But, in my judgement, the potential benefits of European membership incomparably outweigh the price. Principal among those potential benefits is the prospect of economic growth . . .

The propaganda in the previous elections and at the last election made it very clear that not only was I the Labour Party candidate but I was committed in definite and strong terms to fighting for Britain's entry to the European Economic Community.

Yesterday evening the management of my Labour Party . . . reminded me that at my selection conference in 1962 – when the Labour Party was committed against European entry – I told the delegates to that meeting that I was for Europe and, in the foreseeable future, would remain for Europe. I have taken that public stand virtually all my public life for reasons which I can only describe not simply as being consistent with my view of social democracy but essential to that view. My choice is between breaking my word to my constituents and breaking my compact with my constituency party; but also, much more important, denying my judgements and beliefs. That would not be in the interests of the House. With some trepidation I say it would not be in the interests of my party . . .

There are some of us – I do not know how many – who have publicly taken a view which may be wrong but which in all conscience they hold. We may be insignificant members of the Parliamentary Labour Party, but the country as a whole will not admire a party which has a group of men in its midst who, having said constantly that something they believe is still in the national interest, do not have the courage to carry that view into the Division Lobby.

Source: H.C.Deb., vol. 823, cols. 1800–6, passim, 27 October 1971

Document 7.8

The Labour Party entered the 1974 general elections pledged to renegotiate the terms obtained by the Heath government and to give the electorate a vote on whether or not the UK should remain a member of the EEC. In neither the February election manifesto (A) nor that for October (B) was there a definite commitment to hold a referendum.

A

THE COMMON MARKET

Britain is a European nation, and a Labour Britain would always seek a wider co-operation between the European peoples. But a profound mistake made by the Heath Government was to accept the terms of entry into the Common Market, and to take us in without the consent of the British people. This has involved the imposition of food taxes on top of rising world prices, crippling fresh burdens on our balance of payments, and a draconian curtailment of the power of the British Parliament to settle questions affecting vital British interests. This is why a Labour Government will immediately seek a fundamental renegotiation of the terms of entry.

We have spelled out in '*Labour's Programme for Britain*' our objective in the new negotiations which must take place:

'The Labour Party opposes British membership of the European communities on the terms negotiated by the Conservative Government.

'We have said that we are ready to re-negotiate.

'In preparing to re-negotiate the entry terms, our main objectives are these:

Major changes in the COMMON AGRICULTURAL POLICY so that it ceases to be a threat to world trade in food products, and so that low-cost producers outside Europe can continue to have access to the British food market.

'New and fairer methods of financing the COMMUNITY BUDGET. Neither the taxes that form the so-called "own resources" of the Communities, nor the purposes, mainly agricultural support, on which the funds are mainly to be spent, are acceptable to us. We would be ready to contribute to Community finances only such sums as were fair and in relation to what is paid and received by other member countries.

'As stated earlier, we would reject any kind of international agreement which compelled us to accept increased unemployment for the sake of maintaining a fixed parity as is required by current proposals for a European ECONOMIC AND MONETARY UNION. We believe that the monetary problems of European countries can be resolved only in a world wide framework.

'The retention by PARLIAMENT of those powers over the British economy needed to pursue effective regional, industrial and fiscal policies. Equally we need an agreement on capital movements which protects our balance of payments and full employment policies. The economic interests of the COMMONWEALTH and the DEVELOPING COUNTRIES must be better safeguarded. This involves securing continued access to the British market and, more generally, the adoption by an enlarged Community of trade and aid policies designed to benefit not just "associated overseas territories" in Africa, but developing countries throughout the world.

'No harmonisation of VALUE ADDED TAX which would require us to tax necessities.

'If the renegotiations are successful, it is the policy of the Labour Party that, in view of the unique importance of the decision, the people should have the right to decide the issue through a General Election or a Consultative Referendum. If these two tests are passed, a successful renegotiation and the expressed approval of a majority of the British people, then we shall be ready to play our full part in developing a new and wider Europe.

'If renegotiations do not succeed, we shall not regard the Treaty obligations as binding upon us. We shall then put to the British people the reasons why we find the new terms unacceptable, and consult them on the advisability of negotiating our withdrawal from the Communities.'

An incoming Labour Government will immediately set in train the procedures designed to achieve an early result and whilst the negotiations proceed and until the British people have voted, we shall stop further processes of integration, particularly as they affect food prices . . . Thus the right to decide the final issue of British entry into the Market will be restored to the British people.

Source: *Let Us Work Together – Labour's Way Out of the Crisis,*
Labour Party general election manifesto, February 1974

B

THE COMMON MARKET

. . . The Labour Government pledges that within twelve months of this election we will give the British people the final say, which will be binding on the Government – through the ballot box – on whether we accept the terms and stay in or reject the terms and come out . . .

Within one month of coming into office the Labour Government started the negotiations promised in our February manifesto on the basis set out in that manifesto. It is as yet too early to judge the likely results of the tough negotiations which are taking place. But whatever the outcome in Brussels, the decision will be taken here by the British people.

Source: *Britain Will Win With Labour,*
Labour Party general election manifesto, October 1974

Document 7.9

The Wilson government's claim to have largely achieved its renegotiation objectives was challenged not only by the Conservative Opposition, but also by anti-market Labour critics for whom the whole exercise was a hollow sham.

Mr. Douglas Jay (Battersea North): The overriding fact emerging is that renegotiation has changed almost nothing, and almost every Member knows in his heart that this is true. The attempt in this White Paper to turn molehills into mountains is no more convincing than that of the 1971 White Paper, although the special pleading in this is a little less untruthful than that of 1971. All this is not the fault of the negotiators, apart from their failure to attempt to get either of the treaties amended. It is inherent in the nature of the Common Market.

First, renegotiation has not in any way altered the constitutional position, the Treaty of Rome, or the system of authoritarian legislation from Brussels. Secondly, there is no alteration in the Treaty of Accession which forces on this country a series of food taxes on almost every major foodstuff and lays down the actual increases in the prices of those foodstuffs that we have to accept over a

four-year period, much of which is still to come . . . Thirdly, there is no fundamental renegotiation of the common agricultural policy.

Fourthly, even on New Zealand, a subject on which the Prime Minister has
always claimed that there had to be a major improvement, there is at best no
change and at worst a worsening of the situation from the United Kingdom's
point of view. The import duty on New Zealand mutton and lamb still has to go
to 20 per cent. All our cheese imports from New Zealand have to come virtually
to a stop from 1978 onwards, and there is no change except for a pious form of
words that can mean anything or nothing . . .

I turn to the question of the budget contribution . . . On closer examination, it
is not certain whether the new agreement is better or worse for us than the
Commission's proposals of last January. A whole series of conditions still have to
be satisfied before we get any refund. The balance of payments criterion is not
wholly omitted. The system of 'own resources', which the Labour Party
manifesto said was unacceptable, is accepted, and after three years of refunds our
economy has to be supervised by the Commission in any case . . .

I turn next to the Regional Fund . . . We are now offered net, according to the
Foreign Secretary, £20 million a year for the whole of the United Kingdom. That
is less than one-tenth of our expenditure on assisted areas and it is one-hundredth
of our trade deficit with the EEC . . . Indeed, it is such a molehill that the White
Paper . . . does not even attempt to make it into a mountain.

After this further, well-meaning effort in renegotiation, what are we left with
when we strip away all the verbiage? We are left with an authoritarian system of
legislation, taxation and government which is already sapping away not just the
sovereignty of this country as an independent self-governing nation but the
democratic control of our people over the laws and powers of government. To
my mind, that is more important than what is normally called sovereignty.

Source: *H.C.Deb.*, vol. 889, cols. 858–61 *passim*, 7 April 1975

Document 7.10

*The Wilson government's justification for holding a referendum was that membership of the
EEC was an issue of unique constitutional importance on which the British people had not been
given an adequate opportunity to express their view (A). This argument was rejected by
Labour pro-market critics like John Mackintosh, an acknowledged expert on constitutional
affairs (B).*

A

**The Lord President of the Council and Leader of the House of Commons
(Mr. Edward Short)**: Whatever view one may take on Britain's membership of
the European Community, I hope that we would all agree that this is much the
most important issue that has faced this country for many years. Whether we
decide to stay in or come out, the effects on the economy, on our political and
parliamentary system, on our influence in the world and, indeed, perhaps

eventually on our whole way of life will be profound not just for ourselves but for future generations.

How should a decision of this importance be taken? The right hon. Member for Sidcup (Mr. Heath) had it right when he said that such a decision should be taken only with the full-hearted consent of Parliament and the people. In our system we accept decisions with which we do not agree, but only if we are satisfied that they have been arrived at fairly and democratically . . .

Unfortunately, the last Government's handling of the European issue did not match their previous promises. They had no mandate to take us in, merely to negotiate – 'nothing more, nothing less'. The result is that the consent of the British people has not, in fact, been secured. The issue continues to divide the country. The decision to go in has not yet been accepted.

That is the essence of the case for having a referendum. Only by means of a referendum can we find out whether the British people do or do not consent to our continued membership. A General Election could not give us this answer, because this is an issue within the parties, not between them.

How, for example, would a Conservative supporter opposed to our membership have recorded his view in the last two elections? . . . One former Conservative [Enoch Powell] recorded his view most appropriately, but a number of hon. Gentlemen opposite who took his view did not, I believe, follow his example.

The country has not yet had an opportunity to say whether we wish to be in or out. For an issue of this unique magnitude, that is simply not good enough.

I understand and respect the view of those devoted to the sovereignty of Parliament who argue that a referendum is alien to the principles and practices of parliamentary democracy. I respect their view, but I do not agree with it.

Source: *H.C.Deb.*, vol. 888, cols. 291–2, 11 March 1975

B

Mr. John P. Mackintosh (Berwick and East Lothian): In the last 400 years of its history this House has not only exercised sovereignty but has given away sovereignty – not just on the Common Market issue, which is arguable, but when it conceded independence to the Republic of Ireland. This House acquired sovereignty over an Empire of 600 million people, and then gave away that sovereignty country by country . . . These things were done – war, peace and the creation and ending of an Empire – by debate and decision in this House of Commons. This, therefore, is the history of the matter. So one cannot argue that membership of the European Community is in any sense a unique occasion which merits unique treatment . . .

The only serious special reason that has been put forward for bringing in a referendum on this question does not lie in the nature of the problem but in the difficulties faced by the Labour Party in handling the issue within itself. I agree that there is some importance in keeping parties united . . . But to inflict this particular issue on Parliament as a remedy for a party division is entirely monstrous.

Source: *H.C.Deb.*, vol. 888, cols. 411–13 *passim*, 11 March 1975

Document 7.11

In the following extracts Enoch Powell, a leading opponent of continuing UK membership of the EEC, and Edward Heath offer contrasting views on whether such membership posed a threat to parliamentary sovereignty and British independence.

A

The choice now is no other than whether the Parliament and people of this country intend to continue to be a self-governing democracy at all – whether the political decisions under which the British live their lives and the acts to which they are committed in the world shall still be determined by their own representatives, elected by the people and responsible to the people. For a nation such as we are, our whole history dominated by the evolution of Parliament and our very existence inseparable from parliamentary self-government, that choice is nothing less than whether we shall remain a nation at all.

That is why those in all parties who believe that Britain has the will and the power to remain a nation, and the right to continue to rule herself through her own parliamentary institutions, appeal to the electorate across the parties. That is why the opponents of a lifetime now sink their differences, as in the past they have sunk them in the face of external enemies, in order to preserve what is more important than any party policy – the right of the British people to decide in freedom how they will be governed.

Source: Extract from a speech by Enoch Powell at a public meeting in the ABC Cinema, Sidcup, Kent, 4 June 1975

B

Mr. Edward Heath (Sidcup): I come now to the question of sovereignty. Of course, this is a matter which must be treated with the deepest respect, but, whether one is discussing national sovereignty or parliamentary sovereignty, what matters is the purpose of sovereignty. To me, sovereignty is not something to be hoarded, sterile and barren, carefully protected by the right hon. Member for Down South (Mr. Powell) in a greatcoat with its collar turned up. Nor is sovereignty something which has to be kept in a crypt to be inspected by my right hon. Friend the Member for Banbury on the opening of Parliament.

Sovereignty is something for us as custodians to use in the interests of our own country. The question we have to decide, therefore, in carrying through this great political purpose, as I believe it to be, for the peace and freedom of Europe and of our own country, is how we are entitled to use that measure of sovereignty which is required. That, I believe, puts it perfectly fairly. It is a judgement which we have to make, and I answer without hesitation that the sacrifice of sovereignty, if it be put in that extreme form, or the sharing of sovereignty, the transfer of sovereignty or the offering of sovereignty is fully justified. Indeed were we not to do so in the modern world, I believe that as a Parliament, as a party and as a Government we should be culpable in the eyes of history. I believe, therefore, that sovereignty is for this House to use in the way it thinks best.

Source: *H.C.Deb.*, vol. 889, col. 1282, 9 April 1975

Document 7.12

One of Tony Benn's consistent claims during the referendum campaign was that membership of the EEC had been disastrous for the British economy (A). This was dismissed by pro-marketeers like Roy Jenkins (B).

A

In 1971, Mr Heath took us into the Common Market, promising that the EEC would make Britain prosperous, and bring positive, substantial and immediate gains to our industry and our people.

Let us examine the four claims he and his Ministers then made, and see how false they have proved.

They told us in 1971 that the Common Market was 'our most promising export market.' Now, three years later, our trade deficit with the Six stands at over £2 billion. Mr. Heath was wrong then and he is wrong now.

They told us in 1971 the Common Market would provide 'an immediate stimulus to investment.' Now, three years later, our industrial investment is just as low, and falling. Mr. Heath was wrong then and he is wrong now.

They told us in 1971 that joining the Common Market would provide 'jobs for our people.' Now, three years later, unemployment stands at 900,000. Mr. Heath was wrong then and he is wrong now.

They told us in 1971 that inside the Common Market 'prospects would open up for Scotland, Wales, Northern Ireland and all the development areas.' Now, three years later, many factories and plants in these areas have closed down, because they are thought too distant from Europe's industrial heartlands – the golden triangle from which they are excluded. Mr. Heath was wrong then and he is wrong now.

If you bought a new house and moved in, expecting to be secure and warm and within three years the outer walls and roof had collapsed, you would press the architect and master builder of that house for an explanation. Mr. Heath is [the] architect and master builder who took us into the Common Market edifice promising trade, investment and jobs.

Now, after three years, we face an industrial crisis. I am asking him for his explanation.

Source: Speech by Anthony Wedgwood Benn, Secretary of State for Trade and Industry, at the Coventry Police Hall, 16 May 1975

B

The full facts, fairly presented, demolish the argument that entry into the European Community has caused the grave deterioration in our international trade and balance of payments. In the Community or outside, we face a long, grim struggle to get our economy right. A 'Yes' vote on June 5th is vital to that process but it will represent only one step along the road of national survival.

It is equally essential to face the sharp contrasts between the basic alternatives now facing our country in international relations and trading patterns. The European Community is by far the largest and most powerful grouping in world trade . . . Our membership of the Community does not make us, on our own, all-powerful in negotiating international trading and financial arrangements – but it gives us our only realistic chance of protection for ourselves and influence on behalf of others in a rough and increasingly uncertain world.

What are the alternatives if we vote 'No' on June 5th? It is high time everyone understood the genuine and fundamental contradiction in the 'anti' case. If we were to withdraw from the Community the country would have to choose between two profoundly unattractive courses of action. First, there is the 'free trade area' alternative, which finds support from a random selection of individuals dotted around the political landscape. Supporters of this view argue that after withdrawing from the Community and tearing up one treaty we could then, without difficulty, negotiate another one to give us free trade with them. We might be able to achieve this – but it would be a bruising, difficult, long job in the midst of great uncertainty about our future . . .

The 'free trade area' banner raised by many of the anti-marketeers is a tattered flag bearing a false device but there is a separate and entirely different faction in their ranks.

They believe in something which is totally abhorrent to any notion of free trade with anybody, either in our own country or outside it. They believe in a siege economy, relying on direct controls to stop the imports we buy from outside and pray that the rest of the world would go on buying from us. The immediate effect would be a sharp rise in the cost of living in this country as attractively-priced imports were shut out. The poorest consumers would be hardest hit. Our industry would gradually grow even less competitive and efficient as it sheltered behind high tariff walls, while jobs and investment in our export industries would vanish like drops of water in the desert. As a country which consumes 5 per cent more than it produces we are uniquely ill-placed to gamble with policies of this kind.

Source: Speech by Roy Jenkins, Home Secretary,
to a Britain in Europe rally in Edinburgh, 14 May 1975

Document 7.13

Business sentiment was overwhelmingly in favour of Britain remaining in the EEC. In the lead up to the referendum the CBI carried out a survey of its members' views. The resulting report, completed in March 1975, strongly supported continued membership and warned of the dangers of withdrawal.

After only two years of the transitional stage we cannot attempt to draw up anything which might be considered as a balance sheet. However . . . substantial gains can already be identified. Furthermore, the CBI's earlier concern that the Community might prove too inward-looking has already been allayed in several respects. The Common Agricultural Policy is not having the consequences for the British balance of payments that had been expected; on the contrary, it is providing secure access to cheaper food supplies. Both food and crude materials take up a greater share of Britain's total imports than those of other EEC Member States, and a greater proportion of our national product is exported than most of our major European competitors. It is not enough to produce goods; they must also be sold, and industry needs secure access on equal terms to our largest market. The views expressed by a wide cross-section of firms and trade associations confirm the CBI's conviction that withdrawal from the EEC must cost Britain dear in both jobs and living standards.

Some of the consequences of withdrawal would be immediate; Britain's economic situation is such that she is far less well able to stand alone than in the years before accession. Most countries find it desirable to belong to an economic grouping even in times of world expansion; in a recession, Britain with her great dependence on imports of food, fuel and raw materials, will anyway be one of the hardest hit, but particularly if she were struggling to survive on her own.

Membership of the EEC has not only assured us, during our present economic difficulties, of the support of our partners, it has also assisted in maintaining a degree of confidence in sterling. At a time when there are grave doubts about Britain's ability to face her problems alone, probably no step could have such a serious and immediate consequence as a decision to cast away the security of membership of the EEC. Thus outside the Community her dangers would be compounded and her capacity to meet them reduced.

The CBI has long asserted that the chief benefits of membership would be slow to materialise; today it must stress that the disadvantages of withdrawal would come swiftly. It is more than ever convinced of its original view that membership carries a long-term balance of advantage; it is now increasingly conscious of the fearful dangers of withdrawal.

Source: 'British Industry and Europe',
A Report by the CBI Europe Committee, March 1975

Document 7.14

One of the central issues in the referendum debate was the impact of membership of the EEC on food prices. Supporters of the 'yes' campaign insisted that the days of cheap and readily available food on world markets were gone for good (A). Anti-marketeers denied that this was the case and argued that artificially high prices were an unavoidable consequence of the CAP (B).

A

The Minister of Agriculture, Fisheries and Food (Mr. Fred Peart): It is not, I think, in dispute, that our entry into the Common Market coincided with the start of a marked increase in the general level of world prices and a serious shortage of some commodities ...

There are those who assert that this is a temporary phenomenon, that prices are already falling in some cases, and that if we are free from the constraints of continued membership, we should soon find sources of relatively cheap food again ... But there has been something of a revolution in world food supplies and prices comparable to the oil crisis which itself was responsible for major increases in the costs of food production, processing and distribution, through its effects on fertilisers, fuel, transport and shipping costs.

Moreover, the rising world population with increased expectations, and the growing ability of developing countries to make their demands effective, must increase the pressure on available supplies. Also, world stockpiles have been seriously depleted. In these circumstances it is foolish to suppose, much as they value continued access to our markets, that any of our traditional suppliers would be willing to gear themselves primarily to meeting our needs, especially at the expense of other outlets where they could obtain a higher return ...

These considerations lead to two fundamental conclusions. The first is that it makes increasingly good sense to produce as much of our own food as we can efficiently and economically ... Secondly, EEC prices are likely to be much more in line with world prices than in the past, and the CAP system could provide our best assurance of supplies.

Source: *H.C.Deb.*, vol. 889, cols. 1244–6, 9 April 1975

B

Membership of the Common Market has meant and must mean dearer food. If we get out of the Market there will not be cheap food, but there will be cheaper food. It is not a question of seeing that the world's food producers get a reasonable return. The real scandal of the Common Market's agricultural policy is that it taxes food imports from outside the EEC and so makes the prices artificially high. Take these examples:

on butter from New Zealand there is a Brussels tax of 8 pence a lb
on butter from elsewhere outside the EEC a tax of 18p a lb
on cheese from New Zealand a tax of 13p a lb
on cheese from elsewhere a tax of 21½p a lb
on lamb a tax of 4p a lb
on 'canned pigmeat' – ham and so on – a tax of 3p a lb

And worse is to come. Because we are only half way through to paying full EEC taxes, as we shall have to by 1978 ...

The pro-marketeers tell you they are good internationalists. They fail to tell you that none of these taxes goes to the producers of this good. They go into the

Common Market's coffers to help European farmers keep their prices high; to manipulate the food markets of Europe to stop the housewife of Britain from getting a square deal. Since we joined the EEC in 1973 British housewives' and taxpayers' money has been used by Brussels towards the purchase of 628,000 tons of beef to be locked in cold store; of half a million tons of skimmed milk and barley; of over 2 million tons of wheat; of thousands of tons of rye, oilseeds, sugar and tobacco. This food has been locked away because it has been too expensive to consume.

Not only could we get much food from outside the EEC cheaper than it costs inside; but much EEC food is sold cheaper to outside countries than we in the EEC pay for it. In 1973 butter for which the British housewife paid 23p a lb went to the Russians for just 6 pence . . . By courtesy of Brussels the Russians enjoyed butter at a price not seen in Britain for more years than most of us can remember.

For cheaper food for the British housewife there is only one answer – it is 'No' to the EEC.

Source: Barbara Castle, Secretary of State for Social Services,
speaking at the Islington Town Hall, 22 May 1975

8   In transition: 1973–1979

The seven-year period following Britain's entry into the EC in January 1973 put to the test many of the speculative claims and counter-claims of the pro- and anti-marketeers about the likely impact of membership. The substance of these conflicting assessments figured in the previous section. The extracts below deal with how some of the early *actual* effects of membership were represented in various quarters. In addition, these extracts illustrate the often qualified British approach towards EC membership. This stance was shaped by a number of interrelated influences including government reservations, Labour party opposition to the policy consequences of EC membership and public antipathy to the EC.

Pro- and anti-marketeers in this period drew up sharply conflicting cost–benefit analyses of EC membership. Commentators at the time and since, however, have tended to emphasise the difficulty of measuring the precise effects of membership and of addressing the counterfactual question of what British exclusion from the EC might have entailed in this period. Such problems are particularly apparent in any evaluation of the economic and commercial effects of EC membership, especially since that was only one of a range of factors affecting the performance of the British economy in the 1970s. A further complication is that British entry to the EC coincided with the onset of the worst economic recession to affect the Western economies since 1945. The sea-change in economic conditions was precipitated by the collapse of the Bretton Woods fixed exchange rate system in 1971 and the quadrupling in the price of oil during 1973–74. In these circumstances, the British economy experienced a sharp fall in production, a steeply rising rate of inflation and unemployment, and a mounting balance of payments deficit. This period of 'stagflation', culminating in a major sterling crisis in 1976, formed a marked contrast to the relatively low rates of inflation and unemployment and balance of payments surplus at the time of the opening of negotiations for EC membership in 1970.

The Heath government's case for EC membership had relied heavily on the view that the dynamic benefits of membership in the form of faster growth and a more competitive British industry would outweigh the static costs of membership arising out of more expensive food and raw materials imports (see section 7). In the event, Britain's economic growth rate relative to that of the rest of the EC in the years immediately before and after entry to the EC underwent little change (8.1 Table A). In the period 1965–70, for example, Britain's annual average growth rate was 2.2 per cent as compared with 4.9 per cent for the rest of the EC. The comparable figures for the period 1972/73–1978/79, 1.48 per cent and 2.34 per cent, indicated a narrowing of the gap, largely because Britain was less severely affected by the recession of 1974–75 than some of the other EC economies. There was little evidence to suggest that EC membership had had a galvanising effect on the British economy, especially as the other EC states recovered more strongly and quickly from recession than Britain in the later 1970s.

The impact of EC membership on British trade also failed to fulfil the expectations of the Heath government. The government had anticipated an initial upsurge in imports from the rest of the EC as British tariff rates were higher than the EC's, and this proved to be the case (8.1 Table C). It was believed, however, that access to the EC market would facilitate a strong expansion of British exports to the rest of the EC. In the early years of membership at least, the anti-marketeers were able to demonstrate that while the EC accounted for an increasing proportion of British trade, the rest of the EC benefited from this trading pattern more than Britain (8.1 Tables B, C and D). The substance of this argument was that while Britain's trade deficit with the EC accounted for 58.84 per cent of Britain's total trade deficit in the period 1973–78, trade with the rest of the EC as a proportion of Britain's total trade amounted to an annual average of 34.71 per cent in the same period. Against that, however, there was evidence by 1976–77 to suggest that the rate of growth of British exports to the rest of the EC was exceeding the rate of growth of British imports from the rest of the EC (8.1 Table C).

A further aspect of British trade during this period was the continuing significance of extra-EC markets and sources of supply. The EC market was less important for British exports than it was for the exports of the other EC member states (8.1 Table E). This, in turn, had an important bearing on British policy within the EC, especially in the context of EC efforts to promote more stable trading conditions via monetary integration (see below).

Some of the consequences of EC membership were more predictable, if no less contentious, than the economic and commercial effects. For example, membership necessitated acceptance of the powers and jurisdiction of the EC's Court of Justice and thus of an independent legal system distinct from the legal systems of the member states. Under Article 177 of the Treaty of Rome the Court was empowered to interpret the treaty in the event of any doubt over its meaning, to rule on the validity of any action by an EC institution, and to deliver a ruling on request from a national court or tribunal in cases where such a body needed a ruling to enable it to give judgement. These provisions established not only the general scope of EC law but also its precedence in the event of any conflict with national law. It was on the basis of this Article that the

Court of Appeal found in favour of the plaintiff in its first case involving the application of the Treaty of Rome (8.2).

The legal implications of membership attracted less public attention than the financial consequences and the British contribution to the EC budget. The size of this contribution had been fairly predictable at the time of entry with projections of Britain as a net contributor. At this time it had been hoped that the difference between the gross contributions to and receipts from the EC budget (the net contribution) could be reduced by increased EC expenditure on policies such as regional development that were likely to favour Britain. In the event, this proved to be a vain hope, and the principal elements of the EC's funding and expenditure system were to remain unchanged. Both the source of EC funding (all duties on goods entering the EC and up to 1 per cent of VAT collected by the member states) and the large amount of the EC budget consumed by the CAP (approximately 80 per cent) failed to benefit Britain as a large importer of goods from non-EC sources and as a major importer of food. During the later stages of the five-year transition period Britain's contribution to the EC budget rose inexorably (8.3). It was against this background that the Thatcher governments of 1979–84 vigorously campaigned for the introduction of a permanent system of rebates (see section 9).

The detailed implementation of new EC policy initiatives was a further consequence of membership which, like the contribution to the EC budget, intensified public dissatisfaction with the EC. A case in point was the evolution of the EC's Common Fisheries Policy (CFP) which originated in 1970 with an agreement on the right of free access to all EC waters by EC fishermen. While this move heralded the end of the existing system of exclusive zones for national fishing fleets, the new member states at this time – Britain, Denmark and Ireland – negotiated some concessions to cover the first 10 years of membership. In 1976 the EC adopted a 200-mile exclusive fishing zone, and in doing so raised the vexed question of exclusive national fishing rights within this zone. The matter was not to be resolved until 1983, but in the meantime the issue was easily exploited by anti-marketeers like Enoch Powell, one of the most formidable opponents of EC membership in this period (8.4).

The impact of EC membership on British politics and especially on James Callaghan's Labour government of 1976–79 did little to encourage a British lead in the EC or to reconcile the Labour Party to membership. Like Wilson, Callaghan pursued a defensive, semi-detached relationship with the EC. During the renegotiation of the terms of entry episode of 1974–75, he had become convinced of the value of EC membership as a dull necessity rather than a matter of principle. In the foreign policy field, his natural inclination was to cultivate close ties with the US which, in his view, had been damagingly downgraded by the Heath government. In his first major speech as Foreign Secretary in February 1974 he strongly supported Atlantic cooperation at a time when the 1973 'Year of Europe', launched by the Nixon administration to revitalise the Western alliance and to reassert American leadership in the face of an enlarged EC, had resulted in a series of disagreements between the US and the EC (8.5). Callaghan was particularly concerned to allay American fears about the gradual erosion of the Atlantic community and the achievement of European unity at the expense of the Western alliance. This strong 'Atlanticist' strain in his thinking was evident throughout his premiership, most notably in his handling of the sterling crisis of 1976 and in his plan to combat recession in the Western economies (March 1978).

Callaghan ideally wished to limit the extent to which EC affairs intruded into British politics, to avoid association with any plans to increase the EC's powers, and to maintain tolerable relations with the other member states. A major constraint on his treatment of EC matters was his government's precarious position with a tiny parliamentary majority that disappeared altogether in early 1977 and resulted in the making of the Lib–Lab pact in order to remain in power. What principally limited his room for manoeuvre, however, was the fear of widening divisions within the Labour Party and thereby worsening the problem of managing a party in which the left was in the ascendancy and was highly critical of the government's spending cuts of 1975–76. Opposition to EC membership in the Labour Party was only temporarily stilled by the result of the 1975 referendum. On the first anniversary of the referendum, the Labour Common Market Safeguards Committee – the most influential organ of anti-marketeer opinion in the party – issued the first in a series of annual reports detailing the adverse consequences of EC membership (8.6). Party opinion, as expressed through the National Executive Committee (NEC) and the annual conference, increasingly viewed EC membership in a negative light. The manifesto adopted by the NEC for the European elections of 1979 amounted to a damning indictment of EC membership and prepared the ground for the party's subsequent commitment (1981) to negotiate Britain's withdrawal from the EC. (8.7).

British reactions to the EC's most notable innovation during this period – the European Monetary System (EMS) – further highlighted some of the singular features of the impact of EC membership on the country. The centrepiece of the EMS was the Exchange Rate Mechanism (ERM) which, like the earlier ill-fated 'snake' system that had briefly included sterling in 1972, was designed to limit fluctuations between the currencies of the member states. This Franco-German initiative of 1978 was far more modest in scope than the EC's earlier plan for economic and monetary union by 1980. This ambitious scheme had collapsed as a result of the disintegration of the Bretton Woods fixed exchange rate system and the divergent economic performances of the EC economies. The EMS project was immediately viewed by large sections of the Labour Party as a threat to national economic and monetary sovereignty and as a staging-post to full economic and monetary union in the EC. In particular, the possibility of including sterling in the ERM held out the decidedly uninviting prospect of tying the inflation-prone British economy to the low inflation discipline of West Germany and thus involving unpopular deflationary measures for the British economy. Fierce opposition to the plan at the Labour Party conference of 1978 was an important factor in convincing Callaghan of the case for withholding sterling from the ERM. In defence of this decision, which left Britain as the sole EC state outside the ERM, Callaghan emphasised the lack of convergence between the EC economies and also singled out the Conservatives' earlier hapless attempt to include sterling in the 'snake' (8.8).

Apart from party considerations, this decision reflected a wider domestic consensus and a deepening mood of disenchantment with EC membership. The Conservatives, under Margaret Thatcher's leadership, had little interest in repeating the failure of 1972 to keep sterling in the 'snake', and on coming to power in 1979 were to withhold sterling from the ERM for the next 11 years. British industrial, commercial and financial interests, still heavily skewed towards extra-EC interests, were sceptical of the case for including sterling in the ERM in order to reinforce stable trading conditions in the EC. Meanwhile, earlier public support for and interest in EC membership had evaporated. The British turn-out in the first elections for a directly elected European Parliament (1979) was markedly lower than that for any other member state, while opinion polls during this period and into the 1980s regularly reported that the British electorate was least satisfied with EC membership (8.9). On the tenth anniversary of British entry into the EEC, *The Economist*, a long-standing supporter of EC membership, fairly reflected the passage from the heady optimism of the pro-marketeers in the early 1970s to the more subdued assessments 10 years later. Hard pressed to cite many benefits derived from EC membership, it conceded that Wilson, who had been roundly criticised by the press in the first half of the 1970s for his pocket calculator approach to the issue, had after all correctly emphasised the importance of the terms of membership (8.10).

Document 8.1

Table 8.1A GDP growth rates expressed as an annual percentage change (statistics for
1971/72 not available in this series)

	1970 1965	1970 1969	1971 1970	1973 1972	1974 1973	1975 1974	1976 1975	1977 1976	1978 1977	1979 1978
Belgium	4.8	7.1	3.7	6.1	4.3	−1.4	2.0	2.0	2.25	2.4
Denmark	4.4	2.9	3.6	3.9	4.3	−0.8	5.5	1.9	1.0	3.5
France	5.8	6.0	5.0	6.0	3.9	−2.4	5.2	3.0	3.0	3.2
Germany	4.7	4.9	2.7	5.3	0.6	−3.4	5.5	2.6	3.0	4.6
Ireland	4.5	1.4	2.7	7.2	1.0	−2.2	3.0	5.0	6.5	1.9
Italy	5.9	5.1	1.4	6.4	3.4	−3.7	5.6	1.7	2.0	5.0
Luxembourg	3.6	6.1	0.7	7.5	4.4	−7.7	3.0	1.7	2.5	2.7
Netherlands	5.6	5.6	4.3	4.2	2.0	−1.3	4.6	2.4	2.0	2.2
UK	2.2	2.1	1.7	5.7	0.3	−1.6	1.4	0.7	3.0	0.9

Source: OECD (1970–80) *Main Economic Indicators*, OECD Publications, Paris.

Table 8.1B UK balance of trade by area (£million)

	EEC	Rest of Western Europe	North America	ODC	OE	Rest of the world	Total
1970	+39	+178	−488	+147	−114	+199	−42
1971	−191	+115	−175	+221	−188	+479	+261
1972	−591	−41	−82	−157	−131	+280	+722
1973	−1,191	−282	−283	−208	−330	−88	−2,383
1974	−2,042	−358	−703	+98	−2,217	−13	−5,235
1975	−2,412	−71	−662	−15	−714	+638	−3,236
1976	−2,127	−2	−826	+13	−697	+50	−3,589
1977	−1,733	+245	−757	−388	+898	+26	−1,709

ODC: Other developed countries
OE: Oil exporters

Source: *Trade and Industry: News from the Departments of Industry, Trade, Prices and Consumer Protection*, 24 November 1978, London, Her Majesty's Stationery Office (hereafter HMSO).

Table 8.1C UK balance of trade with the EEC, 1970–77, balance of payments basis (percentage change on previous period)

	Exports fob £m	Imports fob £m	Visible balance	Exports as a proportion of imports
1970	2,347	2,308	+39	101.7
1971	2,511 (+7)	2,702 (+17)	−191	92.9
1972	2,835 (+13)	3,426 (+27)	−591	82.7
1973	3,944 (+39)	5,135 (+50)	−1,191	76.8
1974	5,581 (+42)	7,623 (+48)	−2,027	73.2
1975	6,273 (+12)	8,685 (+14)	−2,412	72.2
1976	9,052 (+44)	11,179 (+29)	−2,127	81.0
1977	11,878 (+31)	13,611 (+22)	−1,733	87.3

Note: fob is usually rendered as f.o.b. (free on board) and means that duty is assessed on the value of traded goods at the point of export.

Source: *Trade and Industry: News from the Departments of Industry, Trade, Prices and Consumer Protection*, 24 November 1978, London, HMSO.

Table 8.1D The value of UK visible trade with the EEC as a percentage of total UK trade, 1973–78

	1973	1974	1975	1976	1977	1978
Imports (c.i.f.)	32.93	33.18	36.32	36.49	38.32	40.48
Exports (f.o.b.)	32.43	33.22	32.22	35.56	36.45	37.74

Note: c.i.f. (cost, insurance, freight) means that duty is assessed on the value of the traded good together with transit costs.

Source: *Annual Abstract of Statistics*, London, HMSO, 1980.

Table 8.1E   The value of the intra-EC trade of each EC member state expressed as a percentage of each state's total exports in 1958 and 1980

	1958	*1980*
Belgium/Luxembourg	35	71
Denmark	58	50
Germany	35	48
France	28	51
Ireland	83	74
Italy	32	48
Netherlands	57	73
United Kingdom	20	42

Source: Office for Official Publications of the European Communities, *The Economy of the European Community*, Luxembourg, 1982.

Document 8.2

The following extracts are taken from a judgement by Lord Denning in the Court of Appeal in the case of Schorsch Meier GmbH v. Hennin, 22 November 1974.

Here we see the impact of the Common Market on our law. No one would have thought of it before. A German company comes to an English court and asks for judgment – not in English pounds sterling but, if you please, in German deutschmarks. The judge offered a sterling judgment. But the German company said 'No. Sterling is no good to us. It has gone down much in value. If we accepted it, we would lose one-third of the debt. The debt was payable in deutschmarks. We want deutschmarks. We will accept no other.' The judge refused their request. He had no power, he said, in English law to give any judgment but in sterling. The German company appeal to this court . . .

The currency of the contract was clearly German. The money of account and the money of payment was German deutschmarks. At the time when the sum became due the rate of exchange was £1 = DM8.30. At that rate the sterling equivalent of DM3,756.03 was £452 sterling. Some time later sterling was devalued. As a result £1 sterling was only worth DM5.85 . . .

When the case came before the county court judge, the German company proved the debt owing in deutschmarks, that is, DM3,765.03. They gave no evidence of rates of exchange. They asked for judgment in deutschmarks. They relied on the Treaty of Rome. They submitted that the rule of English law (by which an English court can give judgment only in sterling) is incompatible with art [article] 106 of the treaty. They asked the court to refer the matter to the European Court under art 177(1)(*a*) of the treaty. The judge refused. He held that, applying English canons of construction, art 106 had no bearing on the rule of the common law: and that this was so clear that no reference to the European court was required under art 177(1)(*a*) . . .

I turn now to the Treaty of Rome. It is by statute part of the law of England. It creates rights and obligations, not only between member states themselves, but also between citizens and the member states and between the ordinary citizens themselves; and the national courts can enforce those rights and obligations . . . Whenever the treaty is prayed in aid, the English courts can themselves interpret it, subject always to the European court, if asked, having the last word . . .

This is the first case in which we have had actually to apply the Treaty of Rome in these courts. It shows great effect. It has brought about a fundamental change. Hitherto our English courts have only been able to give judgment in sterling. In future when a debt is incurred by an English debtor to a creditor in one of the member states – payable in the currency of that state – the English courts can give judgment for the amount in that money . . .

I would allow the appeal and adjudge that the debtor do pay to the plaintiff DM3,756.03 or the sterling equivalent at the time of payment.

Source: R. N. G. Harrison (ed.), *The All England Law Reports*, London, Butterworth and Co., 1975, vol. 1, pp. 154–5 and 157–8

Document 8.3

Table 8.3 UK contributions to the EEC budget, 1973–78 (£ million)

	Gross contribution	Receipts	Net contribution
1973	181.1	78.7	102.4
1974	180.5	149.9	30.6
1975	341.7	397.7	+56.0
1976	462.8	295.5	167.3
1977	737.0	368.0	369.0
1978	1285.0	555.0	730.0

Source: Cmd 7405, *The European Monetary System*.

Document 8.4

The following extract is taken from a speech by Enoch Powell. It focuses on the adverse impact of EEC membership on the question of British territorial waters and fishing rights. Powell was convinced that the implications of membership would eventually lead to Britain's withdrawal.

My colleagues in Parliament and I remain implacable in our opposition to Britain's membership of the Common Market. It is not a hopeless rearguard action in which we are participating. This is no Jacobite cause of non-jurors, half tolerated with amusement or pity by a world which has moved on while we stay behind. We are on the winning side, winning a victory which is as assured as the ultimate victory of the laws of biology or dynamics. Scarcely a month now goes by without some event which awakens more of those around us in Parliament to the fact that a gigantic mistake was made in 1972 and that it will have to be reversed – something expressly contemplated by the Government itself when it stated, at the very moment of the referendum, that continued membership would depend on the continuing assent of Parliament.

These reflections are prompted, and the withdrawal of that assent is brought a stage nearer, by the emergence of a subject of which the implications are still too little appreciated by the country at large. That subject is the law of the sea . . .

When the Heath Government hijacked us into the Community we were allowed to keep our national 12-mile fishing limit until the end of 1982; that is all. When the Labour Party before the 1974 Election undertook to renegotiate the Treaty, they forgot all about the sea. The consequence is that the 200 mile zone will be – I quote the Minister again – 'the Community's fishing limits!'. Everything 200 miles and 12 miles belongs to the Community, not us; and after 1982, unless something happens, it will be everything between 200 miles and the beach. The rest of the Community are laughing their heads off at us, because most of the fishing grounds are around these islands and we have 'handed' them to the continentals on a plate. They have us at their mercy: we are on a hiding to nothing which is why we are starting to negotiate – starting, mind you, not finishing – by giving up even a 50 mile zone and asking to be allowed, out of the kindness of their European hearts, to keep our present 12-mile limit and extend it up to 50 miles in 'substantial areas'. I just hope that, even if the Community were to accept these as yet unspecified areas, the fish would be good enough to oblige by staying in them. Did somebody whisper the word 'veto', which we used to be told that we could and would brandish whenever a vital British interest was at stake? No, sir; in this case, the veto works the other way. It works against us; even landlocked Luxembourg could use it.

So every nation which is worth the name – and many which are not – is to have a 200-mile exclusive fishing zone, while we shall be lucky to get anything beyond 12 miles, if that. As for control over conservation and agreements with other non-EEC countries about access to our vital fishing grounds . . . those will not be in the hands of Britain. All that will be handled by the landlubbers at Brussels, who (if the metaphor be not inappropriate) have other fish to fry; and small redress we shall have when our so-called partners in the Community proceed to vacuum-clean our seas as they have ruined their own . . .

Source: Enoch Powell, extract from a speech at
Ardglass, Co. Down, 31 July 1976

Document 8.5

Shortly after Labour returned to power following the general election of February 1974, Callaghan, the Foreign Secretary, set the renegotiation of the terms of entry exercise in the context of relations with the United States.

I should like to say how we propose to begin the process of renegotiation but before doing so I wish to detain the House for a moment with an issue of equal, if not greater, importance; namely the recent speeches and remarks of President Nixon and Dr. Kissinger [US Secretary of State], which have called attention to the unsatisfactory state of repair into which relations between the Community and the United States have fallen. By implication this raises the question with which we, and, I hope, all in the House are much concerned; namely, the political direction that the Community itself seems to be taking . . .

I wish to indicate our approach to these matters. First, our manifesto states: 'A Labour Britain would always seek a wider co-operation between the European peoples'.

I shall enlarge on that a little later. Parallel with that, Britain needs to base her system of alliances for defence and other purposes, as well as our system of trading arrangements, on a much wider foundation.

These two issues need not be in conflict, but in our estimation it is not possible indefinitely to sustain a close alliance with the United States on matters of defence, which involve the closest co-operation and interdependence, without a parallel co-operation on matters of trade, money, energy and so on . . .

I must emphasise that we repudiate the view that Europe will emerge only out of a process of struggle against America. We do not agree that a Europe which excludes the fullest and most intimate co-operation with the United States is a desirable or attainable objective.

That does not mean that European countries become satellites of the United States . . .

Some may have found President Nixon's rough words the other day unduly harsh. But at least they had the effect of introducing a greater sense of realism, and that has been a scarce commodity in much of the discussion over the past two years. The peoples of Europe have been treated to too much high-flown rhetoric and not enough substance. Our belief is that the Community should accept more modest and attainable goals . . .

I must emphasise again that for us the value of political consultation and co-operation will be ruined if it appears to take an anti-American tinge or if consultation with the United States is inadequate. Of course, we do not always expect to agree with the United States. That is not the point. That is a different matter. We shall be ready to start talks and arrangements that may be made between the Community and other groupings.

Source: *H.C.Deb.*, vol. 870, cols. 859–62 and 864, 19 March 1974

Document 8.6

On the first anniversary of the June 1975 referendum, the Labour Common Market Safe-guards Committee issued a pamphlet – The Common Market: Promises and Reality *– which reviewed the impact of Common Market membership on Britain. The following extract from this pamphlet deals with the adverse effects of membership on Britain's balance of payments.*

It was always one of the major contentions of the pro-Marketeers that if tariff barriers between Britain and the original six countries in the Common Market were reduced the result would be a positive and substantial gain for Britain. This was to take the form of a massive increase in British exports of manufactured goods to the fast growing markets of the Six which would more than compensate us for any increases in the cost of food and raw materials as a result of membership, and the reduction in exports following from the loss of our trade preferences in the Commonwealth and EFTA. From the beginning it was exceedingly improbable that this would happen, partly because it was clear that the export record of the main European economies, particularly that of Germany, had for many years been superior to our own, and partly because before we joined the Market the average British level of tariffs on imports of manufactured goods was higher than the Common External Tariff of the EEC countries.

As we joined the Common Market, and the tariffs were progressively reduced, far from our balance of trade with the other EEC countries improving it fell predictably into enormous deficit. The Table below provides the figures for our visible trade both with the EEC and the Rest of the World since 1970:-

Table 8.6

Year	EEC (£m)	Rest of the World (£m)
1970	–47	–56
1971	–183	–468
1972	–583	–95
1973	–1,167	–1,128
1974	–2,026	–3,238
1975	–2,354	–846
1976	–1,816*	+64*

* Annual rates based on First Quarter of 1976.

These raw figures, it is true, need to be interpreted with some care. A proportion of the increased trade deficit with the other EEC countries is accounted for by a switch in our food imports from the rest of the world to Common Market countries, albeit at considerably higher prices, in consequence of the Common Agricultural Policy. However the greater part is accounted for by the fact that the other EEC countries, contrary to all the pro-Market promises and predictions, are selling us far more manufactured and semi manufactured goods than we are selling them. Our deficit in manufactures alone with the original Six EEC countries is now running at just short of £1,000m. per year.

Source: The Labour Common Market Safeguards Committee,
The Common Market: Promises and Reality, London, 1976

Document 8.7

The following extract is taken from the manifesto adopted by the National Executive Committee of the Labour Party for the European elections of 1979. Its criticism of the adverse impact of EEC policies on Britain intensified after Labour's defeat in the general election of 1979, eventually resulting in the formal decision (1981) to seek Britain's withdrawal from the EEC.

Britain has now been in the Common Market for just over six years, and there can be no doubt that the British people have been deeply disillusioned by the experience of EEC membership. In particular, the promises and the forecasts of the benefits that joining the EEC would bring have been shown to be false. Unlike the Tories and Liberals who made those promises so freely, the Labour Party warned the British people in 1975 of the dangers of Common Market membership. Today, we stand by everything we said because it has been proved correct. The Common Agricultural Policy is an expensive farce, forcing us to accept, at one and the same time, high food prices and vast food mountains. Our contribution to the EEC budget is monstrously unfair – with Britain having to pay, during next year alone, nearly £900 million more into the budget than we will get back. And, through the EEC take-over of important powers to make laws and levy taxes, our right to democratic self-government has been gravely weakened.

Labour is determined to change all this. But it will mean tough negotiations and hard bargaining with our European partners. It will also mean a major revision of the Treaty of Rome . . .

We believe that each member state should be free to determine, as far as it is able to do so, the value of its own currency; and we will continue to resist British membership of the European Monetary System. The EMS, we believe, would limit the degree to which member states can alter their exchange rates and encourage, or even enforce, recourse to deflationary policies (and hence increased unemployment and economic stagnation) to overcome the balance of payments difficulties. Similarly, the Labour Party will maintain its opposition to Economic and Monetary Union, the introduction of which would have serious consequences for the level of employment throughout the country . . .

The Community we are seeking is one which is more just, more equal and better adapted to the needs of a rapidly changing Europe. As at present constituted, it helps maintain a capitalist system which rewards the rich and powerful at the expense of traditional socialist goals – jobs for all, an end to poverty, help to the needy, rising living standards and the abolition of privilege.

We recognise and reaffirm that Britain's membership of the EEC depends on the continuing assent of Parliament. We declare that if the fundamental reforms contained in this manifesto are not achieved within a reasonable period of time, then the Labour Party would have to consider very seriously whether continued EEC membership was in the best interests of the British people.

> Source: National Executive Committee of the
> British Labour Party, *European Election Manifesto*, 1979

Document 8.8

At the Brussels European Council meeting of 4–5 December 1978, Callaghan announced that sterling would not be part of the Exchange Rate Mechanism of the European Monetary System. During a Commons debate immediately afterwards, from which the following extracts are taken, he defended this decision in the course of exchanges with Thatcher, leader of the Opposition.

I [the Prime Minister] explained to the Council that I would not be recommending to the Cabinet that the United Kingdom should participate in the exchange rate mechanism when it begins to function. I informed the other Heads of Government that we intend to work for a continuation of the exchange rate stability which sterling has enjoyed for nearly two years . . .

It was agreed that the United Kingdom would be free to join the exchange rate mechanism at a later date if we wish, or, of course, to remain outside it. We shall, of course, join in the development of the ECU and of the European monetary fund . . .

The broad conclusion that I offer to the House is that well-constructed and effective international monetary arrangements can assist those who take part in them in certain circumstances but they can be no more than additional supports, and that in the end it will be the success of our own efforts in restraining inflation, keeping down prices, maintaining the stability of sterling and remaining competitive that will ensure the long-term well-being of our people.

Mrs Thatcher: This is a sad day for Europe, in that nine member countries have been unable to agree on a major new initiative which will affect us all . . . is it not also a sad reflection on the performance of this Government that after four and half years the Prime Minister is content to have Britain openly classified among the poorest and least influential members in the Community, and that along with them we must ask for assistance if we are even to contemplate joining the scheme? . . . what really prevented the Prime Minister from joining the scheme? Was it economic weakness and lack of competitiveness, or are the reasons political, in that, whatever his own view, his party clearly would never have allowed him to join the system? . . .

[**The Prime Minister**]: The right hon. Lady also asked what had kept us out. I suppose that basically it was that we felt that the system as it was devised was too close to the original snake. It gradually acquired more characteristics of the snake as the negotiations went on. The right hon. Lady, who of course likes to draw a veil over her own experience in this matter, might contemplate, in the quietness of this evening, that she herself was part of a Government that went into a similar system and emerged very bedraggled after six weeks. We should at least try to learn from our history, even if the right hon. Lady prefers to forget it.

But I think that basically the final decision not to join was made simply for this reason: when the right hon. Lady's Government negotiated the matter six or seven years ago, they were informed, I am certain in good faith, and they accepted in good faith – I do not blame them for accepting the information; they just happened to be wrong, all of them – that the economies of the Community countries would converge before the transitional period came to an end. That has not happened . . . their convergence required not only action on our part but promises by the other members of the Community that they would take action to achieve it. Both those things have been missing, and therefore we decided that at this stage it would be imprudent to join the exchange rate mechanism.

Source: *H.C.Deb.*, vol. 959, cols. 1421–6, 6 December 1978

Document 8.9

Table 8.9A Eurobarometer opinion poll – spring 1983. Feeling that one's country has benefited from membership of the Community – national results (%)

Belgium	90.7
Denmark	62.2
Germany	76.5
Greece	63.7
France	72.0
Ireland ·	66.7
Italy	83.0
Luxembourg	86.0
Netherlands	87.6
United Kingdom	36.0

Source: Office for Official Publications of the European Communities, *Europe as Seen by Europeans: European Polling 1973–86*, Luxembourg, 1986.

Table 8.9B The turn-out at the election of 1979 for the European Parliament

Belgium*	91.4
Germany	65.9
Denmark	47.0
France	61.3
Ireland	63.6
Italy	85.5
Luxembourg*	85.0
The Netherlands	57.8
United Kingdom	32.6

* Voting is compulsory.

Source: Office for Official Publications of the European Communities, *Steps to European Unity*, Luxembourg, 1987.

Document 8.10

On the tenth anniversary of British membership of the EEC, an article in The Economist *considered the economic impact of membership on Britain.*

In 1971 the government's white paper on EEC membership was extremely bullish. It argued that the EEC would wake up British industry with a cold shower of competition and 'lead to much improved efficiency and productivity'. It also suggested that, if the stimulus of EEC membership added only 0.5 per cent to Britain's growth rate, this would improve the balance of payments by £1.1 billion – quite enough to offset the cost of the common agricultural policy.

This optimism (which *The Economist* shared at the time) proved misplaced – but not because of the EEC. Thanks to the first oil shock, growth spluttered to a standstill . . . It is thus hard to estimate what the effect of joining the EEC has been on the British economy. It has sharply accelerated the growth of British exports to the community, which rose an average 24% per year in value terms in the past decade (compared with a growth of 16% to non-EEC countries); 43% of all British exports now go to the EEC. And British manufacturers have increased their share of all the original Six's markets (in 1980 6.8% of West German manufactured imports came from Britain against 4.8% in 1972; and West Germany has now overtaken the United States as Britain's biggest export market). The trouble is that EEC imports into Britain have risen even faster.

The common agricultural policy . . . has cost Britain heavily – not just in the form of payments to the EEC budget, but because it has worsened the terms of farm trade (making most food imports more expensive) . . .

Against these costs must be set one clear benefit. British membership of the EEC has attracted more direct investment from abroad. Although total American investment in Europe has dropped since the boom days of the 1960s, the proportion of it going to Britain has sharply increased. In 1980, 59% of all direct American investment into the EEC went to Britain . . .

Japanese investment in Britain has also sharply accelerated. The Japanese see Britain . . . as a good base for launching export assaults on the continent and avoiding EEC countries' anti-Japanese controls. And between 1973 and 1979 there was 75% more investment by EEC companies in Britain than by British companies in the EEC.

Whatever assessment is made of the net effect on trade or investment from EEC membership, one thing is clear. The impact is small by comparison with the British contribution to the EEC budget. If Britain had actually paid £1 billion to Brussels in 1981, as it had been expected to do, it would have been hard to say that EEC membership was good for Britain's economy. On treasury figures, membership might have cut Britain's gdp by as much as 1%. But in the event Britain paid only £8m (the commission's estimate) or £60m (the treasury's estimate) to Brussels in 1981. The continuing argument over the budget is therefore central to any calculation of the benefits or losses from British membership. To that extent Sir Harold Wilson was right: the terms of membership are important.

Source: *The Economist*, 25 December 1982 – 7 January 1983, pp. 61–2

9 'No, no, yes': 1979–1990

The 11 years of Margaret Thatcher's premiership (1979–90) saw acute tensions and recurring crises in the UK's relations with its EC partners. Difficulties arose in the first instance over the scale of the British contribution to the Community budget. By 1984 this long-running dispute had been settled. There then followed a more cooperative and harmonious phase. This did not last long, however, and during the latter half of the 1980s an increasingly isolated Thatcher became engaged in a largely unsuccessful struggle against a powerful renewed drive towards deeper integration within the EC. The documentary extracts in this section illustrate these developments. They also bring out the important shift that took place at this time in Labour's policy and attitudes towards the EC.

Between 1979 and 1984 Community affairs were dominated by the British Budgetary Question (BBQ). The problem was one that Thatcher had inherited and that Callaghan too would have needed to address if he had won the 1979 general election. The simple fact was that the financial arrangements which Heath had agreed to in the early 1970s were disadvantageous to British interests. Wilson had tried to improve matters by negotiating a rebate formula in 1975. This was extremely complicated, however, and had proved to be of little practical value. It was therefore left to Thatcher to secure a better deal.

In 1979 the UK was one of only two net contributors to the EC budget – the other being West Germany. Its net payment for that year amounted to around £900 million and the figure was scheduled to go even higher in 1980 when the protection provided during the transitional period came to an end. By then Britain would be making an even bigger net contribution than West Germany, despite the fact that its GDP was much smaller. Thatcher regarded this as an intolerable state of affairs and in characteristic fashion set out to remedy it without delay. The result was a series of acrimonious meetings with other EC leaders, the most notorious of which was the Dublin European Council of November 1979 (9.1B). At Dublin Thatcher rejected as only 'one third of a loaf' an annual rebate of £350 million, holding out for the whole of the difference between Britain's payments and receipts. Her assertive manner and her references to wanting 'our money back' alienated both Giscard d'Estaing, the French President, and Schmidt, the West German Chancellor. The fractious proceedings in Dublin set the tone for subsequent negotiations and it was not until June 1984 that an agreement was reached – at the Fontainebleau European Council – on a permanent mechanism for the British rebate.

Widely differing explanations have been offered as to why the BBQ generated so much rancour and took so long to be resolved. Some accounts have laid particular emphasis on Thatcher's abrasive negotiating style, arguing that its effect was to stiffen the attitude of others. As a variation on this theme, it has further been claimed that Thatcher deliberately exacerbated and prolonged the budget rebate crisis as a way of boosting her flagging domestic popularity and diverting attention from the devastating economic recession of the early 1980s (9.1A). Other interpretations have placed the prime reponsibility for failing to reach a prompt and amicable settlement on Giscard d'Estaing and Schmidt. According to this line of argument, the French and West German leaders, who enjoyed an exceptionally close personal and working relationship, not only treated the relatively inexperienced British Prime Minister as something of an outsider, but were also guilty of a serious tactical blunder in making a grossly inadequate offer at the Dublin European Council (9.2B). Yet another viewpoint is that there were faults on both sides: Giscard in particular was impolite in his dealings with Thatcher, while she for her part contrived to weaken a good case by inept presentation (9.1C).

The resolution of the BBQ at Fontainebleau brought a short-lived improvement in the UK's relations with its Community partners. Differences soon arose, however, over British attempts to curb spending on the CAP. At the same time, a more fundamental divergence began to develop between the UK and a majority of other EC members over proposals for a greater degree of economic and political integration. The impetus to change and reform came from certain key individuals, notably François Mitterrand, who had replaced Giscard d'Estaing in May 1981, and Jacques Delors, the President of the European Commission (1985–92). It also reflected a widespread concern that the EC was becoming increasingly uncompetitive compared to Japan and the US, particularly in the vital field of high technology. The view held in many quarters was that a broad range of far-reaching measures was necessary to tackle this problem. Whilst essential, the elimination of remaining barriers to the free working of the internal market would not of itself suffice. There must also be a substantial streamlining of the EC's decisionmaking procedures, especially through the extension of majority voting in the Council of Ministers and the granting of more powers to the Commission.

The Thatcher government had mixed feelings about such an agenda. On the one hand, it strongly supported efforts to promote the free movement of goods, capital and labour within the EC. On the other, it saw no necessity for a radical overhaul of the Community's institutions and was adamantly opposed to anything which eroded national sovereignty. It set out its own approach in a discussion paper submitted to the Fontainebleau European Council (9.2). The document, entitled *Europe – The Future*, maintained that the best way to deal with the technological gap opened up by Japan and the US was by freeing up the internal market: measures were accordingly proposed to simplify and speed up customs procedures and other formalities which were hindering intra-Community trade. A plea was predictably made for reform of the CAP. On the question of constitutional change, it was stressed that nothing must be done to weaken the existing right of veto enjoyed by each member state. There was also a suggestion that a larger and more diverse Community might need to be more flexible in the event of only some countries wishing to adopt new procedures and practices: in such cases there must be safeguards for the interests of non-participants. This was doubtless a defensive response to remarks by Mitterrand about the possibility of a 'multi-speed' Europe and of pressing on with desirable changes without Britain if necessary.

From the mid-1980s the British government fought a stubborn if ineffective rearguard action against moves towards closer integration. It suffered a major setback at the Milan European Council (June 1985) where Thatcher was unable to prevent the convening of an intergovernmental conference (IGC) to consider basic institutional reforms and a possible revision of the Community's founding treaties. The proposals of the resulting IGC formed the basis of the Single European Act (SEA, 1986). Although the SEA's central objective was to remove all impediments to the free movement of persons, capital and goods by 1992, it also involved substantial institutional changes, including the introduction of more qualified majority voting (QMV). It soon became clear, moreover, that the creation of a genuine single market would entail policy harmonisation over such matters as taxation and border controls.

As the full implications of the SEA sank in, and as the Commission produced a series of ambitious projects for the EC's future development – notably the Delors Report on EMU (April 1989) and the Social Charter (May 1989) – Thatcher became increasingly suspicious and hostile. She was especially mistrustful of Delors, regarding his plans for full economic and monetary union, greater powers for the Commission and comprehensive welfare provisions throughout the EC as a blueprint for the establishment of a centralised European superstate dominated by Brussels. In July 1988 Delors told the European Parliament that in 10 years' time 80 per cent of economic, financial and social legislation affecting members of the EC would emanate from Brussels. Thatcher was furious. Her reaction to his speech to the TUC annual conference in September 1988, in which he talked of the need to protect workers' interests, was even stronger. In an address delivered at the European College in Bruges on 20 September, Thatcher attacked many of the policies advocated not only by Delors but also by most other EEC governments (9.3).

By this stage Thatcher's approach to EC affairs was provoking mounting criticism. Whereas her earlier strident defence of British financial interests had struck a chord with many sections of public opinion, during the late 1980s there were clear signs of disquiet over the perceived extremism of her views. Of particular importance in this respect was her barely concealed dislike and suspicion of the Germans. Thatcher's opposition to the unification of Germany (1990) was a matter of common knowledge. Further indications of her anti-German instincts came from leaked press accounts of a seminar held at Chequers in March 1990 at which the Prime Minister reportedly questioned experts on Germany about the German people's national failings (9.4). In July 1990 Nicholas Ridley, the Secretary for Trade and Industry, was obliged to resign following publication in *The Spectator* of an indiscreet interview in which he insulted not only the Germans, but also the French and members of the European Commission. Few doubted that he was voicing the xenophobic prejudices of his political mistress (9.5).

In 1989 the Conservatives performed disastrously in the European elections following a campaign characterised by deep hostility to Brussels. The message was not lost on the Labour Opposition which had already begun to appreciate the electoral advantage to be obtained from exploiting public unease over Thatcher's European policies. The Labour Party manifesto claimed that Thatcher's confrontational style had left the UK friendless and isolated within the Community and promised a more cooperative approach towards other member states (see 9.6). This stance helped to produce large-scale electoral gains and Labour was encouraged to go further still in abandoning its earlier antagonism towards British membership of the EC. The party's policy in this area had changed out of all recognition over the past few years. In 1983 it had fought the general election on a commitment to negotiated withdrawal from the Community at the earliest opportunity. By the time of the next general election (1987) this commitment had been dropped and Labour was proclaiming its intention to 'work constructively with our EEC partners' (9.7A, 9.7B and 9.7C). Ironically, this shift in policy exposed the Labour leadership to the kind of taunts that had earlier been hurled at Heath by his political opponents (see section 6). Thatcher began to portray Neil Kinnock, who had succeeded Michael Foot as party leader in 1983, as a tool of Brussels (9.8). This set the pattern for the 1990s when John Major routinely used the same tactic against Kinnock and his successors, John Smith and Tony Blair.

Thatcher herself paid a heavy price for her views on Europe. It is arguable, indeed, that the dissatisfaction felt on that score – not least by some members of the Cabinet – played a major part in her fall from power. There were, of course, many other causes of political discontent at the time, including the unpopular poll tax, the high level of interest and mortgage rates, and the Prime Minister's personal style which was increasingly regarded as imperious and unfeeling. Thatcher's stance on EC matters nevertheless cost her much support both generally and within her own party. Furthermore, it was an EC issue – membership of the ERM – which precipitated the crisis that led directly to her resignation. Thatcher was adamantly opposed to sterling's entry to the ERM, believing that the latter was a preliminary step towards full economic and monetary union and that fixed exchange rates were, in any case, inherently unworkable. By the mid-1980s, however, Lawson, the Chancellor of the Exchequer, Howe, the Foreign Secretary, Robin Leigh-Pemberton, the Governor of the Bank of England, and senior Treasury officials had reached the conclusion that going into the ERM would be good for the economy and would provide a more effective weapon for containing inflation than control of the domestic money supply. On 13 November 1985 Lawson submitted a paper proposing entry to a meeting of leading Cabinet ministers and Leigh-Pemberton. Those present were overwhelmingly in favour. After Thatcher threatened resignation, however, the proposal was rejected (9.9). This marked the beginning of a prolonged and increasingly public wrangle between the Prime Minister and her two most senior colleagues, in the course of which Howe was removed from the Foreign Office (July 1989) and Lawson resigned (October 1989) in protest at the role of Thatcher's personal economic adviser, Professor Alan Walters, who was a fierce critic of the ERM.

By the summer of 1990 Thatcher's resistance had been greatly weakened, partly because the collapse of the government's economic strategy seemed to demand a change of policy. Under persistent pressure from John Major, who had replaced Lawson as Chancellor, and Douglas Hurd, the recently appointed Foreign Secretary, Thatcher finally gave her consent to sterling's entry into the ERM on 8 October 1990 – principally as a means of reducing domestic interest rates without undermining confidence in the pound. Even after entry, however, she remained deeply sceptical about the ERM and monetary union. This was reflected in comments made during the Rome European Council (October 1990) and in her report to the Commons on its outcome (9.10). Her perform-ance on the latter occasion dismayed Howe, the Deputy Prime Minister, for whom it was the last straw. No longer able to keep silent about his disapproval of Thatcher's whole approach to the EC, he resigned. His resignation speech (13 November 1990) was a devastating critique (9.11), and it played a major part in producing a challenge to Thatcher's leadership of the Conservative Party and her subsequent resignation.

Document 9.1

During the Thatcher government's first five years in power (1979–84) the UK's relations with its European partners were dominated by a wrangle over the British Budget Question. In the following extracts three first-hand observers – Sir Ian Gilmour, a disgruntled Foreign Office minister in the Thatcher government (1979–81), Christopher Tugendhat, a British Commissioner at the time, and Roy Jenkins, the President of the European Commission (1977–80) – offer contrasting retrospective assessments of the role of Thatcher and other EC leaders in the budget crisis.

A

To my mind there was only one explanation for the Prime Minister's attitude. Her objection was to the fact of the [budget] agreement [Brussels, May 1980], not to its terms. That was not because we had succeeded where she had failed. It was because, to her, the grievance was more valuable than its removal. Not for the last time during her period of office, foreign policy was a tool of party or personal politics. However badly things were going in Britain, Mrs Thatcher could at least win some kudos and popularity as the defender of the British people against the foreigner. Hence a running row with our European partners was the next best thing to a war; it would divert public attention from the disasters at home. Her attitude was of course inflaming British antagonism to the Community, but that did not worry her at all; it probably pleased her.

Source: I. Gilmour, *Dancing with Dogma: Britain under Thatcherism*,
London, Simon and Schuster, 1992, p. 240

B

Then came the June 1979 election victory and a marvellous opportunity to put the relationship between Britain and the rest of the Community on to a new footing . . . The problem was the budget and the fear of becoming a net contributor to the tune of nearly £1 billion a year from 1980 onwards . . .

It was at this point that an act of statesmanship was required and notably from Chancellor Schmidt and President Giscard d'Estaing. They were not simply the leaders of the two most powerful countries in the Community. They were the doyens of the European Council, close personal friends and close allies. Together they could certainly have solved the British budget problem before it got out of hand. What they should have done was to take Mrs Thatcher aside, show understanding for what was after all a genuine problem for which her government was in no way responsible . . .

Instead, as the November 1979 European Council approached, it became apparent that the French and German leaders had decided to embark on a trial of strength with their new British colleague. Mrs Thatcher would be isolated and alone and, it was thought, unable to withstand a combined onslaught from all the rest . . .

Schmidt and Giscard d'Estaing promoted a derisory offer and every pressure was brought to bear on Mrs Thatcher to accept. She responded by demanding 'my money back', a phrase that was widely interpreted as an attack on the whole principle on which the Community's 'own resources' system of financing is based. Schmidt at one point feigned asleep . . . Finally, the meeting ended in deadlock. Already dubbed the Iron Lady by Moscow, Dublin enshrined Mrs Thatcher as 'la Dame de Fer de l'Europe'. From that moment on, in addition to its technical complexities, the British budget problem became inextricably caught up with the pride, prejudices and personalities of the heads of state and government concerned.

Schmidt and Giscard d'Estaing were treating the European Council as a private fief . . . They were 'very patronising, even rude, in their treatment of her', one of my colleagues in the Commission subsequently told an American journalist. 'They made it clear that she, a mere woman, wouldn't be able to stand up to these two experienced and knowledgeable men in hard negotiation.'

I have no doubt that Mrs Thatcher's sex was a complicating factor.

Source: C. Tugendhat, *Making Sense of Europe*, London,
Viking Penguin, 1986, pp. 120–2

C

At Strasbourg [October 1979] she was very oddly treated by Giscard, who was presiding . . . At neither of the small but elaborately contrived banquets did he have her sitting next to him. It was an extraordinary performance for the would-be Sun King of Europe. Merely as a new Prime Minister from one of the four major countries she would have been an obvious choice. As the first woman ever to appear at a European Council the obviousness was at least quadrupled. Yet I do not believe that Giscard did it out of simple anglophobia . . . It was more a certain clumsiness of manners which sat ill with his intelligent, condescending sophistication . . .

Whatever his motive, Mrs Thatcher had every reason to feel offended . . . To her considerable credit, she showed no sign of reacting to the slight. What she did complain about was that he cheated her over the agenda. She told me at luncheon that she had made an arrangement to have the BBQ taken first . . . However, whether with malice or generosity, Giscard did not allow her to open, but began with a report of the working of the EMS over the first three months. Then, at what was in fact the best time to take the difficult issue of substance, he got me to open the convergence/budgetary discussion, which I did in a way as helpful as possible to the British, and which gave Mrs Thatcher the opportunity to come in next and deploy her full case. She nevertheless persisted in the view, which may have been formally true, that Giscard had reneged on an agenda undertaking.

Her presentation of her own case . . . was ill-judged. What she needed at this stage was to get support for our proposition that a problem existed and that the Commission should be charged with bringing forward proposals for dealing with it for the next European Council. Instead she spoke shrilly and too frequently, and succeeded in embroiling not only with Giscard (which maybe was unavoidable) but also in turn with van Agt (Netherlands), Jorgensen (Denmark) and Lynch (Ireland). Then, worst of all, she got in an altercation with Schmidt, whose support was crucial to her getting the outcome she wanted from the meeting . . .

Mrs Thatcher had thus performed the considerable feat of unnecessarily irritating two big countries, three small ones and the Commission within her opening hour of performance at a European Council.

Source: R. Jenkins, *A Life at the Centre*, London, Macmillan, 1991, pp. 494–5

Document 9.2

At the Fontainebleau European Council of 25–26 June 1984 the British government submitted a discussion paper outlining its own distinctive vision of the EC's future development.

STRENGTHENING THE COMMUNITY

6.   If the problems of growth, outdated industrial structures and unemployment which affect us all are to be tackled effectively, we must create the genuine common market in goods and services which is envisaged in the Treaty of Rome

and will be crucial to our ability to meet the US and Japanese technological challenge. Only by a sustained effort to remove remaining obstacles to intra-Community trade can we enable the citizens of Europe to benefit from the dynamic effects of a fully integrated common market with immense purchasing power. The success of the United States in job creation shows what can be achieved when internal barriers to business and trade come down. We must create the conditions in which European businessmen too can build on their strengths and create prosperity and jobs. This means action to harmonize standards and prevent their deliberate use as barriers to intra-Community trade: more rapid and better coordinated customs procedures; a major effort to improve mutual recognition of professional qualifications; and liberalizing trade in services, including banking, insurance and transportation of goods and people. If we do not give our service and manufacturing industries the full benefit of what is potentially the largest single market in the industrialized world, they will never be fully competitive at international level, and will be unable to create much needed jobs within the Community.

7.   At the same time we must do more, and work harder to make actions undertaken within the Community relevant to the lives of our people. A sustained effort will be required further to simplify and speed up customs and other formalities affecting the ease with which our citizens can travel across intra-Community borders. We should aim, for example, to allow European citizens to travel as freely and cheaply as the inhabitants of the United States. Important steps could be taken in that direction by increased competition and the de-regulation of air services.

8.   The Common Agricultural Policy has succeeded in the objective of providing Europe with a strong agricultural base. Remarkable increases in productivity have been achieved. The preservation of the best elements of that policy requires a continuing effort to correct the distortions which manifest themselves in the form of massive and costly surpluses of certain products, imposing high storage costs and the need to dispose of them in ways which complicate relations with our OECD partners and are impossible to defend to our own citizens and tax payers. An important and courageous effort has been made to control surpluses in the dairy sector. A sustained, multi-year effort will be required to achieve a better balance between production and demand, thereby releasing resources for other purposes . . .

A FLEXIBLE EUROPE

13.   European Communities, with their corpus of institutional and legal structures, and their own resources, are and must remain the framework within which Community law applies. Action undertaken in the Community frame-work must continue to be on a basis of equal rights and equal obligations. But a certain flexibility of approach may be necessary in the coming decade, when the Community will have become larger, its membership more diverse, and in some areas of technological development, the industrial structures and interests of

Member States more varied. For such practical reasons, it may make sense for participation in new ventures to be optional. This should not lead to rigid distinctions between different groups of participants. That would be particularly disillusioning for new members who expect to be joining a democratic and homogeneous Community. Where ventures are launched by Member States with limited participation, it should be open to others to join in as and when they are able to do so . . .

ORGANIZATION AND INSTITUTIONS

24. . . .

(e) The *voting provisions* of the Treaty must be fully honoured. Unanimity must be respected in all cases where the Treaty so provides. The same applies for majority voting. At the same time, Member States must be able to continue to insist where a very important national interest is at stake on discussion continuing until agreement is reached. But they should be required in each case to set out their reasons fully.

Source: 'Europe – the Future', *Journal of Common Market Studies*, vol. XXIII, no. 1, September 1984, pp. 73–81

Document 9.3

From the mid-1980s Thatcher found herself battling against a sustained drive for deeper integration within the EC. More specifically, she became embroiled in a running feud with Jacques Delors, the President of the European Commission. On 20 September 1988 she delivered a speech at the College of Europe in Bruges, in which she extolled the value of independent nationhood and attacked what she saw as the centralising tendencies of the Brussels bureaucracy. Although the speech was based on a Foreign Office draft, it had been substantially modified by Charles Powell, Thatcher's foreign policy adviser, and the final version appalled the Foreign Secretary, Geoffrey Howe.

My first guiding principle is this: willing and active co-operation between independent sovereign states is the best way to build a successful European Community.

To try to suppress nationhood and concentrate power at the centre of a European conglomerate would be highly damaging and would jeopardize the objectives we seek to achieve.

Europe will be stronger precisely because it has France as France, Spain as Spain, Britain as Britain, each with its own customs, traditions and identity. It would be folly to try to fit them into some sort of identikit European personality.

Some of the founding fathers of the Community thought that the United States of America might be its model.

But the whole history of America is quite different from Europe. People went there to get away from the intolerance and constraints of life in Europe. They sought liberty and opportunity; and their strong sense of purpose has, over two centuries, helped to create a new unity and pride in being American – just as our pride lies in being British or Belgian or Dutch or German.

I am the first to say that on many great issues the countries of Europe should try to speak with a single voice. I want to see us work more closely on the things we can do better together than alone. Europe is stronger when we do so, whether it be in trade, in defence, or in relations with the rest of the world.

But working more closely together does not require more power to be centralised in Brussels or decisions to be taken by an appointed bureaucracy.

Indeed, it is ironic that just when those countries such as the Soviet Union, which have tried to run everything from the centre, are learning that success depends on dispersing power and decisions away from the centre, some in the Community seem to want to move in the opposite direction.

We have not successfully rolled back the frontiers of the state in Britain, only to see them reimposed at a European level, with a European super-state exercising a new dominance from Brussels.

Certainly we want to see Europe more united and with a greater sense of common purpose. But it must be in a way which preserves the different traditions, Parliamentary powers and sense of national pride in one's own country; for these have been the source of Europe's vitality through the centuries.

Source: Baroness Thatcher's Office

Document 9.4

On 24 March 1990 Thatcher presided over a seminar held at Chequers, one of the main topics of discussion being the potential risk posed by Germany's economic and financial strength. Thatcher herself harboured deep-seated suspicions about Germany, especially in the light of its prospective unification, and wished to consult various experts on German history. The meeting was attended by two American historians, Gordon Craig and Fritz Stern, and three British historians, Lord Dacre (formerly Hugh Trevor-Roper), Norman Stone and Timothy Garton Ash. Also present were Douglas Hurd, the Foreign Secretary, Charles Powell, Thatcher's foreign policy adviser, and George Urban, whose advice was occasionally sought by the Prime Minister. The following account is by Urban.

MT [Margaret Thatcher] took the chair and opened the discussion. We would, she said, first talk about the historical background of Germany and the reliability of Germany as a future partner in Europe: to what extent was Germany, through its freshly won or prospective economic might, likely to become a politically over-powerful and perhaps even aggressive factor? And she made no secret of her conviction that Germany was indeed historically a dangerous power, not only because of the First and Second World Wars, but because of the sheer size of her population, the diligence and discipline of her people, the unreliability (as she called it) of the German character, the likelihood of Germany embracing another 'mission' in Europe and so on. In other words, it was fairly obvious from the moment she began speaking that her gut reactions were anti-German . . .

My impression is that she rather expected our group to endorse her anti-Teutonic preconceptions . . .

But stage by stage, it emerged clearly enough that, collectively, we had very different views from those she [Thatcher] was entertaining and especially those she had, damagingly enough, put on the record since the fall of the Berlin Wall [November 1989] . . .

It was depressing to see that Margaret Thatcher's attitude to the whole problem of Germany was so much that of a novice, despite the learned books she had ostentatiously piled up in front of her on the seminar table. She didn't hide her cordial dislike of all things German (forgetting, it seemed, the Teutonic descent of the English nation, of the English language and of the royal family), aggravated by her distaste for the personality of Helmut Kohl, whom she saw not at all as a fellow-Conservative or a Christian Democrat, but as a German deeply mired in provincialism. The contrast between herself as a visionary stateswoman with a world-view, and Kohl the wurst-eating, corpulent, plodding Teuton, has a long history in MT's imagination. Kohl's effectiveness in Europe was, she thought, due purely to the money in his pocket and the respect money commanded in the world (could this be wrong for a true Thatcherite?). And she was wondering how long it would be before German economic might were translated into political power – in which case she felt Germany would have won the Second World War, because what 'the Germans' could not attain by force of arms 'the Germans' would now be attaining by economic clout. I was appalled. Were these the views of a responsible prime minister? . . .

Not only did the PM display bias against Germany, but she was also taking an odd pride in doing so. Throughout the day she let it be known that she was speaking for the robust, no-nonsense instincts of the great British public, and no continental politician was going to tell her what to think or what to do. She was not going to tolerate German 'domination' or any undue political influence flowing from economic power. She was resentful that the French, the Belgians, the Dutch and others were, she thought, succumbing to this influence. They were over-impressed by Germany's economic might and unwilling to stand up to her . . .

The focal point of the seminar was, of course, MT herself . . . the part of demure understudy was being played by Douglas Hurd, standing or sitting there like a well-disciplined prefect, too nice and too much of a gentleman to make waves, but obviously pained and unhappy . . . It was, for me at least, abundantly clear who was in charge of policy-making, and I am not at all sure whether this is a good thing in matters of European policy either for Britain or for Europe. More Cabinet reponsibility and Cabinet decision-making are now called for. The PM resents Kohl because he is successful and a Teuton to boot; she resents Delors because he is a socialist and a French 'centralizer'; she resents the Benelux leaders because they won't annoy Germany. Where is this taking Britain? . . .

We can only pray and hope that she will be guided, under the influence of Geoffrey Howe and Douglas Hurd, by less irrational ideas than she is now, but that she will not do so willingly I am pretty certain.

Source: G. R. Urban, Diary, *Diplomacy and Disillusion at the Court of Margaret Thatcher: An Insider's View*, London, L. B. Tauris & Co. Ltd, 1996, pp. 120–44 *passim*

Document 9.5

In July 1990 The Spectator published an article by Dominic Lawson based on an interview with Nicholas Ridley. The Trade and Industry Secretary offered some highly unflattering opinions on the Germans, the French and members of the European Commission and was subsequently forced to resign from the government because of the furore caused by his observations. Ridley was known to be a minister whose views were closely attuned to those of the Prime Minister and the automatic assumption of most observers, including Lawson, was that he was uttering thoughts which met with her approval.

In modern political life there is no more brutal practitioner of the home truth . . . Even knowing this, I [Dominic Lawson] was still taken aback by the vehemence of Mr Ridley's views on the matter of Europe, and in particular the role of Germany. It had seemed a topical way to engage his thoughts, since the day after we met, Herr Klaus-Otto [*sic*] Pohl, the president of the Bundesbank was visiting England to preach the joys of a joint European monetary policy.

'This is all a German racket designed to take over the whole of Europe. It has to be thwarted. This rushed take-over by the Germans on the worst possible basis, with the French behaving like poodles to the Germans, is absolutely intolerable.'

'Excuse me, but in what way are moves towards monetary union', "The Germans trying to take over the whole of Europe"?'

'The deutschmark is always going to be the strongest currency, *because of their habits.*'

'But Mr Ridley, it's surely not axiomatic that the German currency will always be the strongest . . . ?'

'It's because of the *Germans.*'

'But the European Community is not just the Germans.'

Mr Ridley turned his fire . . . on the organisation as a whole.

'When I look at the institutions to which it is proposed that sovereignty is to be handed over, I'm aghast. Seventeen unelected reject politicians' – that includes you Sir Leon [Brittan] – 'with no accountability to anybody, who are not responsible for raising taxes, just spending money, who are pandered to by a supine parliament which is also not responsible for raising taxes, already behaving with an arrogance I find breathtaking – the idea that one says, "OK, we'll give this lot our sovereignty", is unacceptable to me. I'm not against giving up sovereignty in principle, but not to this lot. You might just as well give it to Adolf Hitler, frankly' . . .

'But surely Herr Kohl is preferable to Herr Hitler. He's not going to bomb us after all.'

'I'm not sure I wouldn't rather have . . .'

Somehow I imagined . . . that I could hear a woman's voice with the very faintest hint of Lincolnshire, saying 'Yes, Nick, that's right, they *are* trying to take over everything'. I can at least recall, with no recourse to imagination, the account of one of the Prime Minister's former advisers, of how he arrived for a meeting with Mrs Thatcher in a German car. 'What is that *foreign* car?' she glowered.

'It's a Volkswagen', he replied, helpful as ever.

'Don't *ever* park something like that here again.'

The point is, Mr Ridley's confidence in expressing his views on the German threat must owe a little something to the knowledge that they are not significantly different from those of the Prime Minister, who originally opposed German reunification, even though in public she is required not to be so indelicate as to draw comparisons between Herren Kohl and Hitler.

Source: *The Spectator*, 14 July 1990

Document 9.6

In its election manifesto for the European elections of June 1989 Labour accused the Thatcher government of alienating Britain's EC partners and held out the prospect of a less confrontational approach.

Labour wants a change of government, a change of approach, in Britain. But we are also demanding a new deal in Europe.

Mrs Thatcher is out of sympathy with the European agenda. Her ideological obsessions mean that her government refuses to help British industry prepare for the difficult challenges that lie ahead and she refuses for the same reasons to co-operate with the rest of Europe on social and environmental matters. Mrs Thatcher makes enemies more easily in Europe than she makes friends. The Tories are virtually isolated in the European Parliament. Her style is to talk tough, and maximise resentment against Britain, but she has too often given way on issues that matter.

Labour has a different vision of Europe. We see the need for a Europe which is created for the people, not for the multinationals. We need a Europe which is powerful enough to restrain the multinationals and to meet the international competition, but democratic enough to avoid the dangers of excessive centralisation.

We need a Europe with its own role and destiny, but open enough to look beyond its own narrow concerns. We need a Europe freed from the distortions of the Common Agricultural Policy and which concentrates instead on the things it is best at doing – helping to strengthen national and European industries, setting common standards and playing its part in creating a cleaner, safer world, free from poverty, discrimination and the threat of war.

Source: *Meeting the Challenge in Europe*, Labour Party manifesto
for the European elections, 1989

Document 9.7

During the 1980s and early 1990s the Labour Party performed another somersault over Europe, gradually retreating from its hostile stance and adopting an increasingly positive, even enthusiastic, attitude towards membership of the EC. This evolution can be traced in the party's successive general election manifestos between 1983 and 1992.

A

BRITAIN AND THE COMMON MARKET

Geography and history determine that Britain is part of Europe, and Labour wants to see Europe safe and prosperous. But the European Economic Community, which does not even include the whole of Western Europe, was never devised to suit us, and our experience as a member of it has made it more difficult for us to deal with our economic and industrial problems. It has sometimes weakened our ability to achieve the objectives of Labour's international policy.

The next Labour government, committed to radical, socialist policies for reviving the British economy, is bound to find continued membership a most serious obstacle to the fulfilment of those policies. In particular the rules of the Treaty of Rome are bound to conflict with our strategy for economic growth and full employment, our proposals on industrial policy and for increasing trade, and our need to restore exchange controls and to regulate direct overseas investment. Moreover, by preventing us from buying food from the best sources of world supply, they would run counter to our plans to control prices and inflation.

For all these reasons, British withdrawal from the Community is the right policy for Britain – to be completed well within the lifetime of the parliament. That is our commitment. But we are also committed to bring about a withdrawal in an amicable and orderly way, so that we do not prejudice employment or the prospect of increased political and economic co-operation with the *whole* of Europe.

We emphasise that our decision to bring about withdrawal in no sense represents any weakening of our commitment to internationalism and international co-operation. We are not 'withdrawing from Europe'. We are seeking to extricate ourselves from the Treaty of Rome and other Community treaties which place political burdens on Britain. Indeed, we believe our withdrawal will allow us to pursue a more dynamic and positive international policy – one which recognises the true political and geographical spread of international problems and interests. We will also seek agreement with other European governments – both in the EEC and outside – on a common strategy for economic expansion.

Source: *The New Hope for Britain*,
Labour Party general election manifesto, 1983

B

Labour's aim is to work constructively with our EEC partners to promote economic expansion and combat unemployment. However, we will stand up for British interests within the European Community and we will seek to put an end to the abuses and scandals of the Common Agricultural Policy. We shall, like other member countries, reject EEC interference with our policy for national recovery and renewal.

Source: *Britain Will Win*, Labour Party general election manifesto, 1987

C

The Labour government will promote Britain out of the European second division into which our country has been relegated by the Tories. Our first chance will be the United Kingdom's six-month presidency of the Community, starting on 1 July. We shall use that presidency to end the Tories' opt-out from the Social Chapter, so that the British people can benefit from European safeguards. We will also use our presidency to help ensure that poorer countries are not disadvantaged as a result of the Single Market.

We shall play an active part in negotiations on Economic and Monetary Union. We shall fight for Britain's interest, working for Europe-wide policies to fight unemployment and to enhance regional and structural industrial policy. The elected finance ministers of the different countries must become the effective political counterpart to the central bank whose headquarters should be in Britain . . .

We shall seek fundamental changes in the wasteful Common Agricultural Policy. Savings can help finance other Community projects.

We shall make the widening of the Community a priority, and shall advocate speedy admission for Austria, Sweden, Finland and Cyprus, whose membership applications have been or are about to be lodged. We shall seek to create conditions in which, at the appropriate time, the new democracies of Central and Eastern Europe can join the Community.

Source: *It's Time to get Britain Working Again*,
Labour Party general election manifesto, 1992

Document 9.8

During the late 1960s and early 1970s Heath was portrayed by Labour as a poodle of Brussels. After Labour's stance on Europe changed during the latter part of the 1980s, the tables were turned and successive Labour leaders – Neil Kinnock (1983–93), John Smith (1993–94) and Tony Blair (1994–) – faced the same criticism. In the following extract Thatcher accuses Kinnock of subservience during her statement on the Rome European Council.

The Prime Minister: It is our purpose to retain the power and influence of this House, rather than denude it of many of its powers. I wonder what the right hon. Gentleman's [Kinnock's] policy is, in view of some of the things that he said. Would he have agreed to a commitment to extend the Community's powers to other supplementary sectors of economic integration without having any definition of what they are? One would have thought, from what he said, that he would. The Commision wants to extend its powers and competence into health matters, but we said no, we would not agree to that.

From what the right hon. Gentleman said, it sounded as though he would agree, for the sake of agreeing, and for being Little Sir Echo, and saying, 'Me, too.' Would the right hon. Gentleman have agreed to extending qualified majority voting within the Council, to delegating implementing powers to the Commission, to a common security policy, all without any attempt to define or limit them? The answer is yes.

Source: *H.C.Deb.*, vol. 178, col. 872, 30 October 1990

Document 9.9

For several years – until October 1990 – Thatcher fought a stubborn rearguard action against sterling's entry to the ERM. In effect, she exercised a veto against a policy favoured by most senior ministers, the Treasury and the Bank of England. The following extract records a critical meeting in November 1985 called to discuss a paper favouring membership prepared by Nigel Lawson, the Chancellor of the Exchequer.

The colleagues Margaret had invited to the meeting were Willie Whitelaw, Geoffrey Howe [Foreign Secretary], Norman Tebbitt, who had recently been moved from Secretary of State for Trade and Industry to Party Chairman, Leon Brittan, Norman's successor at Trade and Industry, John Biffen, the Leader of the House of Commons and John Wakeham, then Chief Whip.

Of these six, three – Willie, as Deputy Prime Minister, Geoffrey and Leon as head of the second economic Department of Government – were there because she could scarcely exclude them. The other three had been chosen largely because she felt sure they would support her, either on political grounds or, in John Biffen's case, on economic grounds. Apart from Geoffrey and myself [Lawson], none of them had given any previous indication of support for ERM membership. Biffen was a committed free-floater of long standing, and I regarded him as a lost cause . . .

I opened the meeting by summarizing the main points of my paper . . . It recalled that the Government's clearly stated policy was to join the ERM when the time was right, and argued that that time had now come . . . It concluded with these words:

> My judgement that the advantages of joining now outweigh the risks is shared not only by the Governor of the Bank of England, but also by senior officials in both the Treasury and the Bank. They all believe that it makes operational sense to join, and that they can now deliver our policy objectives more effectively in the EMS than if we remain outside it.

From then on the discussion did not go as Margaret had expected. Geoffrey, of course, spoke in favour, along the lines that he had done at the 30 September seminar. But then Leon Brittan said that while he had been opposed to ERM membership in the past, because of the problems of sterling's petrocurrency status, since the importance of this factor had diminished and given the declining credibility of the monetary aggregates, he now believed we should join. Norman Tebbit, who was to turn against the ERM later when it was seen as part of the essentially political argument about European monetary union and the single currency, also declared himself in favour if I thought it would be helpful politically; and added that, as Party Chairman, he felt that it would be easy to carry the Party and that a decision now might silence some of the back-bench critics of our economic policy . . .

John Biffen unsurprisingly declared himself very doubtful of the merits of ERM membership. Robin Leigh-Pemberton [Governor of the Bank of England] then had his say arguing that the difficulties of sterling outside the ERM were greater than they would be inside the ERM.

Margaret then weighed in. She recited what had become a familiar litany of objections. The United Kingdom had low foreign-exchange reserves and a more open capital market than anyone else. The Government would be left with no discretion on interest rates; and the UK could not pull out of the ERM, even on a very temporary basis, in advance of an election, without looking as if it had lost all faith in its own policies. A 'rigid grid' would deprive the Goverment of all freedom of manoeuvre.

Willie, as was his custom, had held himself back to the end . . . having listened attentively to the discussion he declared, 'If the Chancellor, the Governor and the Foreign Secretary are all agreed that we should join the EMS then that should be decisive. It has certainly decided me.' I suspect he was as surprised as the rest of us when Margaret instantly replied, 'On the contrary: I disagree. If you join the EMS, you will have to do so without me.' There was an awkward silence, and the meeting broke up.

Source: Nigel Lawson, *The View From No. 11: Memoirs Of A Tory Radical*, London, Bantam Press, Transworld Publishers, 1992, pp. 497–9 *passim*

Document 9.10

On 30 October 1990 Thatcher gave the Commons a report on the outcome of the Rome European Council of 27–28 October. At the Council Community leaders had discussed preparations for EMU and the forthcoming IGC on institutional reform. Thatcher's increasingly extreme attitude in response to persistent questioning was a factor in precipitating the resignation of the Deputy Prime Minister Geoffrey Howe.

Mr. Neil Kinnock (Islwyn): . . . On the central matter discussed in Rome, is it not clear that last weekend the Prime Minister managed to unite the rest of the European Community against her, to divide her own party and, more importantly, further to weaken the influence that Britain needs in order properly to uphold our national interests in the European Community? . . .

The Prime Minister says that the Government would not surrender the use of the pound sterling as our currency. Perhaps she will therefore tell us how she regards the advice of her fellow Conservative, Commissioner Brittan, when he said:

> 'You don't have to lose the pound sterling under the single currency plan. You can perfectly well have a note or a coin which states its value in pounds . . . and its fixed equivalent in ecus . . .'

The Prime Minister: . . . Leon Brittan is a loyal member of the Commission. Yes, the Commission wants to increase its powers. Yes, it is a non-elected body and I do not want the Commission to increase its powers at the expense of the House, so of course we differ. The President of the Commission, Mr. Delors, said at a press conference the other day that he wanted the European Parliament to be the democratic body of the Community, he wanted the Commission to be the Executive and he wanted the Council of Ministers to be the Senate. No. No. No.

Perhaps the Labour party would give all those things up easily. Perhaps it would agree to a single currency and abolition of the pound sterling. Perhaps, being totally incompetent in monetary matters, it would be only too delighted to hand over full responsiblity to a central bank, as it did to the IMF . . . What is the point of trying to get elected to Parliament only to hand over sterling and the powers of this House to Europe? . . .

Mr. Nigel Spearing (Newham, South): Despite what the Prime Minister has just said, is it not clear that it is the wish of our partners that there should be a loss of national identity on currency? Is it not true that even the hard ecu, coupled with fixed exchange rates, would lead inexorably to economic and monetary union and to government either of bankers for bankers or to a strong political central government that would usher in a new Euro-state? If the Prime Minister is to save Britain as a self-governing nation, had she better not make that clear and galvanise the people of this country and all parties in Parliament to say a very polite no to economic and monetary union?

The Prime Minister: If I believed that, I would do just as the hon. Gentleman says, but I do not believe his interpretation is correct. I accept that many in the Economic Community would like to have their version of economic and monetary union, which would lead to passing powers away from national Parliaments to a non-elected body – in fact, to a central board of bankers – to majority voting and to the giving of more legislative power to the European Parliament. That is their version, but it is not the version that we have accepted. The Single European Act defined economic and monetary union as

> 'Co-operation in Economic and Monetary policy'.

That is all you need, in my view. The hard ecu is a proposal that does not require a central bank, which would make it an inflation-proof currency and which could be used if people chose to do so. In my view, it would not become widely used throughout the Community – [*Interruption*] – possibly most widely used for commercial transactions. Many people would continue to prefer their own currency.

Therefore, I do not believe that the fears of the hon. Member for Newham, South (Mr. Spearing) will happen. I am pretty certain that most people in this country would prefer to continue using sterling. If, by their choice, I was wrong, there would come a time when we would have to address the question. However, that would not be for us but for future generations in the House.

Source: *H.C.Deb.*, vol. 178, cols. 871–8, 30 October 1990

Document 9.11

The pro-European Deputy Prime Minister and former Foreign Secretary, Howe, found himself increasingly out of sympathy with Thatcher's policy on Europe and finally decided that he must leave the government. His resignation speech was highly damaging to Thatcher and was instrumental in precipitating the challenge to her leadership which led to her downfall.

Let me first make clear certain important points on which I have no disagreement with my Right Hon. friend, the Prime Minister. I do not regard the Delors Report as some kind of sacred text that has to be accepted, or even rejected, on the nod. But it is an important working document. As I have often made plain, it is seriously deficient in significant respects.

I do not regard the Italian Presidency's management of the Rome Summit as a model of its kind – far from it. It was much the same . . . in Milan some five years ago.

I do not regard it as in any sense wrong for Britain to make criticisms of that kind plainly and courteously, nor in any sense wrong for us to do so, if necessary, alone . . .

But it is crucially important that we should conduct those arguments upon the basis of a clear understanding of the true relationship between this country, the Community and our Community partners. And it is here, I fear, that my Right Hon. friend the Prime Minister increasingly risks leading herself and others astray in matters of substance as well as style . . .

We must at all costs avoid presenting ourselves yet again with an over-simplified choice, a false antithesis, a bogus dilemma, between one alternative, starkly labelled 'co-operation between independent sovereign states', and a second, equally crudely labelled alternative, 'centralised federal super-state', as if there were no middle way in between.

We commit a serious error if we think always in terms of 'surrendering' sovereignty and seek to stand pat for all time on a given deal – by proclaiming, as my Right Hon. friend the Prime Minister did two weeks ago, that we have 'surrendered enough'.

The European enterprise is not and should not be seen like that – as some kind of zero-sum game. Sir Winston Churchill put it much more positively forty years ago, when he said: 'It is also possible and not less agreeable to regard' this sacrifice or merger of national sovereignty 'as the gradual assumption by all the nations concerned of that larger sovereignty which can alone protect their diverse and distinctive customs and characteristics and their national traditions.'

I have to say that I find Winston Churchill's perception a good deal more convincing, and more encouraging for the interests of our nation, than the nightmare image sometimes conjured up by my Right Hon. friend, who seems sometimes to look out upon a continent that is positively teeming with ill-intentioned people, scheming, in her words, to 'extinguish democracy', to 'dissolve our national identities' and to 'lead us through the back-door into a federal Europe'. What kind of vision is that for our business people, who trade there each day, for our financiers, who seek to make London the money capital of Europe, or for all the young people of today? . . .

The tragedy is – and it is for me personally, for my party, for our whole people and for my Right Hon. friend herself, a very real tragedy – that the Prime Minister's perceived attitude towards Europe is running increasingly serious risks for the future of our nation. It risks minimising our influence and maximising our chances of being once again shut out. We have paid heavily in the past for late starts and squandered opportunities in Europe. We dare not let that happen again. If we detach ourselves completely, as a party or a nation, from the middle ground of Europe, the effects will be incalculable and very hard ever to correct.

Source: *H.C.Deb.*, vol. 180, cols. 461–5 *passim*, 13 November 1990

10 Staying in but opting out: 1990–1997

When Major succeeded Thatcher as Prime Minister in 1990 one of his principal objectives was to mend fences with other members of the Community, especially the Germans, and repair the damage inflicted by his predecessor. His intention was that the UK would be 'at the very heart' of the EC instead of on the sidelines. In the event, his aspirations were not realised. Indeed, by the time of the 1997 general election most of Britain's European partners were so disillusioned with the Major government that they were eager for a Labour victory and the opportunity to work with Blair. The extracts in this section illustrate the mounting domestic and external difficulties Major encountered over Europe, with attention being focused on the impact of the Treaty of Maastricht, sterling's enforced departure from the ERM, the ban imposed on British beef exports and strife within the Conservative Party.

Like Thatcher, Major was faced throughout his premiership by the problem of how to deal with a sustained drive for greater economic and political integration, spearheaded by France, Germany and the European Commission. Like her, moreover, he found that it was impossible to halt the process and that attempting to do so led to friction and isolation. Major's difficulties were compounded by his perceived lack of personal authority and the government's small and dwindling parliamentary majority: in April 1996 it fell to one. Above all, Major had to cope with the existence of warring Eurosceptic and Europhile factions, not only within the Conservative Party at large, but also within the Cabinet itself. His efforts to fashion a common position on which these two tendencies could unite became increasingly desperate and ended in complete failure. The exasperation induced by these conflicting pressures was reflected in a series of angry outbursts, notably against the Eurosceptic 'bastards' in the Cabinet.

Although Major's negotiating style was different from that of Thatcher, the substance of his policies on Europe was essentially the same. He shared both her enthusiasm for the creation of a genuine single market and her hostility to any further ceding of national sovereignty. Major's views on the future development of the Community were expounded in an article which he wrote for *The Economist* in September 1993 (10.1). The piece, sceptical and sombre in tone, represented a strong plea against 'ever tighter political and economic integration'. Its timing was significant. It appeared shortly after the British government had finally secured parliamentary approval for the Treaty of Maastricht after a long and arduous struggle. It also followed closely on a serious crisis within the ERM which had only been resolved by a substantial widening of the permitted fluctuation bands. Both the ERM and Maastricht had a profound influence on Major's thinking.

At the Maastricht European Council (9–10 December 1991) Major's basic aim had been to prevent changes leading to closer integration. He was only partially successful. The resulting treaty, which provided for the establishment of the European Union (EU), extended the scope of QMV and gave greater powers to the European Parliament (EP). It envisaged progress towards a common defence policy. In addition, it set out a procedure and timetable for achieving full economic and monetary union. This last was wholly unacceptable to Major and he negotiated an opt-out allowing the UK to defer a decision on participation in the third and final stage of EMU. A similar opt-out was obtained from the Social Protocol or Chapter. Taken as a whole, the arrangements reached at Maastricht went somewhat further in a supranational direction than Major had wished. He took some comfort from the anti-Maastricht backlash which quickly developed throughout the Community and which found its most obvious expression in the treaty's rejection in a Danish referendum (June 1992) and its near rejection in a French one (September 1992). Although he denied it, Major also derived comfort from the problems experienced by the ERM in 1993 (10.1).

On 16 September 1992 sterling was forced out of the ERM by intense speculative pressure. Major had a record of fluctuating views on the ERM. In the traumatic aftermath of 'Black Wednesday' he underwent another change of mind. Beforehand, he and Norman Lamont, the Chancellor of the Exchequer, had insisted that membership of the ERM was an indispensable part of the government's macro-economic strategy. Now both dismissed the possibility of re-entry, arguing that the system was fundamentally flawed. Major saw the general turbulence that affected it in August 1993 not only as a vindication of his viewpoint, but also as a salutary warning of the pitfalls that lay ahead on the road to EMU (10.1).

Such a jaundiced view of the ERM and EMU was common currency in Conservative Eurosceptic circles, where 'Black Wednesday' soon became known as 'White Wednesday' – the day when the British government had escaped from the shackles of an overvalued currency and needlessly high interest rates. As committed supporters of free-market economics the Eurosceptics objected in principle to a sysem based on fixed exchange rates. They were also opposed to EMU because they believed it to be an essentially political project designed to promote the creation of a European superstate dominated by the French and the Germans. This thesis received support from an influential book, *The Rotten Heart of Europe: The Dirty War for Europe's Money*, by Bernard Connolly. The book caused a considerable stir when it appeared in 1995, not least because its author was the former head of the unit in the European Commission responsible for the EMS and monetary affairs. Connolly had been dismissed from his post for criticising the EMS, and in his book he launched a scathing attack on EMU as a politically driven venture which was bound to end in economic disaster (10.2). Such 'revelations', coming from such a source, provided Conservative Eurosceptics with powerful ammunition for their attack on the Maastricht Treaty.

Having flexed their muscles over Maastricht, the Eurosceptics were ready for the next stage of their battle against deeper integration. The Maastricht Treaty contained a provision that it should be reviewed by another IGC which was to begin in 1996. In the lead-up to this IGC, the Major government set out the line it intended to take, notably in a White Paper (March 1996) whose title – *A Partnership of Nations* – reflected its strong preference for an inter-governmental approach (10.3 and 10.4). Other interested parties likewise made their views known. On 14 March the government of Alain Juppé issued an official statement of the French negotiating position for the IGC which proposed, among other things, greater use of QMV and real progress towards a common defence policy. The German Chancellor, Helmut Kohl, advocated similar policies. Kohl was passionately committed to closer political union, seeing it as the most effective antidote to a revival of destructive, old-style nationalism in Germany and elsewhere. He explained his views in a highly emotional speech delivered at the Catholic University of Louvain (2 February 1996), warning that the only alternative to further integration was war (10.5). Kohl's speech contained a pointed remark which was obviously directed at the UK: it was not acceptable, he said, that 'the slowest ship in the convoy' should be allowed to dictate its speed. A paper produced by the European Com-mission, *Reinforcing Political Union and Preparing for Enlargement*, echoed this reproach and expressed concern about a tendency to opt out from common obligations, citing the case of the Social Protocol as an example. Another unpalatable aspect of the Comission's paper, from the British standpoint, was a recommendation that QMV should become the norm in order to avoid the danger of deadlock in an enlarged EU (10.6).

Many of the ideas put forward by the Commission, the French and the Germans were distinctly at variance with current official thinking in London. In general terms, the Major government was opposed to any further economic and political integration (see 10.3). Thus it intended to resist the introduction of QMV into sensitive areas like defence and foreign policy. Michael Portillo, the Defence Secretary, rejected the idea of a European army and a centralised command structure in a typically rumbustious and jingoistic performance at the 1995 Conservative Party annual conference (see 10.7). The same message was conveyed in a more measured fashion in *A Partnership of Nations*. The White Paper also came out forcefully against the WEU being placed under the political control of the EU, as suggested by Bonn and Paris (10.4).

There was a number of other areas in which the UK occupied a distinctive position (see 10.4). First, the Major government was determined to curb the powers of the European Court of Justice (ECJ) which had delivered unfavourable verdicts against Britain over 'quota-hopping' by Spanish fisher-men and the EU's 48-hour working-week directive, and which was felt to be extending the influence of Brussels through 'political' judgements. Second, the government insisted on retaining Britain's opt-out from the Social Chapter, taking the view that the latter imposed obligations and costs on employers which were damaging to competitiveness. Third, it intended to postpone until the last possible moment a decision on participation in the final stage of EMU. Of the other EU members, only the Danes took a comparable line, having secured special arrangements for themselves at the Edinburgh European Council (December 1992). Finally, there was the potential minefield of 'flexibility'.

The accession of Austria, Finland and Sweden in January 1995 took the number of EU members to 15. In addition, there was a long queue of further applicants whose admission would double the EU's population and create enormous administrative difficulties. The UK's suggested answer to the challenge posed by the growing size and diversity of EU membership was to replace uniformity by flexibility or 'variable geometry', so as to allow individual states to decide for themselves the pace at which they wished to share sovereignty in different areas. The risk in this approach – highlighted by the Commission's references to a two-speed Europe – was that the French and the Germans in particular would seize the opportunity to press ahead with an integrationist agenda, the end result being the emergence of a dominant inner core from which the UK was permanently excluded. The Major government was fully alive to this danger and demanded safeguards for the interests of those states which chose not to integrate (10.3).

By the time the IGC opened in Turin on 29 March 1996, it was evident that Britain would find itself out of step with most other EU countries, as well as the Commission, on a broad range of important issues. Major faced an uphill task. His primary concern was to block any moves towards further integration. At the same time, he could not afford to become isolated. This was a balancing act which in itself required great diplomatic and political skill. What made it more complicated still, however, was the need to secure an outcome which could be sold to both the Europhile and Eurosceptic wings of the Conservative Party. All the indications were that the latter would not be easily satisfied. Shortly before the IGC began, Thatcher fired one of her periodic warning shots across Major's bow in a speech combining encouragement and thinly veiled menace in equal measure (10.8).

In the period leading up to and during the IGC the Eurosceptics exerted intense pressure on Major to halt, indeed reverse, what they saw as a remorse-less drive towards the creation of a European superstate. They demanded assurances that the government would defend the national veto, prevent an extension of QMV, uphold Britain's opt-out from the Social Chapter, resist attempts to give greater powers to the European Commission and EP and clip the wings of the ECJ. Most important of all, Major was urged to stand firm against British participation in EMU. The Eurosceptics wanted this to be ruled out once and for all. At the very least, they insisted, there should be a referendum on the matter. Major was not prepared to countenance the first option, preferring to follow a policy of 'wait and see', which would enable Britain to continue playing a role in the crucial preparatory negotiations for EMU, as well as postponing civil war within the Conservative Party and rows with other EU states. As far as a referendum was concerned, Major's initial reaction was unfavourable. In the end, however, he was unable to hold out against the various pressures that were brought to bear on him, not least from the formation of the Referendum Party – an organisation founded and generously financed by the Anglo-French billionaire businessman and MEP Sir James Goldsmith which posed an electoral threat to the Conservatives in particular.

The main obstacle to a government concession over demands for a referendum was concern at the possible resignation of Kenneth Clarke, the Chancellor of the Exchequer, who was a staunch supporter of the single currency and firmly against the idea of a referendum. The Foreign Office devised a formula which Clarke was willing to accept, however, and in April 1996 the government announced its commitment to holding a referendum. For the Eurosceptics it was a hollow victory. There would only be a referendum if and when it had been decided by the Cabinet and Parliament that Britain should join the single currency. Moreover, in a departure from the 1975 arrangements, ministers who were opposed to the decision would have to resign if they wished to campaign for a 'no' vote. Finally, critics soon began to complain that the referendum would only be concerned with the single currency, with the Referendum Party arguing that voters should be given the opportunity to express their views on the much broader question of Britain's future in the EU (10.9).

Although the Eurosceptics had not achieved all that they wanted, the referendum episode had nevertheless demonstrated the strength of their position at all levels of the Conservative Party and the leverage they were able to exercise over a weak government. The crisis that developed over 'mad cow disease' from the spring of 1996 gave a further boost to their influence. It also cast a long shadow over Britain's relations with other EU states. The origin of the crisis was an admission by Stephen Dorrell, the Health Secretary, on 20 March of a possible connection between bovine spongiform encephalopathy (BSE) in cattle and Creutzfeldt-Jakob disease (CJD) in humans. Dorrell's Commons statement led shortly afterwards to the EU's imposition of a world-wide ban on all exports of British beef and beef derivatives.

Initial British expectations of a speedy end to the ban were quickly dashed, the main problem being that the various packages of measures for eradicating BSE proposed by Douglas Hogg, the Agriculture Minister, were judged to be completely inadequate by continental governments. In British official circles there was intense anger – shared to the full by Major – at the alleged failure of the UK's European partners to translate early promises of help, financial and otherwise, into concrete action. This was accompanied by the conviction that the ban could not be justified on scientific grounds and was, in any case, of doubtful legality (10.10). Outside official circles, the tabloid press and

Conservative Eurosceptics embarked on an orgy of xenophobic hysteria, clamouring for retaliatory trade sanctions and a suspension of British payments to the EU, and using the issue to whip up feelings against Britain's partners and even against British membership of the EU. It was the Germans who bore the main brunt of the onslaught, as crude gibes about Kohl's girth mingled with references to the Second World War and the emergence of a 'Fourth Reich' (10.11 and 10.12). Such hostile sentiment stemmed in part from an underlying resentment of Germany's dominant position in the EU, symbolised by the decision to site the European Central Bank (ECB) in Frankfurt. It also reflected the fact that Bonn was a leading opponent of lifting the beef export ban. Major himself felt that Kohl had let him down.

On 21 May 1996 Major informed the Commons that the government would seek an interim order from the ECJ for the ban to be lifted. He also announced its intention to block all EU business involving unanimous voting until the export ban on beef derivatives was ended and the UK received 'a clear framework leading to a lifting of the wider ban' (10.10). There followed several weeks of systematic obstruction, the only effect of which was to harden the resolve of other EU governments and the Commission not to give way. Kohl in particular was determined that Major should not be offered any concessions which might be of assistance to him in the forthcoming general election. This was a telling indication of the extent to which Anglo-German relations had deteriorated since the early days of the Major government.

After threatening to disrupt the Florence European Council, which was due to start on 21 June, Major chose a policy of stealthy retreat instead, accepting a deal on the beef ban which conceded nothing of substance to the UK. Major's claim that the agreement negotiated in Florence represented a great success was derided by the Opposition (10.13A). Paradoxically, however, Conservative Eurosceptics did not seek to exploit the government's climb-down, praising the effectiveness of its tough tactics and calling for them to be used in other areas (10.13B). This cooperative approach was to prove short-lived.

Document 10.1

One of John Major's main goals after becoming Prime Minister was to repair relations with the UK's European partners and ensure that the British government occupied a leading role in the Community's decision-making process. In an upbeat speech at the Konrad Adenauer Institute in Bonn on 11 March 1991 he spoke of Britain being 'at the very heart' of the EC. His initial optimism did not survive the battle to secure parliamentary acceptance of the Maastricht Treaty and sterling's humiliating exit from the ERM. In the aftermath of these events he wrote an article for The Economist *(September 1993) in which he struck a less conciliatory note and adopted a tone which harked back to the last days of Thatcher's premiership.*

In the past year there has been a sense of malaise within Europe. The recession has played a large part in this. So has the debate in many countries about the

Maastricht Treaty. So has Bosnia. But I believe the causes go deeper. The European Community has become ill at ease with itself and, for the time being, uncertain about its future course.

A powerful view – still dangerously fashionable among some continental politicians – is that the fault of Maastricht lay in not going far enough; that economic problems require corporatist solutions that the free market cannot supply; that instability, East and West, requires further progress towards further integration; and that full federation is the grand vision of the future.

I believe profoundly that this view is wrong. It does not carry the hearts and minds of the electorates of Europe. They believe that decision-making in the Community must be brought closer to the people, not taken further away. Unless the Community is seen to be tackling the problems which affect them now, rather than arguing over abstract concepts, it will lose its credibility . . .

So I believe it is time to look afresh at the Community and consider the way ahead. Time to put away the old slogans, dreams and prejudices. All over Europe, what are people worrying about? Not to reduce the number of currencies, but to increase the number of jobs . . .

I do not want to caricature a debate full of subtle shades of opinion. But the prevalent view within the Community has been that unless the Community continued to march towards ever tighter political and economic integration, ever greater uniformity, then its existing achievements would be eroded. The demons of nationalism would reassert themselves. Europe's ability to compete with the United States, Japan and the Pacific rim would be undermined. The very future of the enterprise would be in jeopardy. Clinging to a false transatlantic analogy, they wanted to create a 'United States of Europe'.

There are, of course, some in Britain too who hold that view. There are, however, many more, myself amongst them, who do not; and not only in Britain. I believe it is that centralising vision that alarms so many voters in the applicant countries of Norway, Sweden, Finland and Austria . . .

Successive Conservative governments have . . . supported the European Community as a way of securing peace, ensuring stability and increasing our standard of living. But we have opposed the centralising idea. We take some convincing on any proposal from Brussels. For us, the nation state is here to stay.

Some differences in the Community are stark and simple. We counted the financial cost of our membership. Others counted their financial gain. We subjected each proposal to the scrutiny of Parliament. They relaxed in the sure knowledge that their public opinion uncritically endorsed the European idea. Hang the detail. Never mind the concession of power to Brussels.

Maastricht changed all that. For the first time the sort of questions that Britain had been asking were asked in other countries as well. The Danes wanted the safeguards for Denmark that I had secured for Britain. The German people did not want their government to sacrifice the D-mark. The French came within a whisker of saying 'no' to the treaty their goverment had signed.

Since then, the old complacency has taken a further jolt. Last autumn, when the pound left the ERM, I warned of the fault lines throughout the system. Some scoffed. The fault line was in British policy, they said. Not so. These policy fault lines lie across Europe; the ERM as a whole has foundered.

I take no satisfaction in that. Exchange-rate stability is in the interests of business and thus prosperity. But I am not prepared to sit down in Brussels in a few weeks' time and pretend that Humpty Dumpty is whole and well. I care too much about the European Community to pursue sellotape policies – patching together the unmendable – or to play the politics of illusion – pretending that it was never broken. The good European does not cling to old nostrums, but seeks solutions to new problems.

Source: *The Economist*, 25 September 1993

Document 10.2

In the period following sterling's exit from the ERM in September 1992 Conservative opinion hardened against re-entry. 'Black Wednesday' soon came to be called 'White Wednesday' – the day when sterling was freed from the constraints of the ERM and the British government recovered its freedom to determine monetary policy. Such thinking was profoundly influenced by a book which appeared in 1995, written by Bernard Connolly, a former senior Brussels official who had headed the Commission unit responsible for the EMS and monetary policy. Connolly had been dismissed for expressing critical views about the EMS. The following extract is from the preface to the second edition of the book.

Normal people in the Community countries are clearly thirsting for knowledge about what their leaders are doing and why they are doing it; they fear that they are having the wool pulled over their eyes: they suspect that hidden agendas are being implemented; they are fed up with the establishment sloganizing that has replaced analysis; they are coming to understand that the myths propagated by the supporters of EMU have no foundation; above all, they now realize that monetary union is a political project – an attempt to create a European superstate.

There are reasons for believing that the publication of this book in September 1995 played a part in opening people's eyes to the realities of European monetary politics . . . And when it became clear even to the wilfully blind that the economic policies followed in the pursuit of monetary union were destroying jobs, not creating them, ravaging the public finances, not restoring them, devastating confidence, not fostering it, a whole slew of European politicians changed tack and proclaimed the essentially political, not economic, ambition underlying the single currency idea.

Moreover, the divisiveness of the monetary union project can no longer be hidden. There will be a European political and economic 'hard core'. Its members will be those existing countries, present and future members of the Community, that together made up the empire of Charlemagne. The southern, western and northern 'peripheries' of the Community will be tributaries of the hard core. In economic terms, they will be expected to join a new ERM, one in which they will face only burdens and responsibilities, expected to manage their policies (under surveillance) not in their own interests, nor even in the interests of the Community, but in the interests of the hard core – to all intents and purposes in the interests of France and Germany. If they jib at this, they will be reminded that they must do as they are told. President Chirac expressed it clearly in March 1996: the union (that is the hard core) must give itself means of 'punishing' those countries outside the hard core that 'do not respect the common discipline'.

Even within the so-called hard core (whose underlying economic performance is now, as was predicted in this book, clearly deteriorating relative to other Community countries and the world as a whole) the atmosphere of mutual distrust and suspicion has become palpable. French politicians make it clear that they fear German dominance; certain German politicians, and most of all Helmut Kohl himself, warn of a return to Balance of Power politics and war in Europe if their ideas on monetary and political union are not accepted lock, stock and barrel. Yet European union can only enshrine German dominance, whether voluntary or – much more likely as far as the German people are concerned – involuntary. That is something the French elite currently seem prepared to accept, in the name of giving 'Europe' greater muscle against the Anglo-Saxon, Asian and Latin-American worlds. But once economic and geopolitical developments make it clearer even to French technocrats that the 'European model' will bring nothing more than continued economic decline and a further deterioration in the quality of political and democratic life, the new empire of Charlemagne will split asunder – and much more rapidly than its eighth century forerunner and model.

Source: Bernard Connolly, The Rotten Heart of Europe: The Dirty War
for Europe's Money, London, Faber and Faber, 1996, pp. viii–ix

Document 10.3

The Major government's basic opposition to further integration was reflected in the position paper which it prepared for the 1996 IGC. The following extract sets out the government's general approach.

4.   Despite its substantial achievements, the European Union is experiencing a period of uncertainty and self-doubt. The Maastricht process polarised opinion in several Member States, and exposed a level of public unease and alienation which must concern all those, like the Government, who want the European Union to fulfil its potential. Europe as a whole has continued to fall behind the best performing countries in terms of its international competitiveness. The Single Market has not yet delivered all the benefits which it should and could. There has been an over-emphasis on social regulation, which has led to rigidities in the labour market and some examples of ill-conceived, intrusive and unnecessary legislation. The results, especially for job creation, are a source of major concern. In the last 20 years the US has created 36 million new jobs, of which 31 million were in the private sector. In the same period only 8 million new jobs have been created within the EU, with no increase at all in total private sector employment.

5.   The classic approach of many politicians on the continent to such problems has been to press for 'more Europe': tighter political integration; more centralisation; more uniformity; and corporatist economic solutions to perceived deficiencies in the free market. The Government has always resisted such demands and today it has become clearer that such a response does not command popular support across Europe. The Treaty on European Union, like the original Treaty of Rome, calls for an 'ever closer union among the peoples of Europe', (not, let it be noted, among the states of Europe, or among their Governments). This Treaty aspiration for strengthened cooperation and friendship across the whole of Europe is a noble one, fully shared by the Government. But it does not mean an ever closer Political Union in the sense of an inexorable drift of power towards supra-national institutions, the erosion of national parliaments, and the gradual development of a United States of Europe. The Government rejects that conception of Europe's future. We are determined to safeguard the powers and responsibilities of the nation states that are signatories to the Treaty . . .

The British Approach

6.   The Government is clear about the sort of Europe it believes in. We are committed to the success of the European Union, and to playing a positive role in achieving that success. We are confident that it can be achieved if the EU develops as a Union of nations cooperating together under the Treaties freely entered into and approved by the national Parliaments of every Member State; a Union which respects cultural and political diversity; which concentrates single-mindedly only on what needs to be done at a European level, and doing it well; which does not interfere where it is not needed; and which is outward-looking, free-trading, democratic and flexible. We shall not accept harmonisation for its own sake, or further European integration which is driven by ideology rather than the prospect of practical benefit. Above all, we shall be guided by a cool assessment of the British interest. Common European decision-making, as opposed to cooperation, can only be justified where it brings benefits for British security, prosperity and quality of life which are so significant that they justify some loss of unfettered national control over decision-making in the area concerned, or where common action enables nation states to exercise joint control which is not open to them individually . . .

8.   The Government believes that, especially with the prospect of enlargement, the European Union should be able to respond more sensitively to the needs of an increasingly diverse membership. The Union needs to accept a degree of flexibility or, as it has sometimes been called, 'variable geometry', without falling into the trap of a two-tier Europe with a hard core either of countries or of policies. The pillared structure introduced at Maastricht was welcome recognition that structures which work well for the single market are inappropriate for the Common Foreign and Security Policy or Justice and Home Affairs issues. Strict disciplines are right and necessary in certain areas, such as

the rules which govern international trade and the single market. But conformity should never be sought for its own sake. There may be areas in which it is perfectly healthy for some Member States to integrate more closely or more quickly than others. It is important however that such policies only become Union policies and draw on the Community's institutions, including the budget, where this is agreed by all. In addition, no Member State should be excluded from an area of policy in which it wants to participate, and is qualified to do so. Policies must be open to all . . .

Source: Cmd 3181 (March 1996), *A Partnership of Nations: The British Approach to the European Union Intergovernmental Conference 1996*

Document 10.4

This extract deals with the British government's views on the key issues to be addressed at the 1996 IGC.

Qualified Majority Voting

22.　　The weighted voting system (or 'qualified majority voting') works against the background of a political agreement known as the Luxembourg Compromise whereby, in the last resort, a Member State may insist that where it has a very important national interest at stake in a particular decision, discussion should continue until its fundamental problem has been resolved. There is no question of weakening this national safeguard at the IGC . . .

26.　　The scope of majority voting was extended by the Single European Act of 1986 and at Maastricht. Majority voting now applies to a wide range of issues such as the single market, agriculture, transport, external trade questions and most decisions on research and development and environmental issues. Unanimity has been retained, however, for areas of particular national sensitivity . . .

27.　　At a time when there is serious public concern about the centralisation of decision-making, the case has not been made for making it easier to override the objections of Member States in matters of particular sensitivity. The Government will therefore oppose further extension of qualified majority voting . . .

The European Court of Justice

36.　　The IGC will provide an opportunity to examine the role of the European Court of Justice (ECJ) . . .

37.　　 . . . There have been judgements in recent years that have given cause for concern, particularly where they have imposed disproportionate costs on Governments or business, even when they have made every effort to meet their EC obligations. There is concern that the ECJ's interpretation of laws sometimes seems to go beyond what the participating Governments intended in framing these laws. The Government is working up a number of proposals to enable the Court to address these concerns better . . .

Common Foreign and Security Policy; defence issues

44.   . . . questions of defence go to the heart of national sovereignty . . . They are not matters for decision in the European Union. Member States must be free to act in defence of their national interests. Our proposals are rooted in that conviction. They are also based on our belief in the overriding importance of the Atlantic Alliance as the bedrock of our future security . . . But in the case of smaller peacekeeping, humanitarian or other crisis management operations, it will not always be reasonable to expect the United States or Canada to participate. European defence cooperation must therefore be organised in such a way that . . . European countries are also able to act on their own when necessary.

45.   In the Government's view, the WEU provides the best framework for the further development of this cooperation . . .

47.   The Government therefore believes that the WEU should be maintained as an autonomous organisation with its own Treaty base, and that its operational capacity should be developed to enable it to operate effectively in peacekeeping, humanitarian and other limited crisis management tasks . . .

Justice and Home Affairs

49.   As in the field of foreign and security policy, these are matters of high domestic political sensitivity involving questions of national sovereignty such as the rules governing the admission of third country nationals to member States, operations of police and customs authorities and the criminal justice system. There can be no question of supra-national solutions imposed on Member States in these areas, regardless of national sentiment or varying social and legal traditions. This area of work therefore requires special procedures. These are provided for in the so-called 'Third Pillar' introduced by Title VI of the Maastricht Treaty, which is subject to unanimity, and where the Government is firmly of the view that all decisions must continue to be taken on that basis . . .

Employment and the Social Protocol

59.   The need to create more jobs is one of the highest priorities in Europe. But the Government will oppose extending Community competence over employment, as some are advocating. It is businesses which make jobs . . . No-one should pretend that jobs can be wished into being simply by legislating for them in the Treaty. The key to creating new employment in Europe is to improve competitiveness and productivity . . .

60.   It is no secret that other Member States wish to see the UK's Social Chapter 'opt-out' removed at the IGC. The Government's position, however, is well known and equally constant. To accede to the Social Chapter could generate a one-way process in which European employment laws were increasingly imposed on the UK . . . The potential costs, in money and in jobs, are enormous. The UK will not give up its opt-out and cannot be forced to do so . . .

The Common Fisheries Policy

65.   . . . 'Quota-hopping' has been a particular problem, not least because it prevents fishing communities from enjoying a secure benefit from national quotas, thereby undermining the whole intention of the quotas. The Government is determined to address this and other problems in the Common Fisheries Policy and will explore every avenue for that purpose. If Treaty changes are needed, we shall seek them.

Source: Cmd. 3181 (March 1996), *A Partnership of Nations: The British Approach to the European Union Intergovernmental Conference 1996*

Document 10.5

The German Chancellor Kohl believed passionately in the necessity of continuing moves towards closer integration, arguing that Europe would otherwise be prey to disastrous national conflicts.

Ladies and gentlemen, there is no reasonable alternative to ever closer integration among the European peoples. We all need a united Europe. I would like to single out three reasons for this here:

First, the policy of European integration is in reality a question of war and peace in the 21st century. My deceased friend François Mitterrand shared this view. He stated before the European Parliament in Strasbourg on 17 January 1995 that nationalism is war.

I know that some people do not like to hear this. My warnings may come as an unpleasant truth. However, it is no use burying one's head in the sand. If there is no momentum for continued integration this will not only lead to standstill but also to retrogression. But we have no desire to return to the nation state of old. It cannot solve the great problems of the 21st century. Nationalism has brought great suffering to our continent – just think of the first fifty years of this century.

Second, we need Europe to ensure that our common views count in the world. We can only protect our common interests if we speak with one voice and pool our resources.

Third, we all need Europe in order to remain competitive on the world markets. Only together can we hold our own in international competition with the other major economic areas of East Asia and North America. Latin America, too, is entering into this competition with the Mercosur Pact . . .

Ladies and gentlemen, the intergovernmental conference which is to review the Maastricht Treaty concluded in February 1992 is due to commence shortly. I venture to say that if we suffer a setback now on the road to Europe it will take considerably longer than one generation before we are given such an opportunity again . . .

Economic and monetary union is certainly one of the greatest challenges facing us in the European Union at the present. The current preparatory phase is a period of uncertainty, a period in which the very continuation of European integration is being questioned. Have the Europeans become tired of Europe again?

I do not believe that this really is the case. However, the road mapped out at Maastricht not only signifies great progress but also calls for considerable efforts on everybody's part to achieve a major step forward.

I am confident, however, that at the Intergovernmental Conference the ultimately prevailing view will be that without the further development of the Maastricht Treaty the European Union would be incapable of mastering the challenges of the next century.

No one wants a centralized superstate. It does not and never will exist . . .

I would regard it as a disastrous development if Europe's strength were to diminish with its enlargement. However, I would find it equally disastrous if Europe were only able to derive its strength from keeping others out.

During the next few years we will have to prove that a viable Europe can be built with 15 and more states. At the same time, however, the slowest ship in the convoy should not be allowed to determine its speed. If individual partners are not prepared or able to participate in certain steps towards integration the others should not be denied the opportunity to move forward and develop increased cooperation in which all partners are welcome to take part.

> Source: Address by Kohl on receiving an honorary doctorate
> from the University of Louvain, 2 February 1996,
> Embassy of the Federal Republic of Germany, London

Document 10.6

The European Commission's approach to the 1996 IGC was radically different from that of the British government.

1. Promoting the European social model

The social dimension

The social dimension should be one of the central themes of the Conference. Above all there has to be a common base of social rights for all Union citizens. The Commission believes that to achieve this the Social Protocol must be integrated into the Treaty, and clearer provisions laid down concerning cooperation between Member States on matters of social policy, such as the fight against marginalization or against poverty . . .

Employment

13.   Unemployment is undermining the foundations of our societies, affecting nearly 20 million people, many of them young . . .

In its 1993 White Paper on growth, competitiveness and employment, the Commission proposed a series of measures aimed at mobilising all sections of society. This strategy is still relevant today: growth, competitiveness and employment go hand in hand. Only a competitive economy can create lasting jobs.

Structured and coherent action by the Union has to contribute to restoring a high level of employment, which is already a Treaty objective.

To this end, the Commission proposes that specific provisions on employment be written into the Treaty. They would be grounded on experience accumulated by the Community and treat employment as a matter of common interest; they would aim at:

(i)   establishing the conditions for a common strategy for employment;
(ii) stimulating cooperation between the interested parties;
(iii) consolidating the arrangements for multilateral surveillance of Member States' multinational programmes;
(iv) taking employment into account in all Community policies . . .

2. Making majority voting the general rule

44.   In an enlarged Union, adherence to unanimity would often result in stalemate. Indeed, the difficulty of arriving at unanimous agreement rises exponentially as the number of members increases.

The Commission accordingly proposes that qualified majority voting becomes the general rule.

Two additional observations are then warranted:

(i)   Unanimity need not necessarily be replaced by qualified majority voting as defined at present. In particularly sensitive fields, decisions could be taken by 'super-qualified' majority voting, for example.
(ii) What holds true for Community legislation also holds true for the Treaty itself and amendments to it: if in future the Treaty could, as at present, be amended only by unanimity, it would be in danger of stagnating in the state in which the 1996 Conference left it, making future progress in the direction of European integration an unlikely prospect . . .

The Commission considers that in future it should be possible to amend at least provisions that are not of a constitutional nature by a procedure which imposes fewer constraints than the one currently in force.

3. Organizing flexibility

45.   The European Union must not be forever bound to advance at the speed of its slowest members.

This is even more true in an enlarged Community . . .

The Commission observes that, already, organized flexibility is the route sometimes to be followed for deepening the Union, as the example of economic and monetary union shows.

On the other hand, the Commission firmly rejects any idea of a 'pick-and-choose' Europe (e.g. the Social Protocol) which flies in the face of the Common European project and the links and bonds which it engenders.

The Commission takes the view, however, that the European Union must make it possible to have forms of cooperation or integration between those of its members wishing to progress faster and further in the attainment of the Treaty's objectives. This should be envisaged only after exhaustion of all other possible forms of action involving all the Member States under the Treaty ...

Source: *Intergovernmental Conference 1996 Commission Opinion Reinforcing Political Union and Preparing for Enlargement.*

Document 10.7

At the Conservative Party annual conference of October 1995 Michael Portillo, the Eurosceptic Defence Secretary, gave a characteristically audience-pleasing speech. Its main thrust was opposition to the idea of a common defence policy or a European army, but the speech also represented a blistering attack on the influence of Brussels.

The Atlantic Alliance is the rock of our defence policy.

That alliance requires European nations to shoulder their responsibilities. We have fought alongside the French and Dutch on the slopes above Sarajevo, together demonstrating that we recognise that obligation.

But the defence of Europe involves more than the European Community: Norway, the countries of eastern and central Europe, Turkey and Russia.

It would be absurd, as some of our partners are urging, to try to merge our defence cooperation into the European Community.

Brussels. You knew I'd mention it.

Imagine.

The European Commission might want to harmonise uniforms and cap badges. Or even to metricate them.

The European Court would probably want to stop our men fighting for more than 40 hours a week.

They would send half of them home on paternity leave.

There are those in the Labour party and across Europe, sleep walking their way along the dreamy road to a European superstate.

We will not allow Brussels to control our defence policy.

With a Conservative Government Britain will not join a single European Army.

While John Major is Prime Minister, Malcom Rifkind is at the Foreign Office, and I am Secretary of State for Defence, the foreign and defence policies of this country will not be dictated to us by a majority vote of a council of ministers.

Would it have given Britain permission to re-take the Falkland Islands? No way.

Britain will not be told when to fight and when not to fight.

Mr Blair has said that he will never let Britain be isolated in Europe. An extraordinary statement.

Never willing to be isolated means never willing to stand up for our vital national interests.

Never to use the veto.

Never to stand alone.

Britain is blessed with very brave soldiers, sailors and airmen willing to give their lives.

For Britain.

Not for Brussels . . .

New Labour would hand over Britain's security to union convenors.

Not new Labour, real Labour.

We know their defence policy.

Withdrawal, retreat, surrender. Withdrawal from the world. Retreat from our responsibilities. Surrender to European federalism.

You can't trust Labour on defence . . .

Let us teach our children the history of this remarkable country . . .

I mean the real history of heroes and bravery, of good versus evil, of freedom against tyranny.

Of Nelson, Wellington and Churchill.

The history that created a sovereign nation. The defence that protected our parliamentary democracy when every country in continental Europe fell to the dictators. The defence that will sustain that sovereignty yet.

Source: *Conservative Party News*, Press Office, Conservative Central Office

Document 10.8

Major came under exteme pressure to resist any moves towards further integration. He was faced with constant sniping from his predecessor who fired occasional warning shots across the bows.

"OUR NEW EUROPEAN MASTERS"

But today the main challenge to limited government comes not from within these shores, but rather beyond them – from the European Union. There is, of course, also a challenge to *self*-government – and the two are closely connected.

The activity of the European Court, which can only ultimately be checked by amending the European Communities Act itself, is increasingly undermining our judicial system and the sovereignty of our Parliament. Proposals are being made for common European defence – proposals which Michael Portillo has roundly and rightly attacked. They are a threat to national independence. But most important, of course, is the proposed single European currency which, as John Redwood has argued, 'would be a major step on the way to a single European nation'.

The Prime Minister will have the support of all of us who wish to see these dangerous and damaging proposals resisted, and the present trends reversed, as he argues Britain's case at the forthcoming intergovermental council. And we look forward to a successful outcome.

But vital as the issue of *self*-government is, it is *limited* government that concerns me today. For the European Union not only wishes to take away *our* powers; it wishes to increase its *own*. It wants to regulate our industries and labour markets, pontificate over our tastes, in short to determine our lives. The Maastricht Treaty, which established a common European citizenship and greatly expanded the remit of the European Commission, shows the outlines of the bureaucratic superstate which is envisaged. And Maastricht is the beginning, not the end of that process . . .

Self-goverment, limited goverment, our laws, our Parliament, our freedom.

These things were not easily won. And if we Conservatives explain that they are now in peril, they will not be lightly surrendered.

Source: The Keith Joseph Memorial Lecture, delivered by
Baroness Thatcher on 11 January 1996, Baroness Thatcher's Office

Document 10.9

Major's reluctant concession of a referendum on the single currency was treated with scorn by the Referendum Party.

What Major's and Blair's referendum will do:
* Decide whether or not we join the single currency.

What Major's and Blair's referendum *won't* do:
* It *won't* stop laws made in Parliament being overturned in Europe.
* It *won't* stop the wanton destruction of our fishing industry.
* It *won't* stop Britain being forced to run her economy, not for the benefit of her own people, but for the benefit of Europe.
* It *won't* stop Britain being forced to set the exchange rate of the pound, not to suit Britain's economy, but to suit that of Europe.
* It *won't* stop the tide of new regulations that are crippling our small businesses.
* It *won't* stop VAT being imposed on children's clothes, books, travel and even houses.
* It *won't* stop the fraudulent waste and huge expense of Europe's bureaucratic institutions.
* It *won't* stop British taxpayers facing the threat of having to subsidise pensions in the rest of Europe.
* It *won't* stop Brussels telling us how many hours a week we should work.
* It *won't* stop plans for Britain to give away control of her borders, national security and foreign policy.
* It *won't* stop European law being the supreme law of this land.
* It *won't* stop the politicians surrendering Britain's future as an independent nation without seeking the views of the British people.

This is our last chance. We must have a *full* referendum on Europe now. And with your support we can get one.

REFERENDUM PARTY
It's now or never – Let the people decide
Source: *The Independent*, 12 January 1997

Document 10.10

The beef crisis caused a sharp deterioration in relations between Britain and its EU partners, especially the Germans. It also gave a boost to Eurosceptic sentiment within the Conservative Party. The government believed that the ban was unjustified on scientific grounds and also illegal. In the absence of any progress towards ending it, Major announced a policy of non-cooperation on 21 May 1996.

The Prime Minister (Mr. John Major): . . . As the House will know, we have been making every effort with the European Commission and with the member states to lift the ban on beef and beef products imposed two months ago by the European Union. We appreciate the difficult situation on the beef markets of a number of member states, the fragile state of consumer confidence throughout Europe, and the political pressures faced by a number of Governments, but we have put in place a wide range of measures to ensure that all products reaching the market are safe on any normal definition of the word.

As a result of controls on feed, the incidence of bovine spongiform encephalopathy in Britian is falling rapidly, and will continue to do so. There can no longer be any conceivable justification for the ban remaining in place. It is having a hugely damaging effect on the beef industry throughout Europe.

We have explained very clearly the extent of the measures that have been taken – going well beyond those in many other European Union member states – to ensure the safety of British beef and beef products . . .

As a result, the Commission recently made a proposal to lift the ban on gelatine, tallow and semen. That is based on scientific evidence . . . A majority of member states supported that proposal when it was put to the standing veterinary committee yesterday, but it did not attract the required qualified majority vote to enable it to take effect . . .

President Santer and Commissioner Fischler have confirmed that they stand by the proposal . . . However, the present position is clearly unacceptable. A balanced proposal based on the best scientific advice has been ignored by a number of member states, in some cases despite prior assurances of support. I must tell the House that I regard such action as a wilful disregard of Britain's interests, and, in some cases, a breach of faith.

Moreover, we have still been unable to reach agreement on further steps towards a progressive lifting of the wider ban, which is clearly our main objective . . .

Important national interests for Britain are involved in this matter. I cannot tolerate those interests being brushed aside by some of our European partners, with no reasonable grounds for doing so . . .

We have a strong legal case against the ban as a whole, and particular aspects of it. We made it clear from the outset that we believed the ban to be unlawful and disproportionate, and that we would therefore be bringing proceedings. The proceedings will begin this week . . .

But those legal steps are not in themselves sufficient. We shall continue to press the scientific case on our partners and pursue our own programme to eradicate BSE. I have to tell the House that without progress towards lifting the ban, we cannot be expected to continue to co-operate normally on other Community business.

I say this with great reluctance, but the European Union operates through good will. If we do not benefit from good will from our partners, clearly we cannot reciprocate. Progress will not be possible in the intergovernmental conference or elsewhere until we have agreement on lifting the ban on beef derivatives and a clear framework in place leading to a lifting of the wider ban.

We will raise the question of the ban at all Councils, including the Foreign Affairs Council. If necessary, we shall seek special Councils. I shall make it clear that I expect agreement on how to deal with these problems to be behind us by the time the European Council meets in Florence on 21 and 22 June. If it is not, the Florence meeting is bound to be dominated by the issue. It could not proceed with normal co-operation unless it faced up to the crisis of confidence affecting not only consumers but Governments throughout Europe.

That is not how we wish to do business in Europe – but I see no alternative. We cannot continue business as usual in Europe when we are faced with the clear disregard by some of our partners of reason of common sense and of Britain's national interests.

Source: *H.C.Deb.*, vol. 278, cols. 99–101 *passim*,
21 May 1996

Document 10.11

Teresa Gorman, one of the 'whipless eight' Eurosceptic MPs whose refusal to toe the official line on Europe caused the Major government enormous difficulties, applauded the decision to block EU business until the ban on British beef exports was eased. The following article which she wrote for The Sun *was characterised by strong anti-Germanism.*

Don't you love seeing Agriculture Minister Douglas Hogg grovelling to Europe? Doesn't it give us a feeling of national pride?

Have you seen it all before when Chamberlain came down the steps of the aeroplane waving a piece of paper after trying to appease the Germans? **And look what happened then.**

We are in danger of doing to our farmers what we have already done to our fishermen, destroying their livelihood on the altar of European union – and it's got to stop . . .

The Germans won't be content until every cow in the country has been killed . . .

They are destroying public confidence while expanding their own domestic production. To add insult to injury they are banning us from selling worldwide. What kind of country would put up with this?

At last the Prime Minister is going to stand up to them . . .

Negotiation doesn't work. What the Europeans are doing is illegal but they don't care.

We should retaliate. Cutting our budget contribution will make them take notice . . .

Appeasement doesn't work. If we do not benefit from goodwill from our partners we clearly cannot reciprocate.

You can't appease a bully determined to put the boot in.

We should stick to the scientific evidence that our beef is healthy, go back to selling in world markets and tell the Europeans to get stuffed.

Source: *Sun*, 22 May 1996

Document 10.12

The Sun *also welcomed Major's tough action. In this extract too the anti-German sentiment is pronounced.*

MAJOR SHOWS BULLS AT LAST

He tells EU: It's war.

John Major declared war on Europe for refusing to lift the ban on British beef.

He pledged to bring the EU to its knees by blocking **ALL** community business until his demands are met . . .

The furious PM triggered the biggest flashpoint in our 23-year membership by accusing fellow leaders of breaking their promise.

He condemned them for agreeing to end the two-month blockade and then going back on their word . . .

Mr Major's decision to go to war followed our latest Brussels humiliation.

On Monday [20 May 1996], EU agriculture chief Franz Fischler told vets to lift part of the ban affecting beef products. Germany, Portugal, Spain, Luxembourg, Holland and Belgium all privately told the PM the deal would be rubber-stamped – but their experts blocked it.

Mr Major is particularly furious at what he sees as a betrayal by 20-stone German Chancellor Helmut Kohl.

Kohl privately assured Mr Major he would help lift the ban. But Germany's veterinary chief voted to **KEEP** it.

A senior Tory source said: 'Don't underestimate the PM's anger towards Germany. Certain countries have been speaking with forked tongue, and they are one.'

Source: *Sun*, 22 May 1996

Document 10.13

After the Florence Council of 21–22 June 1996, Major announced that he had achieved his objectives on the beef ban through his non-cooperation policy. His claim was ridiculed by the Opposition parties (A). By contrast, Conservative Eurosceptic backbenchers approved of the result and called for the tactic to be applied in other areas where there was a disagreement between Britain and its EU partners (B).

A

Mr. Paddy Ashdown (Yeovil): I am glad that the puerile policy of posturing masquerading as war on Europe is now over. When the Prime Minister announced it, I told him it would achieve nothing that could not be achieved by other means. The damage that has been done to Britain's influence and respect will be great . . .

It is perfectly clear that the Prime Minister – like a previous Prime Minister – has returned from Europe claiming a victory, the cost of which we shall feel increasingly over the months ahead. This has been a policy of folly abroad and chaos at home, which has left Britain damaged both at home and abroad.

Source: *H.C.Deb.*, vol. 280, cols. 26–7, 24 June 1996

B

Mr. John Redwood (Wokingham): I am glad that my right hon. Friend has had success in getting our EC partners to see the difficulties facing our beef industry. I trust that people in this House will think twice before jeopardising more livelihoods and businesses in the beef industry.

Does my right hon. Friend have equally persuasive ways of raising the issues of the powers of the European Court of Justice and the plight of our fishing industry, which are also in our minds?

Source: *H.C.Deb.*, vol. 280, col. 27, 24 June 1996

extended. Only two directives were currently in force: one relating to unpaid parental leave and the other to works councils. The Commission was drawing up plans for more, however, and, speaking at an EU mini-summit at Noordwijk (23 May 1997), Blair warned that he was not prepared to tolerate a mass of additional regulations under the Social Chapter which might undermine the competitiveness of British industry (11.1). This was an early pointer to difficulties ahead.

The most urgent item on the Blair government's agenda for Europe was preparation for the Amsterdam European Council. This was scheduled to meet in mid-June to complete the work on a new EU treaty which had begun in Turin in March of the previous year. As various drafts emerged from the IGC during May and early June, it became apparent that the Blair government shared many of the reservations felt by its predecessor about closer integration. The French, German and most other EU governments continued to press for greater use of QMV. They also wanted to see a pooling of sovereignty in spheres that were currently in the second and third pillars of the Maastricht Treaty's complicated three-pillared structure and therefore on an intergovernmental basis: defence, foreign policy, justice and home affairs. The British response was predominantly negative. Britain was totally opposed to the idea favoured by Bonn and Paris that the WEU should be absorbed into the legal and constitutional framework of the EU. Nor was it prepared to countenance the elimination of all border restrictions between members states, demanding a legally binding guarantee, written into the new treaty, of the UK's right to retain permanent control over its own frontier checks. In the event, the British case on both these points was accepted at Amsterdam. According to Blair, indeed, the Amsterdam agreement as a whole was a triumph for his government and for the UK: the new flexibility mechanism that was to permit selective integration by some member states contained safeguards to protect the interests of non-participants, as the British government had demanded; the unemployment chapter and a supplementary resolution on economic growth and unemployment both reflected the British emphasis on the encouragement of job skills and labour market flexibility; and an exchange of letters between Blair and Jacques Santer, the European Commission President, provided a basis for the introduction of measures to combat 'quota-hopping' by foreign fishermen operating with British-registered vessels in UK waters (11.2).

Blair's claims were overstated, but no more so than Conservative allegations that the Treaty of Amsterdam constituted yet another massive step towards a European superstate. The truth is that there was only modest progress at Amsterdam in carrying out the ambitious reforms – many of them integrationist in intent – that were envisaged when the IGC began. The EP acquired some minor extra powers. QMV was extended to such areas as countering fraud and was also to apply to policy on immigration, asylum, visas and related matters five years after the treaty came into force. In the case of intended changes to the weighting of votes in the Council, it proved impossible to reach agreement and the issue was simply shelved (11.3). Overall, then, the institutional changes brought about by the Amsterdam Treaty were of a more limited nature than originally expected and certainly less substantial than those agreed at Maastricht.

A key issue which was not considered at the Amsterdam European Council was EMU. Unlike its predecessor, the Blair government was basically favourable to the single currency and to British membership on the grounds that it would probably yield financial and economic benefits. For a variety of reasons – both practical and political – there was never any serious possibility that the UK would join as part of the first wave. The government was unwilling to admit this publicly, however, wanting to retain as much influence and leverage as possible during the critical preparatory phase. Thus the official line was that nothing had been ruled out but that British entry to the single currency area in January 1999 was very unlikely. Despite mounting pressure from Britain's EU partners, the Conservative Opposition and business interests for a clarification of its policy, the government stuck to this vague formula until 27 October 1997 when Brown, the Chancellor, was obliged to give the Commons an authoritative statement of policy because of politically damaging press speculation triggered off by an article in the *Financial Times*. In his statement, Brown ruled out British participation in EMU for the rest of the current Parliament – 'barring some fundamental and unforeseen change in economic circumstances'. At the same time, he made it clear that the government had no objection to it in principle and announced the start of an intensive campaign to prepare business for entry in the event of a decision to go ahead at some point during the next Parliament. A central feature of Brown's statement was that it set out five economic tests on which the government would base its judgement on whether it was in Britain's interest to adopt the euro (11.4).

In the period after Brown's statement, there remained considerable uncertainty about government intentions. During the rest of 1997 and throughout 1998 the government refused to commit itself unequivocally to entry to the euro zone and fix a definite date. In effect, it adopted a 'wait and see' policy of the kind that Blair had derided when his predecessor had pursued it. This stance was determined partly by the undeniable difficulty of forecasting precisely when the five economic tests would be met. There can be little doubt, though, that senior members of the Blair government were also impressed by the potential political risks involved in giving a firm commitment to abandoning the pound and adopting the euro. The consistent message from opinion polls conducted during 1997–98 was that a clear majority of the British public was opposed to such a course (11.5). This was also the line taken by a substantial section of the tabloid press, including the *Daily Mail*, the *Daily Express*, and the *Sun*, as well as broadsheets like *The Times* and the *Daily Telegraph*.

It was the attitude of the *Sun*, whose proprietor Rupert Murdoch was a staunch opponent of the single currency, that presented the greatest potential danger to the government. The *Sun*, which had recently switched its support from the Conservatives to Labour, was reputed to be able to have a significant effect on the outcome of elections. It is not surprising, therefore, that Blair should have shrunk from the prospect of holding a referendum on the euro in which the *Sun* was to be found campaigning against the government's recommendation. He received a taste of what lay in store at the time of the Cardiff European Council (June 1998) when some relatively favourable comments that he made about the euro provoked a series of typically out-rageous articles, one of which posed the question whether the Prime Minister was 'the most dangerous man in Britain' (11.6).

Because of the critical attitude of much of the press, as well as the lukewarm or hostile mood of the public, the Blair government was unwilling to risk an early referendum on joining the euro zone. It opted instead for a gradual approach, waiting for a change in the general climate of opinion and in the meantime doing everything possible to bring that about. In essence, its strategy was to build up an unstoppable momentum in favour of entry. This involved two complementary elements. On the one hand, the government encouraged close cooperation between Whitehall and industry in preparing the latter for adjustment to the new regime: this approach was reflected in the National Changeover Plan (November 1998). On the other hand, Blair in particular sought to forge, in advance of the promised euro referendum, a cross-party, pro-European grand coalition on the lines of the one that had proved so effective in 1975. Here he was favoured by circumstances. The Liberal Democrats were ardent supporters of UK membership and therefore receptive to his overtures. Blair also found willing allies among pro-European Conservatives, prominent amongst whom were Clarke, Heseltine and Howe. In January 1998 these three joined with other Tory 'grandees' in writing an open letter to the *Independent* expressing support for the Blair government's policy towards the EU, and especially for its positive line on the euro (11.7).

This gesture came as a response to the increasingly hard-line Eurosceptic stance of the Conservative Party, exemplified by its opposition to membership of the single currency area for the lifetime of the current and next parliament. Major's resignation immediately after the disastrous election defeat of May 1997 had been followed by the election of William Hague as his successor. This choice represented an unmistakable victory for the Eurosceptic tendency and was indicative of a shift in the balance of power within the Conservative Party. Under Hague's leadership the party moved in a strongly anti-European direction. Hague himself was fundamentally opposed to the single currency. He regarded it as both inherently unworkable and a threat to national sovereignty, and by the summer of 1998 his pronouncements on the subject were assuming apocalyptic proportions. In a speech at Fontainebleau on 19 May he compared the risks of membership of the single currency to those of being trapped in a burning building with no exits (11.8).

Hague's strong stand against joining the euro derived to some extent from a belief that it would win votes. Blair's suspicion that this might well be the case only reinforced his determination to rely on a long-haul strategy. However understandable, this cautious approach gave rise to growing impatience in pro-European circles where there was disappointment that the government was not taking advantage of its huge parliamentary majority, as well as its own and the Prime Minister's continuing popularity with the electorate, to act more decisively and set a date for membership of EMU (11.9A). Such criticism was to come to a head at the time of the 1999 European elections when Labour's dismal showing was attributed to Blair's alleged failure of political will over the euro. The complaint from Eurosceptics was completely different: Blair was accused by them of being engaged in a devious exercise which was designed to take Britain into EMU by stealth (11.9B).

In the event, Britain decided not to join the euro zone at its inception in January 1999. Denmark and Sweden likewise chose to stay out, while Greece alone of the 15 EU states was judged to be ineligible on the grounds that it did not satisfy the economic criteria laid down in the Maastricht Treaty (11.10). The upshot was that 11 countries were scheduled to take part in the launch of the euro. The final preparations for the launch were completed during the UK presidency, and the consequence of Britain's self-exclusion was that the British government played a more limited role in key decisionmaking about EMU than would otherwise have been the case.

The British presidency began with a glittering prospectus. Blair spelled out his government's main objectives in a speech delivered at the Eurostar terminus at Waterloo station (11.11). One of its main themes was the need for economic reform via a 'third way' – an approach said to be located somewhere between old-style intervention and *laissez faire*, with an emphasis on improving workers' employability. There was a promise of progress towards common action on crime, drugs and the environment, and much was made of building a Europe which served the interests of its people. The UK would work constructively with its partners to ensure that EMU began successfully. It would also ensure that negotiations for the EU's enlargement got off to 'a flying start'. During the presidency (January–June 1998) it was these last two items which figured most prominently.

Enlargement produced no immediate problems. At the Luxembourg European Council (December 1997) it had been confirmed that negotiations would begin with Cyprus, the Czech Republic, Estonia, Hungary, Poland and Slovenia on 31 March 1998. Negotiations duly started on the scheduled date, but had not proceeded very far when the British presidency ended. There were already, however, some worrying signs of difficulties ahead. In July 1997 the European Commission had issued a document entitled *Agenda 2000: For a Stronger and Wider Union* proposing sweeping reforms in the CAP, structural (regional) funding and EU finances as an essential accompaniment to enlargement. It was generally agreed that there must be radical changes if the EU was to avoid being bankrupted by admission of new member states which were for the most part economically backward. The Commission's proposals therefore received a broad welcome. This consensus began to break down, however, when it came to detailed consideration of how each existing member's interests might be affected. Enlargement would inevitably involve huge costs and the Germans were determined not to play their customary role of picking up the bill. Both Kohl and his Social Democrat successor, Gerhard Schröder, complained that Germany's net contribution to the EU budget was already disproportionately high and called for a fairer system based on GDP (11.12). Ironically, they demanded a rebate comparable to that obtained by Thatcher in 1984. Other EU leaders gave no sign of being prepared to help in lightening Germany's burden. The uncompromising line from Blair was that, whatever else happened, there could be no question of giving up the British rebate.

From the standpoint of the British government, it was EMU which proved the most troublesome of the issues with which it had to deal during its presidency, as well as the acid test of its claim to be playing a leading role in EU decision-making. There was a row over Britain's unwillingness to serve a two-year probationary period in the ERM as a precondition of joining the euro. Far more serious was a bitter triangular power struggle that developed between the French, Germans and Dutch over who should head the ECB. Blair attracted considerable criticism for the way he handled this crisis in his capacity as President of the European Council. Indeed, the verdict on his personal performance and that of his government during the British presidency as a whole was at best a mixed one (11.13). The assessment offered by senior ministers was predictably flattering (11.14). Credit was claimed for a successful launch of the single currency and enlargement negotiations, and also for the lifting of the ban on beef exports from Northern Ireland recommended by the EU veterinary committee in March 1998. Beyond that, it was alleged that a broad consensus had emerged among member states in favour of the British agenda on modernisation and decentralised decisionmaking. A joint letter sent to Blair by Chirac and Kohl on the eve of the Cardiff European Council, in which the German and French leaders ruled out any idea of a European superstate, was cited as evidence of this (11.14 and 11.15). More disinterested observers rightly expressed a certain degree of scepticism as to what the Blair government had actually achieved during the British presidency.

Document 11.1

Within days of coming to power the Blair government announced its intention to end the UK's opt-out from the Social Chapter. It was made clear from the outset, however, that the new government was opposed to the introduction of a swathe of new directives under this Chapter.

Question: Prime Minster, would it be an accurate summary to describe your attitude to the social chapter being one that you are willing to sign up to it in its present form, but that you don't want anything adding to it and that you wouldn't want it used by leaders of other countries to end what they call social dumping by countries which have lower non-wage costs?

Prime Minister: I don't believe there is any appetite in the rest of Europe to have great rafts of additional legislation under the social chapter. I think that what there is an acceptance of, certainly on our part, is that it is sensible for us to be part of the social chapter so that we are part of the discussions on any legislation there, but we have made it very clear, as you know, that for example we would not allow other countries' social security systems to be imported into Britain as part of the social chapter. I have to say to you I don't believe there is any appetite to do that in the rest of Europe, and quite right too.

In fact I would say that one of the things we stressed today, and I think there is an increasing acceptance of, is the need to focus the attention of the European Union very, very closely indeed on job creation and on employability, on making sure that we have markets that actually assist the reduction of unemployment and the creation of jobs for the future, and that is obviously one of the things that we were pressing on and I think we found a very welcoming audience.

Source: Press Conference on Europe at Noordwijk, 23 May 1997,
EU Information Centre Release

Document 11.2

Blair faced the first major test of his policy on Europe at the Amsterdam European Council held on 16–17 June, only a month after forming his government. His report on the outcome presented a picture of complete success for the British government.

The Prime Minister (Mr. Tony Blair): . . . Our aims in the negotiations were to protect our essential interests over immigration, foreign policy, defence and a central role for Britain in Europe, to promote changes of real interest to the British people and to move Europe on to a new and positive agenda. We also promised to bring a fresh and constructive approach to Europe and to the negotiations.

I am happy to tell the House that those objectives have been fully achieved – and they were achieved while at the same time improving both our standing in Europe and our relationships with our European partners.

First, we have obtained legal security for our frontier controls, through a legally binding protocol to the treaty . . . We have ensured that we, and only we, decide border policy, and that policies on immigration, asylum and visas are made in Britain, not in Brussels.

Others may choose to have different arrangements, to suit their traditions and geographical position. I see no reason for preventing them from doing so, although such arrangements will continue to be governed by unanimity. Under the treaty, the United Kingdom can also participate in areas of interest to us if we so choose, at our option. That is not an opt-out but an opt-in, as we choose.

In the justice and home affairs area, we have agreed better arrangements for co-operation on police matters, crime and drugs . . . However, such co-operation will remain intergovernmental and subject to unanimity . . .

We have also ensured continued protection for our essential interests in all areas in which we sought it. We have maintained, as we said we would, the veto on matters of foreign policy, defence, treaty change, Community finances and taxation.

We have prevented the extension of qualified majority voting in areas where it might cause damage. Others wanted to extend QMV in the social chapter, which would have affected our companies even if we had not been party to the chapter. Because we were in it, we were able to stop that . . .

In addition, we secured a veto over flexibility arrangements which could otherwise have allowed the development of a hard core, excluding us against our will.

Second, for the first time in a decade Britain is setting a positive agenda for Europe . . . completion of the single market, a new emphasis on flexible labour markets and education and skills, reform of wasteful policies in agriculture and elsewhere, enlargement and a more effective common foreign and security policy. Each of these elements was reflected at Amsterdam, in the intergovernmental conference or the Council conclusions. In particular, we successfully promoted support for a new action plan for the single market that echoes key British concerns . . .

Third, we have put jobs at the top of Europe's agenda, where they belong. The new treaty chapter on employment recognises the importance of job creation and sets member states and the Community the task of promoting flexible labour markets, and education and skills . . .

Fourth, the treaty makes Europe more relevant to people: it ensures greater openness; it increases powers to combat fraud and waste; it creates power to act against discrimination . . . it gives subsidiary . . . real teeth through a binding protocol . . .

Fifth, the treaty prepares the institutions of the Union for enlargement. Not as much progress was made on that as there might have been, but we have ensured that, at the time of enlargement, the Council's voting system will be changed to give Britain and other large countries more votes . . . The European Council is committed to decisions on the opening of enlargement negotiations at its meeting in December. We shall play a leading role in those negotiations, particularly during our presidency.

Sixth, while retaining our veto, we have taken steps to improve the effectiveness of foreign policy co-operation with better planning and co-ordination . . . but getting Europe's voice heard more clearly in the world will not be achieved through merging the European Union and the Western European Union or developing an unrealistic common defence policy. We therefore resisted unacceptable proposals from others. Instead, we argued for – and won – the explicit recognition, written into the treaty for the first time, that NATO is the foundation of our and other allies' common defence . . .

We also made real progress in Amsterdam on the problem of quota hoppers – fishermen from other member states who fish against British quotas – even though it was not part of the IGC.

We have secured an agreement with the Commission on our two central concerns. First, we are entitled to put into law a clear economic link between boats using our quotas and Britain. Economic benefits from boats flying the British flag should go to British ports, for example through a proviso that 50 per

cent of a boat's catch should be landed locally. Second, the Commission agreed
to bring forward new tougher measures of enforcement to ensure that fishermen
landing their catches abroad cannot escape controls. Those measures are agreed
by qualified majority voting and so cannot be blocked by another member state.

Source: *H.C.Deb.*, vol. 296, cols. 313–15, 18 June 1997

Document 11.3

*In the IGC of 1996–97 the UK sought to obtain an increase in the votes allotted to the four big
EU states under QMV. It proved impossible to reach any agreement on this question at the
Amsterdam European Council and the position therefore remained the same. The QMV
arrangements, and also those for representation on the Commission and in the EP are set out in
the following table.*

Table 11.3

	Qualified majority votes	Number of members of the European Parliament	Commissioners	Population (millions)
Austria	4	21	1	8.1
Belgium	5	25	1	10.1
Denmark	3	16	1	5.2
Finland	3	16	1	5.2
France	10	87	2	58.0
Germany	10	99	2	81.6
Greece	5	25	1	10.4
Ireland	3	15	1	3.6
Italy	10	87	2	57.1
Luxembourg	2	6	1	0.4
Netherlands	5	31	1	15.4
Portugal	5	25	1	9.4
Spain	8	64	2	39.2
Sweden	4	22	1	8.8
United Kingdom	10	87	2	58.2
Total	87	626	20	370.7

Source: Cmd 3181 (March 1996), *A Partnership of Nations: The British Approach to the European Union
Intergovernmental Conference 1996.*

Document 11.4

An article in the Financial Times *of 26 September 1997 precipitated intense speculation
in the foreign exchange markets and a crop of press rumours about the Blair government's
intentions on membership of the single currency area. Brown, the Chancellor of the Exchequer,
gave a statement to the Commons clarifying government policy.*

We conclude that the determining factor as to whether Britain joins a single
currency is the national economic interest, and whether the economic case for
doing so is clear and unambiguous.

I turn now to the Treasury's detailed assessment of the five economic tests that define whether a clear and unambiguous case can be made . . .

Of these, the first and most critical is convergence: can we be certain that the United Kingdom business cycle has converged with that of other European countries, so that the British economy can have stability and prosperity within a common European monetary policy? That convergence must be capable of being sustained and likely to be sustained. In other words, we must demonstrate a settled period of convergence . . .

The Treasury's assessment is that, at present, the UK's economic cycle is not convergent with our European partners, and that this divergence could continue for some time. To demonstrate sustainable convergence will take a period of years.

The Treasury assessment on the second test – flexibility – is that, in Britain, persistent long-term unemployment and lack of skills, and in some areas lack of competition, point to the need for more flexibility to adapt to change and meet the new challenges of adjustment. The Government have begun to implement a programme for investing in education and training, helping people from welfare to work and improving the workings of our markets.

Of course, other European countries need to tackle unemployment and inflexibility to make sure that Europe as a whole is able to withstand any shocks that arise . . .

The third test is investment, whether joining monetary union would create better conditions for business to make long-term decisions to invest in Britain. The Treasury assessment is that, above all, business needs long-term economic stability and a well-functioning European single market. It concludes that membership of a successful single currency would help us to create the conditions for a higher and more productive investment in Britain. The worst case for investment would be for Britain to enter EMU without proper preparations and without sufficient convergence, with all the uncertainty that that would entail.

The fourth test asks what impact membership of the single currency would have on our financial services industry. EMU will affect that industry more profoundly and more immediately than any other sectors of the economy. The Treasury's assessment is that we can be confident that the industry has the potential to thrive, whether the United Kingdom is in or out of EMU, so long as it is properly prepared. However, the benefits of new opportunities from a single currency could be easier to tap from within the euro zone, and that could help the City of London to strengthen its position as the leading financial centre in Europe.

For millions of people, the most practical question is whether membership of a successful single currency would be good for prosperity, and particularly for jobs. The Treasury's assessment is that our measures to create employment and for welfare reform must accompany any move to a single currency.

Ultimately we conclude that whether a single currency is good for jobs in practice comes back to the question of sustainable convergence. A successful single currency would provide far greater trade and business in Europe. The

Treasury assessment is that, in vital areas, the economy is not yet ready for entry, and that much remains to be done . . .

To sum up, we believe that, in principle, British membership of a successful single currency would be beneficial to Britain and Europe: the key factor is whether the economic benefits of joining for business and industry are clear and unambiguous. If they are, there is no constitutional bar to British membership of EMU.

Applying the economic tests, it is not in this country's interest to join the first wave of EMU starting on 1 January 1999, and, barring some fundamental and unforeseen change in economic circumstances, making a decision in this Parliament to join is not realistic. To give ourselves a genuine choice in the future, it is essential that Government and business prepare intensively during this Parliament so that Britain should be in a position to join a single currency, should we wish to, early in the next Parliament.

On Europe, the time of indecision is over. The period of practical preparation has begun.

Source: *H.C.Deb.*, vol. 299, cols. 584–8 *passim*, 27 October 1997

Document 11.5

All surveys of British public opinion during 1997–98 indicated that there was a clear majority opposed to UK entry into the single currency area. The majority against taking part in the launch of the euro on 1 January 1999 was a bigger one.

Table 11.5A

Q. If there were a referendum now on whether Britain should be part of a single European currency, how would you vote?

	Agree	*Disagree*	*Don't Know*
November 1997	30%	52%	18%
January 1998	32%	52%	16%
March 1998	30%	54%	15%
May 1998	31%	54%	15%
July 1998	33%	50%	17%

Q. If the government were to strongly urge that Britain should be a part of a single European currency, how would you vote?

	In Favour	*Against*	*Don't Know*
November 1997	38%	47%	15%
January 1998	38%	47%	14%
March 1998	36%	51%	13%
May 1998	36%	50%	14%
July 1998	39%	46%	16%

Source: MORI for stockbrokers Salomon Smith Barney, July 1998.

Table 11.5B

Q. Which of the following statements about British membership of the European single currency most closely represents your view?

Membership will offer advantages and Britain should join as soon as possible	14%
Membership could offer advantages but Britain should only join when the economic conditions are right	57%
Britain should rule out the possibility of membership for at least 10 years	20%
Don't know/no opinion	8%

Source: MORI for the European Movement, January 1998.

Document 11.6

One of the biggest obstacles to the Blair govermnment's commitment to signing up for the euro was opposition from media tycoon Rupert Murdoch and his newspaper the Sun. *At the Cardiff European Council of June 1998 Blair made some comments seen as favourable to the single currency. The response from the* Sun *was vitriolic.*

IT IS the question we never dreamed we would ask.
Is Tony Blair the most dangerous man in Britain? In most respects he is a fine Premier. But he seems determined to scrap the Pound and take Britain into the European single currency.

And that we believe will be the biggest gamble any Prime Minister has ever taken.

The result could be disastrous for this country. That is why *The Sun* has vowed to fight it all the way.

Blair is a charming and persuasive politician. He thinks fast and outflanks his opponents with a smile that conceals a touch of steel.

These are the qualities which propelled him to election triumph and cement his position as the world's most popular politician.

Coupled with a massive Commons majority and a futile Opposition, they give this Prime Minister awesome power.

And make him a potential threat.
It is too early yet to say if absolute power will corrupt him. But it is already clear that Blair is determined to have his own way.

Much of it, like peace moves in Northern Ireland and ruthlessly modernising Labour, has been applauded by Sun readers.

Other decisions, like cutting the age for gay sex to 16, fly in the face of public opinion.

But they pale compared to the biggest issue of all: Our membership of the single currency.

Eleven key European states are committed to this dangerous gamble which could put the world economy in peril.

Their decision, taken under Mr Blair's presidency, removes any doubt that the euro will be up and running next January.

The Prime Minister, once a sceptic and now a convert, has decided that since Euro-land is inevitable, Britain cannot afford to be left out.

He has decided the Pound must go.

And, almost imperceptibly, he has shifted stance to become an advocate for the revolution.

The Sun backed him at the election because we believed he was the best man for the job. We still believe that.

But our support, as we made plain at the time, did not give him a blank cheque. If he is determined to propel us into the single currency, he will find The Sun a determined opponent.

We know Blair has had his doubts. He agrees with President Clinton that Europe's outdated but powerful labour and welfare lobbies could wreck the euro.

He knows British and German industrialists have grave fears about a system which could lead to economic disaster.

Blair also knows that the majority of British voters – and perhaps most other EU countries – are deeply unhappy about this gigantic experiment.

But he has decided to use his popularity to cajole, seduce and persuade the voters to back him.

Maybe Blair feels he can get away with sliding us into the euro because there has been no serious debate.

Well, there is now.

The Sun will not flinch from opposing the euro. We are against it economically, politically and constitutionally.

We will fight, fight, fight.

And even if we lose, we hope people will use the words of one of the greatest of our statesmen, Winston Churchill, and say . . .

This was their finest hour.

Source: *Sun*, 'Page One Opinion', 24 June 1998

Document 11.7

Conservative Europhiles became increasingly alienated by their party's line on Europe under the leadership of William Hague. Their dissatisfaction was reflected in an open letter sent to the Independent *by a group of prominent pro-European Conservatives expressing support for the Blair government's policy on EU affairs, and especially on the single currency.*

Sir: Twenty-five years ago this month, Britain joined the European Community. After refusing to participate in the creation of the new Europe in the 1950s, and having been spurned twice by De Gaulle in the 1960s, we finally found our rightful place in 1973, as full and equal partners in the European enterprise.

In the quarter-century membership to date, we have as a country gained much from Europe, and achieved much in Europe. The European Union today, with its emphasis on the single market, monetary and fiscal discipline, agricultural reform, enlargement, and increasingly open trade, owes as much to a distinctively British agenda as to that of any other country. We have helped to create the largest integrated market place in the world, and are helping to ensure that the EU's real economic and political power is used to advance liberalism and multilateralism around the globe.

Despite these achievements, Britain's membership has been marred by a lack of ambition and self-confidence. Too often, Europe has been seen not as an opportunity, but as a threat. We have failed to grasp fully the chance for Britain to play a truly leading role in Europe, and through Europe to magnify our influence worldwide. A positive European vision is critical to the nation's future success.

This month also marks the start of the fifth UK presidency of the European Union. A new government, with a large majority, aspiring to lead in Europe, now has the chance to convert its positive rhetoric into action. Conservatives committed to Britain at the heart of Europe will support Tony Blair and his colleagues in making the right decisions on the difficult challenges which lie ahead – during the next six months and beyond.

Nowhere will the choices be harder and the need for support greater than on economic and monetary union (EMU). Ensuring that Britain is not marginalised in Europe depends, more than anything else, on safeguarding our right to enter a single currency at any time, and ensuring that we suffer as little as possible from (once again) choosing not to be in from the start. We believe it important that EMU should succeed and for Britain to prepare now to join a successful single currency, when the British people freely vote to do so. This is the right policy for our country, and it is one we shall continue to commend with conviction to the Conservative Party and the nation as a whole.

Signed: Geoffrey Howe, Sir Leon Brittan, Peter Carrington, Kenneth Clarke, David Curry, John Gummer, Sir Edward Heath, Michael Heseltine, Chris Patten, Ian Taylor, Christopher Tugendhat.

Source: *Independent*, 5 January 1998

Document 11.8

Hague ruled out UK entry to the euro zone during the lifetime of the current and next Parliaments, generally interpreted as being for a 10-year period. His concerns about membership were expressed in a speech to the INSEAD Business School at Fontainebleau in May 1998.

On 1 January 1999 eleven Western European countries will take a momentous step. They will adopt a single currency between them and accept the authority of a single central bank.

But momentous as this step will be, it will create as many problems as it solves. And the most important is the danger that the single currency will lead to an increasingly centralised Europe . . .

I have to tell you that there is a limit to European integration. We are near that limit now. Push political union beyond its limits and you jeopardise the very peace, stability and prosperity which Europe's post-war statesmen were so anxious to secure.

My fear is that the creation of a single currency will take European political union well beyond its acceptable limits . . .

The effect of imposing a one size, fit all, single interest rate on a set of different economies with different cycles, structures and circumstances could be disastrous.

The single currency is irreversible. One could find oneself trapped in the economic equivalent of a burning building with no exits. But I am also concerned about the effects of EMU on the workings of our democracy and our institutions.

Some may wish it otherwise but voters today live their lives in nation states. Voters expect national governments to be accountable to them for the state of their economy: growth, employment, interest rates, mortgages and inflation. If a government is thought to have performed badly it can be changed by the ballot box. That is the essence of our democracy, and underpins its stability.

Under the single currency the one size, fit all interest rate may affect different countries differently. In some countries it might produce rising unemployment. But if it does the voter cannot change the government or the policy. Indeed the government cannot change the policy.

In Asia those countries that have had the most violent reactions to the financial crisis have been those countries that do not have the safety valve of democratic elections. How will the peoples of Europe react to a recession without the electoral means of changing the people responsible? . . .

Countries that are concerned about unemployment more than inflation will be critical of the European Central Bank for not pursuing a more expansionary policy. On the other hand, if the German public sees inflation rise, it will become antagonistic towards EMU, and towards the countries that vote for inflationary monetary policy.

But with a single currency these governments would suffer the frustration of not being able to decide for themselves and of being forced to accept the common monetary policy. If the governments are likely to feel frustrated how much more frustrated will the voters be? . . .

These are what one might call the political risks of the economic consequences of EMU. But I am also concerned about the direct political consequences of EMU.

The British Prime Minister and his Chancellor of the Exchequer have attempted to argue that the introduction of the Euro has no constitutional implications whatsoever, and is a purely technical question. I find it difficult to believe they really believe this. The Euro has potentially huge political consequences.

Some continental European politicians are quite frank that the purpose of the single currency is political. A single currency was always seen as fundamental to the creation of European political union. Chancellor Kohl has said quite openly that 'if there is no monetary union, then there cannot be political union and vice versa'. The 1992 Maastricht Treaty that creates EMU calls explicitly for the evolution to a future political union. But even without that language, the shift to a single currency would be a dramatic and irreversible step towards that goal . . .

In any economy, monetary policy on the one hand, and on the other hand tax and spending policy, that is fiscal policy, have to be closely coordinated. In order to make the single currency work I fear the European Union will be forced to intrude more and more into the spending and taxation decisions of individual states. Even if the EU does not actually raise the taxes or spend the money itself, it will increasingly control the decisions.

The powers to raise taxes from one's citizens and to spend the money on their behalf are defining features of a sovereign state. I believe that to delegate powers over taxation and spending to the EU would take us beyond the limits of political union towards the creation of what would be in effect a European state . . .

That is why I fear the political consequences of the single currency. For this reason the British Conservative Party is against British membership of the single currency now, and, subject to a ballot of Party members, intends to oppose it at the next General Election.

Source: William Hague's speech to the INSEAD Business School,
Fontainebleau, 19 May 1998

Document 11.9

Europhiles – including the former Chancellor, Kenneth Clarke – chided the Blair government for not moving quickly enough towards entry to the euro zone (A). By contrast, the opponents of British membership suspected that the government was pursuing a strategy designed to present the electorate with a fait accompli *(B).*

A

In a welcome development, the new Labour government declared last autumn that it had no objection in principle to EMU entry. It said, quite sensibly, that it saw no constitutional bar to UK membership and would judge the issue solely on whether the economic conditions were right. Tony Blair even went so far as to say that he wanted Britain to be a member of a successful single currency, a view which I myself firmly share.

However, in a statement to the House of Commons [27 October 1997] which he may yet come to regret, Chancellor Gordon Brown also announced that the government did not wish or expect Britain to participate in EMU during the life-time of the current parliament, which theoretically could run until June 2002 . . .

I myself have never taken the view that Britain should join EMU at the start in January 1999, and few people ever have. But many, including myself, have been equally opposed to ruling out UK entry on any inflexible timetable beyond that date. There is certainly no reason why we should now necessarily exclude the possibility of membership very early in the next century, most notably in January 2002, when notes and coins begin to circulate. Strictly speaking, the government has not done that. But Gordon Brown came perilously close to foreclosing such an option by the language he used in announcing his EMU policy. It represented, I fear, not the confident assertion of a popular government with a large majority, and at least four and a half years ahead of it, but the voice of a strangely intimidated government afraid to use its position of strength to assert controversial positions in the national interest. It is difficult to escape the view that, in its handling of the EMU issue at a critical time, the Blair government suffered something of a failure of nerve, and one which may have serious long-term consequences . . .

The big risk in the British government's current approach to EMU is that it underestimates the serious difficulties which may cloud its room for manoeuvre at home in respect of UK entry say four, five or six years from now. Will the government be as popular in the next parliament as this one? Will there be as big a pro-EMU majority in the House of Commons? Will the domestic economy be doing as well? However much public support there may be for EMU at some future date, there is no guarantee that an unpopular government could actually win the vote. And if Labour is not confident enough now, with so much going for it, to risk a referendum in this parliament, will it be sufficiently confident, when the time comes to risk one in the next? There are legitimate reasons for doubt.

Source: Foreword by Kenneth Clarke, in A. Duff (ed.), *Understanding the Euro*, London, Federal Trust, 1998, pp. 12–15 *passim*

B

BRAZEN EURO RUSE

Does the Government know something the rest of us don't, indeed can't – such as the result of the referendum on abolishing the pound? If not, why are Ministers so busily and brazenly trying to hustle us into the single currency?

The National Changeover Plan the Chancellor announced yesterday is supposed to accelerate preparations for the euro so that we can act quickly once a decision to join has been taken. A cross-party committee of MPs will monitor the progress of those preparations.

It all sounds most plausible. In fact it is a sham.

The real purpose of the exercise is obviously to prepare the ground for membership so thoroughly – using money from the taxpayer and Brussels – that the prospect of a NO vote is greatly reduced when the public gets the chance to have its say.

The Euro-enthusiasts in all parties are acting like a husband who sells the house, arranges for the furniture to go into store and then, with a straight face, tells his wife that no decision on moving has been made. They are ruthlessly set on Britain joining the single currency, come what may.

That tells us a great deal about their determination. Even more about their lack of respect for democracy.

Source: *Daily Mail*, 'Comment', 8 November 1998

Document 11.10

On 25 March 1998 the European Commission and the European Monetary Institute reported that only Greece of the 15 EU countries had failed to satisfy the economic criteria stipulated by the Maastricht Treaty as a precondition of entry to the single currency area. Reservations were expressed, though, about the high level of Belgian and Italian public debts. This judgement, which was confirmed by EU leaders in early May, was based upon statistical reports that were formally filed by member states on 27 February 1998.

Table 11.10

Country	Budget deficit (as % of GDP)	Debt (as % of GDP)	Inflation
TARGET	3.0	60.0	2.7ᵉ
Austria	2.5	66.1	1.2ᵖ
Belgium	2.1	122.2	1.5
Denmark	0.7	64.1	2.0
Finland	0.9	55.8	1.2
France	3.02	58.0	1.3
Germany	2.7	61.3	1.5
Greece	4.0	108.7	5.4
Ireland	0.9	66.3	1.2ᵉ
Italy	2.7	121.6	1.9
Luxembourg	1.7	6.7	1.4
Netherlands	1.4	72.1	1.9ᵖ
Portugal	2.45	62.0	1.9
Spain	2.6	68.3	1.9
Sweden	0.4	76.6	1.9
UK	1.9	53.4	1.9

e – estimated
p – provisional
Source: Keesings 1998, p. 42076 (from *Financial Times*, *Daily Telegraph*, and *The Times*).

Document 11.11

Britain exercised the presidency of the EU from January to June 1998. Blair set out the main objectives of the presidency in an inaugural speech at Waterloo railway station.

In outline, these are our Presidency themes:

First, we must build support for what we call the third way in Europe. The focus for economic reform should be a social model based on improving the employability of the European workforce.

This means education not regulation, skills and technology, not costs and burdens on business, and open competition and markets, not protectionism. There is a way between the old-style intervention and laissez-faire and we must take it. The crucial tests will be in completing the Single Market and in labour market reform.

Second, we will work constructively with our partners to ensure that Economic and Monetary Union is successfully launched.

It is in all our interests that monetary union works. We will play our part to ensure it does.

Third, we want to secure peace, democracy and security in a wider Europe by starting enlargement negotiations.

I want to use our Presidency to ensure that the negotiations get off to a flying start. It is an historic mission on which prosperous Western Europe cannot turn its back. We will also press for the start of reform in the Common Agricultural Policy, Structural Funds and European institutions necessary to make enlargement a success.

Fourth, we will take forward common action on crime, drugs and the environment.

Drug traffickers and money launderers do not respect borders. We must work together, if we are to have any hope of tackling these problems . . .

On the environment we need to ensure that Europe takes the lead . . .

Fifth, we will demonstrate that Europe can work together effectively and be a force for good in its relations with the outside world.

Europe must play a major role on the world stage . . . As the Presidency, we will work hard to build a stronger common foreign and security policy that is robust in the face of the threats that Europe faces.

There will, of course, be many other issues on the table during our Presidency . . . One problem we will certainly not lose sight of is the ban on the export of British beef, where we have to see some practical progress soon.

Finally, I want to involve the British people in our Presidency. A theme running throughout it will be geater openness and transparency . . .

We can only make Europe work for the people of Europe, if in turn the people of Europe feel they have a stake in what Europe does. Our Presidency is an opportunity to demonstrate that Britain now has a strong voice in Europe. That the indecision, vacillation and anti-Europeanism of the past have gone. And that we can at last play our part in building a Europe that works for the people and the people's priorities.

Source: 'Europe Working for People', speech by Tony Blair at the launch of the
UK presidency of the European Union, Waterloo station, 5 December 1997

Document 11.12

The fundamental reforms proposed by the European Commission in Agenda 2000 *raised questions about the existing distribution of the burden of EU finance. The Germans, already nursing a deep-seated grievance about their net contribution to the budget, began to demand a rebate comparable to that obtained for the UK by Thatcher at Fontainebleau in 1984. Kohl took up the issue at the Cardiff European Council of June 1998 (A) and his successor Gerhard Schröder adopted a similar stance (B).*

A

At 28% Germany makes the largest contribution to the EU budget (in 1997 DM 42.3 Billion) and is also the largest net contributor.

In the future we will remain a major net contributor. However, we seek a fair and more just allocation of this burden. In Cardiff our European partners acknowledged for the first time that our concern was justified.

Recognition of the principle of a fair system is one thing. It is quite another to address the question of the practical consequences of such recognition.

Unsurprisingly, opinion was divided in Cardiff on this issue. Some believe that the current rates of contribution should be maintained. If we take into account the future expansion of the European Union, it is evident that things cannot remain as they are.

Occasionally (and also in connection with EU funding) I am warned that we should not represent the interests of Germany so forcibly. I do not understand such statements.

Our partners in the other European states are quite content to represent their own national interests. Furthermore, they automatically assume that we will do the same.

Europeanism is not achieved by the suppression of one's own national interests, but rather by seeking to harmonize those interests with those of one's partners and thus to advance the concept of European integration.

Source: Statement by Kohl to the Bundestag on the
Cardiff European Council, 18 June 1998

B

Without a doubt, the most demanding task of our Presidency will be to start agricultural and structural policy reform. Moreover, we want to reach agreement on a fair and adequate financial structure for the period 2000 to 2006.

These three reform plans, grouped under the heading Agenda 2000, are prerequisites if the European Union is to be effective in the future. Without this reform, the accession of new members is inconceivable.

I want to be quite clear about this: without a fairer way of assessing contributions, we are going to distance the people in our country further from Europe rather than winning them over to deeper integration.

Let me quote a few figures to explain why we want to solve this problem urgently. In 1997, Germany paid . . . 22 billion marks more to the EU than we received from the community coffers as contributions.

To draw a comparison, the second largest net contributor after Germany is the Netherlands with a net burden of a mere 4.5 billion. Germany bears 60 percent of net contributions to the European budget.

Now we know as well that the European Union is not a bank where money is invested in the hope of the highest possible interest rate. But when countries such as Luxembourg, Denmark or Belgium, which according to the criteria of the European report on own resources enjoy higher per-capita prosperity than we do, when these countries are net recipients, while we remain far and away the largest net contributor, there is something not quite right with the calculation.

We cannot and will not continue a policy which aims to buy the goodwill of our neighbours with an intolerable budgetary burden at home. We cannot and will not solve Europe's problems with Germany's chequebook.

We will place these questions at the very top of our list of priorities for the Presidency of the Council.

Source: 'Preview of the European Council in Vienna on 11 and 12 December 1998 and of the German Presidency in the first half of 1999' – Policy Statement by Gerhard Schröder in the Bundestag, 10 December 1998. Translation by W. Jurk, German 2000, 1999

Document 11.13

The verdict of the Conservative Opposition on the UK presidency was a harsh one, as is seen from the following remarks by Michael Howard, the Shadow Foreign Secretary.

Mr. Michael Howard: . . . No one has ever accused the Foreign Secretary [Robin Cook] of false modesty, but the speech that we have just heard was one of insufferable complacency and self-congratulation, born more of fantasies than of the real world. Let us now return to the real world.

A couple of weeks ago, he addressed the European Parliament . . . The very next day, Members of the European Parliament voted on a motion that congratulated the United Kingdom presidency on its achievements, a motion tabled by the Labour Members of the Parliament, who form the largest group of the party of European Socialists. That party and its allies, has an overall majority in the Parliament, so the prospects for the motion must have seemed auspicious. Yet such was the impact of the Foreign Secretary's speech that the motion was lost.

The Foreign Secretary had done it again. The man who single-handedly bungled the royal visit to India, who caused grave offence during his visit to Israel and who has done more than anyone to bring the concept of ethics into disrepute had once more snatched defeat from the jaws of victory . . .

The vote of the European Parliament two weeks ago was a humiliation for the Foreign Secretary. Behind that humiliation lies another truth: the presidency has been a flop. What a contrast with the high hopes set out six months ago. The Prime Minister and the Foreign Secretary were going to transform the continent . . .

Nowhere was that disparity more marked than in the half-term report that the Government published in March . . . The report was a British innovation. There is no tradition of half-term reports, but the Foreign Secretary was so keen to trumpet his achievements that he was determined to break new ground . . .

What were the 45 successes attributed to the British presidency in that report? The Secretary of State for Education and Employment had chaired a meeting about life-long learning. The need for measures to lower telephone bills was highlighted. A seminar of Government press officers was held, at which agreement was reached to disseminate more information on the EU via the internet. And what of the Foreign Secretary? Well, he was praised for 'injecting new impetus' into the middle east peace process. Not a lot of people saw it that way at the time.

The whole ludicrous, self-serving exercise was viewed with incredulity by our European partners. One German diplomat said:

'It's funny, we always thought the British style was understated.'

It is little wonder that we are now told . . . that the Government have abandoned their intention to follow up the ludicrous half-time report with a full-time assessment of their performance . . . The Government have at last recognised the only appropriate verdict on their presidency – the least said the better.

Source: *H.C.Deb.*, vol. 313, cols. 1236ff., 11 June 1998

Document 11.14

Not surprisingly perhaps, the picture of the UK presidency presented by Foreign Secretary Robin Cook was one of uninterrupted achievement.

Mr. Robin Cook: As I look back over the months of our presidency, I believe that the achievement of greatest significance was the successful launch that we gave the enlargement process . . .

In January, I made giving enlargement a flying start one of the objectives of our presidency – we have done that, which will be of long-term credit to Britain. Over the next decade, all the countries involved will become member states with full voting powers at the Council of Ministers . . .

Enlargement is not the only historic step that is being taken under our presidency. Last month, the Heads of Government agreed that 11 member states could proceed to the final stages of economic and monetary union. Britain has not joined the first wave. We will judge whether we are ready to join on the basis of a hard-headed assessment of the economic interests of the British people . . .

In his Paris speech two months ago, my right hon. Friend the Prime Minister set out his vision for Europe. He stressed the importance of reconnecting Europe to its citizens and of striking a better balance to respect not only the advantage of Europe acting in unity, but the individual identity of each member state.

The letter from Chancellor Kohl and President Chirac, which was released earlier this week, demonstrates that those arguments are winning the debate on the future of Europe. It represents a powerful statement of the case for subsidiarity, which the two leaders demand must be 'strictly respected and applied' even more rigorously . . .

That statement is unequivocal. It exposes the Euro-sceptics' fears of a centralised, federalised European state for the fantasies that they are . . .

When we launched the UK presidency, we stressed that its theme would be to make Europe work for the people and that we would focus on issues of popular concern, such as jobs, crime and the environment. Over the past six months, we have made solid progress on all three fronts.

On jobs we were the first member state to produce a national action plan on employment, and Cardiff will be the first European summit at which the action plans which have now been developed by every member state will be reviewed . . .

We have acted to implement the commitment in the Amsterdam Treaty to integrate the protection of the environment across the broad range of European policies . . .

In our presidency, it has been our job to speak for all the member states. I am happy to say that that does not prevent us, and has not prevented us, from also speaking for Britain . . .

On 1 June, only a fortnight ago, the ban was lifted on exports of cattle from Northern Ireland under the certified herds scheme, and yesterday, the Commission agreed to propose to lift the ban on the export of beef under the date-based scheme for cattle born after August 1996.

We are not over the obstacle course yet . . . but the fact remains that we now have in sight an end to the beef ban for the British mainland, as well as for Northern Ireland.

The fact that we have got this far is a striking illustration of how much better the Labour Government have been able to promote British interests through their constructive and positive approach to Europe. By contrast, the policy of confrontation pursued by the previous Government left Britain on the sidelines of Europe, with neither influence nor respect, and did nothing to further Britain's interests on beef or anything else . . .

This is a record of achievement in which the whole of Britain is welcome to share our pride, including even the Conservative party, if it chooses to come out of the bunker, blinking into the light of the modern Europe.

Source: *H.C.Deb.*, vol. 313, cols. 1229–34 *passim*, 11 June 1998

Document 11.15

Shortly before the Cardiff European Council (15–16 June 1998) President Chirac and Chancellor Kohl sent a joint letter to Blair as President of the European Council. Blair and Cook later claimed that the views expressed in the letter showed that the French and German leaders had accepted many aspects of the British government's views on the future development of the EU.

Mr President,

The intention of Germany and France with this letter is to put forward our first joint deliberations and suggestions for increasing the European Union's scope for action and efficiency as well as its public acceptability.

It cannot be the goal of European policy to establish a European central state, that is to say, a centrally structured Europe. We must rather do all we can to create a strong European Union with the necessary scope for action and the capacity to preserve and foster the diversity and richness of Europe's political, cultural and regional traditions and characteristics.

Even in the future Europe there must be an assurance that decisions are taken as closely as possible to the citizen. Citizens will only become more strongly committed to the common Europe if decision-making processes are clearly understandable and transparent and they have the feeling that 'Europe is there for them', that it is helping them safeguard their interests. Local regional or national characteristics must receive adequate consideration in such decision-making.

Thus it will be necessary in future to be more consistent than hitherto in applying the principle of subsidiarity, which we agreed in the Treaties of Maastricht and Amsterdam should be strictly observed. In doing so, aberrations must be corrected and national constitutional and administrative structures respected.

Citizens will accept decisions at European level only if they are certain that the matter in hand cannot be adequately decided at the local, regional or national level and it is also clear that a decision at European level is absolutely necessary and in the interests of the people.

Considering that some European institutions are becoming increasingly remote from the citizens and their day-to-day problems, it is from our point of view important that the members of the European Council initiate a discussion on the implementation of the subsidiarity principle in order to achieve a clearer demarcation of authority as between the European Union and Member States and to examine how far the present mass of regulatory instruments is commensurate with requirements.

Correcting this situation has nothing to do with renationalization but would be consistent with the principles of proportionality, closeness to the citizen and efficiency, and would help rectify aberrations in the direction of overcentralization. In this connection we ought, where regulatory decisions are taken at European level, to revert increasingly to the use of directives in the original sense so as to leave institutions at national level greater scope when implementing them.

On the other hand it is in our view beyond question that in some areas a larger measure of integration is urgently necessary. This applies especially to the common foreign and security policy. The Treaty of Amsterdam provides for substantial progress and opens up new perspectives with regard to internal security and judicial affairs. We therefore suggest that the home affairs and justice ministers be asked to draw up a plan of action ready for our December meeting in Vienna showing how the new provisions can best be implemented.

Source: Joint letter from Chirac and Kohl to Blair, 5 June 1998, Service de Presse et d'Information, Ambassade de France à Londres

Appendix
The institutions of the European Community/European Union

This appendix provides a brief overview of the main institutions of the EC/EU. The European Communities (commonly referred to as the European Community) were founded in the 1950s and comprised the European Coal and Steel Community (ECSC) based on the Treaty of Paris (1951) and the European Economic Community (EEC) and the European Atomic Energy Community (EAEC) founded on the Treaties of Rome (1957). The Treaty on European Union of 1993 (Maastricht Treaty) established a three-pillar structure for what is now designated the European Union. The first pillar, known as the European Community, replaced the EEC and incorporated the economic dimension and policies of the EU including the single market and economic and monetary union. The second and third pillars established the framework for a Common Foreign and Security Policy (CFSP) and cooperation on justice and home affairs respectively.

The EC/EU has four main institutions which exercise the following functions and powers:

- *The Commission* acts as guardian of the treaties, initiates proposals, implements decisions and negotiates for the EC/EU on external economic relations. There are currently 20 commissioners including the President of the Commission who is responsible for general supervision of the Commission's activities. Commissioners are appointed by the governments of the member states but are required to exercise complete independence in the performance of their duties. Their appointment is for a five-year period and is subject to the approval of the European Parliament. They can be removed from office and then only en bloc as a result of a censure motion commanding a two-thirds majority in the European Parliament.
- *The Council of Ministers* (known as the Council of the European Union since the Treaty on European Union) is the decisiontaking body. It is representative of the governments of the member states. The Council comprises one minister from each of the member states, the composition of the Council depending on the subject under discussion. The presidency of the Council is held by each member state for six months at a time. Until the 1980s Council decisions usually required unanimity, and a single member state was

therefore able to veto any proposal. Since the Single European Act (1986), however, the Council has adopted a system known as Qualified Majority Voting (QMV) which applies to most, though not all, Council business.

- *The European Parliament*, originally known as the Common Assembly, was for many years a consultative body lacking substantive powers apart from that of dismissing the Commission. The Common Assembly was appointed by the parliaments of the member states until the first direct elections to the European Parliament were held in 1979. In recent years and especially as a result of the Single European Act, the Treaty on European Union and the Treaty of Amsterdam (1997), the Parliament has increasingly shared the decisionmaking role (co-decisionmaking) with the Council. There are currently 626 Members of the European Parliament (MEPs) who serve for a fixed term of office of five years (previously four years).

- *The Court of Justice* has played an important role in establishing a new legal order independent of the member states. Its particular responsibilities are to provide final rulings on interpretations of the EC/EU treaties, to determine the validity of the actions of an EC/EU institution, and to offer rulings on request from a court or tribunal of a member state. The Court is empowered to settle disputes between EC/EU institutions, member states, commercial organisations and any other parties. Its judgements are enforceable. The Court comprises 15 judges and nine advocates general who are appointed by the member states and are required to act independently of national governments.

Further reading

This highly selective guide to further reading contains general studies of the subject (including works on European integration) and also some of the relevant literature for particular sections in this book. There are extensive and extremely useful bibliographies in most of the undermentioned books, some of which also indicate recent articles on the subject in academic journals.

GENERAL

Baker, D. and Seawright, D. (eds), *Britain For and Against Europe: British Politics and the Question of European Integration*, Oxford, Clarendon Press, 1998.

Brivati, B. and Jones, H. (eds), *From Reconstruction to Integration: Britain and Europe since 1945*, Leicester, Leicester University Press, 1996.

Charlton, M., *The Price of Victory*, London, BBC Publications, 1983.

El-Agraa, A. M. (ed.), *The European Union: History, Institutions, Economics and Policies*, London, Prentice Hall, 1998.

George, S., *An Awkward Partner: Britain in the European Community*, Oxford, Oxford University Press, 1990.

Gowland, D. and Turner, A., *Reluctant Europeans: Britain and European Integration 1945–1998*, London, Longman, 2000.

Greenwood, S., *Britain and European Integration since the Second World War*, Manchester, Manchester University Press, 1996.

Henig, S., *The Uniting of Europe: From Discord to Concord*, London, Routledge, 1997.

Urwin, D. W., *The Community of Europe: A History of European Integration since 1945*, London, Longman, 1995.

Young, H., *This Blessed Plot: Britain and Europe from Churchill to Blair*, London, Macmillan, 1998.

Young, J. W., *Britain and European Unity, 1945–1992*, London, Macmillan, 1993.

SECTION 1
RECONSTRUCTION AND EUROPEAN UNITY: 1945–1949

Barnett, C., *The Lost Victory: British Dreams, British Realities, 1945–1950*, London, Macmillan, 1995.

Becker, J. and Knipping, F. (eds), *Power in Europe? Great Britain, France, Italy and Germany in the Postwar World, 1945–1950*, Berlin, W. de Gruyter, 1986.

Blackwell, M., *Clinging to Grandeur: British Attitudes and Foreign Policy in the Aftermath of the Second World War*, London, Greenwood Press, 1993.

Brivati, B. and Jones, H. (eds), *What Difference Did the War Make?*, Leicester, Leicester University Press, 1993.

Bullock, A., *Ernest Bevin: Foreign Secretary, 1945–1951*, London, Heinemann, 1983.

Croft, S., *The End of Superpower: The British Foreign Office Conceptions of a Changing World, 1945–51*, Aldershot, Dartmouth, 1994.

Hogan, M. J., *The Marshall Plan: America, Britain and the Reconstruction of Western Europe, 1945–1952*, Cambridge, Cambridge University Press, 1987.

Milward, A. S., *The Reconstruction of Western Europe, 1945–1951*, London, Methuen, 1984.

Morgan, K. O., *Labour in Power, 1945–1951*, Oxford, Oxford University Press, 1984.

Young, J. W., *Britain, France and the Unity of Europe, 1945–1951*, Leicester, Leicester University Press, 1985.

SECTION 2
'LOST OPPORTUNITIES': 1950–1957

Dell, E., *The Schuman Plan and the British Abdication of Leadership in Europe*, Oxford, Oxford University Press, 1995.

Di Nolfo, E. (ed.), *Power in Europe? II: Great Britain, France, Germany and Italy and the Origins of the EEC, 1952–1957*, Berlin, W. de Gruyter, 1992.

Dockrill, M. and Young, J. W. (eds), *British Foreign Policy, 1945–56*, London, Macmillan, 1989.

Dockrill, S., *Britain's Policy for West German Rearmament, 1950–1955*, London, Macmillan, 1991.

Milward, A. S., *The European Rescue of the Nation-State*, London, Routledge, 1992.

Schwabe, K. (ed.), *The Beginnings of the Schuman Plan*, Baden-Baden, Nomos, 1987.

Stirk, P. M. R. and Willis, D. (eds), *Shaping Postwar Europe: European Unity and Discord, 1945–1957*, London, Pinter, 1991.

Young, J. W. (ed.), *The Foreign Policy of Churchill's Peacetime Administration, 1951–1955*, Leicester, Leicester University Press, 1988.

SECTION 3
THE 'SPECIAL RELATIONSHIP': 1945–1963

Bartlett, C. J., *'The Special Relationship': A Political History of Anglo-American Relations since 1945*, London, Longman, 1992.

Baylis, J., *Anglo-American Defence Relations, 1939–1984: The Special Relationship*, London, Macmillan, 1984.

Baylis, J. (ed.), *Anglo-American Relations since 1939: The Enduring Alliance*, Manchester, Manchester University Press, 1997.

Dobson, A. P., *The Politics of the Anglo-American Economic Special Relationship, 1940–1987*, Brighton, Wheatsheaf, 1988.

Edmonds, R., *Setting the Mould: United States and Britain, 1945–1950*, Oxford, Clarendon Press, 1986.

Louis, W. M. R. and Bull, H. (eds), *The 'Special Relationship': Anglo-American Relations since 1945*, Oxford, Clarendon Press, 1986.

Manderson-Jones, R. B., *The Special Relationship: Anglo-American Relations and Western European Unity, 1947–56*, London, Weidenfeld and Nicolson, 1972.

Ovendale, R., *The English-Speaking Alliance: Britain, the United States, the Dominions and the Cold War, 1945–1951*, London, Allen and Unwin, 1985.
Ovendale, R., *Anglo-American Relations in the Twentieth Century*, London, Macmillan, 1998.

SECTION 4 KITH AND KIN:
THE COMMONWEALTH AND EUROPE, 1945–1961

Camps, M., *Britain and the European Community, 1955–1963*, Princeton, Princeton University Press, 1964.
Darwin, J., *Britain and Decolonisation: The Retreat from Empire in the Postwar World*, London, Macmillan, 1988.
Kent, J., *British Imperial Strategy and the Origins of the Cold War, 1944–49*, Leicester, Leicester University Press, 1993.
Sanders, D., *Losing an Empire, Finding a Role: British Foreign Policy since 1945*, London, Macmillan, 1990.
Schenk, C. R., *Britain and the Sterling Area: From Devaluation to Convertibility*, London, Routledge, 1994.

SECTION 5
KNOCKING AT THE DOOR: 1959–1963

Aldous, R. and Lee, S. (eds), *Harold Macmillan and Britain's World Role*, London, Macmillan, 1996.
Beloff, N., *The General Says No: Britain's Exclusion from Europe*, Harmondsworth, Penguin, 1963.
Griffiths, R. T. and Ward, S., *Courting the Common Market: The First Attempt to Enlarge the European Community, 1961–1963*, London, Lothian Foundation Press, 1996.
Horne, A., *Macmillan*, volume II: 1957–86, London, Macmillan, 1989.
Kaiser, W., *Using Europe, Abusing the Europeans: Britain and European Integration, 1945–1963*, London, Macmillan, 1996.
Lamb, R., *The Macmillan Years 1957–1963: The Emerging Truth*, London, John Murray, 1995.
Macmillan, H., *Pointing the Way, 1959–1961*, London, Macmillan, 1972.
Tratt, J., *The Macmillan Government and Europe: A Study in the Process of Policy Development*, London, Macmillan, 1996.
Turner, J., *Macmillan*, London, Longman, 1994.

SECTION 6
ANOTHER VETO: 1964–1969

Brivati, B., *Hugh Gaitskell*, London, Richard Cohen Books, 1996.
Brown, G., *In My Way*, London, Gollancz, 1972.
Coopey, R., Fielding, S. and Tiratsoo, N. (eds), *The Wilson Governments, 1964–70*, London, UCL Press, 1993.
Kitzinger, U., *The Second Try*, Oxford, Pergamon, 1968.
Lieber, R. J., *British Politics and European Unity: Parties, Elites and Pressure Groups*, Berkeley, University of California Press, 1970.
Newman, M., *Socialism and European Unity*, London, Junction Books, 1983.
Pimlott, B., *Harold Wilson*, London, HarperCollins, 1992.

Robins, L. J., *The Reluctant Party: Labour and the EEC, 1961–1975*, Ormskirk, G. W. and A. Hesketh, 1979.

Wilson, H., *The Labour Government, 1964–1970*, London, Weidenfeld and Nicolson, 1971.

SECTION 7
ENTRY AND RENEGOTIATION: 1970–1975

Benn, T., *Against the Tide: Diaries, 1973–77*, London, Arrow, 1989.

Butler, D. and Kitzinger, U., *The 1975 Referendum*, London, Macmillan, 1976.

Castle, B., *The Castle Diaries, 1964–1976*, London, Macmillan, 1990.

Goodhart, P., *Full-Hearted Consent: The Story of the Referendum Campaign*, London, Davis-Poynter, 1976.

Heath, E., *The Course of My Life: My Autobiography*, London, Hodder and Stoughton, 1998.

Jowell, R. and Hoinville, G., *Britain into Europe: Public Opinion and the EEC, 1961–1975*, London, Croom Helm, 1976.

Kitzinger, U., *Diplomacy and Persuasion: How Britain Joined the Common Market*, London, Thames and Hudson, 1972.

Lord, C., *British Entry to the European Community under the Heath Government of 1970–4*, Aldershot, Dartmouth, 1993.

Wilson, H., *Final Term: The Labour Government, 1974–1976*, London, Weidenfeld and Nicolson, 1979.

SECTION 8
IN TRANSITION: 1973–1979

Bulmer, S., George, S. and Scott, A. (eds), *The United Kingdom and EC Membership Evaluated*, London, Pinter, 1992.

Callaghan, J., *Time and Chance*, London, Collins, 1987.

Cohen, C. D., *The Common Market: Ten Years After*, Deddington, Philip Allan, 1983.

Coopey, R. and Woodward, N. (eds), *Britain in the 1970s: The Troubled Economy*, London, UCL Press, 1996.

El-Agraa, A. M., *Britain within the European Community*, London, Macmillan, 1983.

Gregory, F. E. C., *Britain and the EEC*, Oxford, M. Robertson, 1983.

Morgan, K. O., *Callaghan, A Life*, Oxford, Oxford University Press, 1997.

Wallace, W. (ed.), *Britain in Europe*, London, Heinemann, 1980.

SECTION 9
'NO, NO, YES': 1979–1990

Byrd, P. (ed.), *British Foreign Policy under Thatcher*, Oxford, Philip Allan, 1988.

Evans, E. J., *Thatcher and Thatcherism*, London, Routledge, 1997.

Gilmour, I., *Dancing with Dogma: Britain under Thatcherism*, London, Simon and Schuster, 1992.

Howe, G., *Conflict of Loyalty*, London, Macmillan, 1994.

Jenkins, R., *European Diary, 1977–81*, London, Collins, 1989.

Lawson, N., *The View From No. 11: Memoirs of a Tory Radical*, London, Bantam Press, 1992.

Thatcher, M., *The Downing Street Years*, London, HarperCollins, 1993.

Young, H., *One of Us: A Biography of Margaret Thatcher*, London, Macmillan, 1991.

SECTION 10
STAYING IN BUT OPTING OUT: 1990–1997

Anderson, B., *John Major: The Making of a Prime Minister*, London, Headline, 1992.

Connolly, B., *The Rotten Heart of Europe: The Dirty War for Europe's Money*, London, Faber and Faber, 1995.

Duff, A., Pinder, J. and Pryce, R. (eds), *Maastricht and Beyond: Building European Union*, London, Routledge, 1994.

Lamont, N., *In Office*, London, Little, Brown, 1999.

Major, J., *The Autobiography*, London, HarperCollins, 1999.

Stephens, P., *Politics and the Pound: The Conservatives' Struggle with Sterling*, London, Macmillan, 1996.

Chronological table

1945	May	End of the Second World War in Europe (8 May).
	July	Labour Party under Clement Attlee won the general election.
	July/August	Potsdam conference of American, Soviet and British leaders.
1947	January	Merging of British and American occupation zones in Germany (Bizonia).
	March	UK/France Treaty of Dunkirk signed.
		Announcement of the Truman doctrine.
	June	Announcement of the Marshall Plan.
	October	General Agreement on Tariffs and Trade (GATT) signed.
1948	March	Brussels Treaty signed by UK, France and the Benelux states.
	April	Organisation for European Economic Cooperation (OEEC) established to administer the European Recovery Programme (Marshall Plan).
	May	Congress of Europe at The Hague.
	June	Berlin blockade began.
1949	April	North Atlantic Treaty signed.
	May	Statute of the Council of Europe signed by ten states.
1950	May	Announcement of the Schuman Plan.
	June	Outbreak of the Korean War.
	October	Announcement of the Pleven Plan for a European army.
1951	April	European Coal and Steel Community (ECSC) Treaty of Paris signed by Belgium, France, Italy, Luxembourg, the Netherlands and West Germany.
	July	ECSC began to function.
	October	Conservative Party under Winston Churchill won the general election.
1952	May	European Defence Community (EDC) Treaty signed by the six ECSC states.
1954	August	French National Assembly rejected the EDC Treaty.
	October	Signature of the Paris Agreements and the formation of the Western European Union (WEU).
	December	Treaty of Association between UK and ECSC.

1955	April	Anthony Eden succeeded Churchill as Prime Minister.
	June	Messina conference of the six ECSC states.
	July	Spaak committee convened to consider plans for further European integration.
1956	March	Spaak report on the creation of a common market.
	October/November	Suez crisis.
	November	Announcement of British plan for a free trade area (FTA).
1957	January	Harold Macmillan succeeded Eden as Prime Minister.
	March	Treaties of Rome signed establishing the European Economic Community (EEC) and the European Atomic Energy Community (EAEC).
	October	Formation of the Maudling committee under the aegis of the OEEC to consider the plan for an FTA.
1958	January	Treaties of Rome came into operation.
	December	France blocked further discussion of the FTA plan.
1959	January	First EEC tariff reductions and increases in import quotas.
1960	January	European Free Trade Association (EFTA) Convention signed in Stockholm by Austria, Denmark, Norway, Portugal, Sweden, Switzerland and the UK.
	May	Failure of four-power summit in Paris.
	December	OEEC reorganised into the Organisation for Economic Cooperation and Development (OECD).
1961	August	First UK application to join the EEC.
1962	January	Agreement on the main features of the EEC's common agricultural policy (CAP).
	December	Kennedy/Macmillan meeting at Nassau and the Polaris agreement.
1963	January	De Gaulle vetoed UK membership of the EEC.
	October	Alec Douglas-Home succeeded Macmillan as Prime Minister.
1964	October	Labour Party under Harold Wilson won the general election.
1965	April	Merger Treaty of the European Communities (EC) signed. It entered into force on 1 July 1967.
	July	France began a boycott of EC institutions.
1966	January	Luxembourg Agreement ended French boycott of EC institutions.
	March	Labour Party won the general election.
	May/July	EEC negotiated an agreement on the CAP.
1967	May	Second UK application for EC membership.
	November	De Gaulle vetoed UK membership of EC.
1968	July	Completion of the EEC customs union.
1969	April	De Gaulle resigned as President of the Fifth French Republic.
	December	The Hague summit of EC leaders agreed in principle to enlarge the EC and to devise a plan for economic and monetary union.

1970	April	EC agreement on new arrangements for financing the budget through automatic revenue ('own resources').
	June	Conservative Party won the general election under Edward Heath.
		EC opened membership negotiations with Denmark, Ireland, Norway and the UK.
	October	Publication of the Werner Report on Economic and Monetary Union and the Davignon Report on European Political Cooperation.
1971	March	EC Council of Ministers agreed to embark on the first of three stages towards economic and monetary union by 1980.
1972	January	Conclusion of EC membership negotiations and signature of Treaties of Accession by Denmark, Ireland, Norway and the UK.
	October	UK Parliament voted in favour of the principle of UK membership of the EC.
		Paris summit of EC leaders reaffirmed the goal of achieving economic and monetary union by 1980.
1973	January	Accession of Denmark, Ireland and the UK to the EC.
1974	March	Labour government under Wilson returned to power after general election with a commitment to renegotiate the terms of entry to the EC.
	December	Paris summit of EC leaders agreed to establish the European Council.
1975	March	Conclusion of the UK's renegotiation of the terms of entry to the EC.
	June	UK referendum resulted in a majority for the renegotiated terms of entry and continued membership of the EC.
	December	Rome European Council meeting agreed to hold direct elections to the European Parliament.
1976	April	James Callaghan succeeded Wilson as Prime Minister.
1977	November	Direct elections to the European Parliament postponed until 1979 due to UK failure to meet the original deadline.
1978	July	Franco-German proposal for a European Monetary System (EMS) announced at the Bremen European Council meeting.
	December	Formal announcement of UK decision not to participate in the Exchange Rate Mechanism (ERM) of the EMS.
1979	March	EMS began to function.
	May	Conservative Party under Margaret Thatcher won the general election.
	June	First direct elections to the European Parliament.
1980	May	EC Council of Ministers agreed to reduce UK contribution to EC budget for two years.
1981	January	Accession of Greece to the EC.
	November	Genscher–Colombo Plan.
1982	January	Common Fisheries Policy agreement.

1983	June	Conservative Party under Thatcher won the general election.
		Stuttgart European Council meeting adopted the Solemn Declaration on European Union.
1984	January	Free trade area established between the EC and the EFTA.
	June	Fontainebleau European Council meeting agreed a formula for reducing the UK contribution to the EC budget.
		British paper entitled *Europe – the Future*.
1985	January	Jacques Delors appointed President of the Commission.
	June	Milan European Council meeting agreed in principle to establish a single market by the end of December 1992 and to convene an intergovernmental conference (IGC) on EC reform.
	December	Luxembourg European Council meeting agreed on the principles of the Single European Act.
1986	January	Accession of Spain and Portugal to the EC.
	February	Single European Act signed in Luxembourg.
1987	June	Conservative Party under Thatcher won the general election.
	July	Single European Act came into force.
1988	June	Hanover European Council meeting instructed a committee chaired by Delors to consider plans for the achievement of economic and monetary union (EMU).
	September	Thatcher's speech at the College of Europe in Bruges.
1989	January	Delors reappointed President of the Commission.
	April	Delors report on a three-stage progression towards the achievement of EMU.
	June	Madrid European Council meeting agreed to begin first stage of EMU on 1 July 1990.
	December	At the Strasbourg European Council meeting all EC states except UK approved the Charter of Basic Social Rights for Workers (Social Charter) and also agreed to establish an IGC on EMU at the end of 1990.
1990	June	Dublin European Council meeting agreed to convene an IGC on political union.
	July	First stage of EMU came into effect.
	October	UK entered the ERM of the EMS.
		Rome European Council meeting agreed to implement the second stage of the Delors Plan for EMU by 1994.
	November	John Major succeeded Thatcher as Conservative Party leader and Prime Minister.
	December	The two IGCs on EMU and political union opened in Rome.
1991	December	Maastricht European Council meeting agreed the Treaty on European Union (Maastricht Treaty). UK government secured opt-outs covering the Social Chapter and the third and final stage of EMU.

1992	February	Treaty on European Union signed in Maastricht.
	May	Conservative Party under Major won the general election. EC and EFTA signed a treaty establishing the European Economic Area (EEA).
	June	Danish voters rejected the Treaty on European Union in a referendum.
	September	UK withdrew from the ERM.
1993	January	Single market came into effect.
	February	EC opened negotiations with Austria, Finland and Sweden (and Norway – April 1993) on their applications for membership.
	May	Danish voters approved the Treaty on European Union after Denmark obtained opt-outs from the Treaty.
	July	UK ratified the Treaty on European Union.
	November	Treaty on European Union formally came into effect.
1994	January	Second stage of EMU came into effect with the establishment of the European Monetary Institute (EMI) in Frankfurt.
1995	June	Cannes European Council meeting recognised that the introduction of a single currency by 1997 was unrealistic.
1996	March	IGC convened to review the Treaty on European Union.
	December	Dublin European Council meeting agreed a single currency stability pact.
1997	May	Labour Party under Tony Blair won the general election and announced its intention to accept the European Social Chapter.
	June	Amsterdam European Council meeting agreed the Treaty of Amsterdam following the IGC review of the Treaty on European Union. William Hague elected leader of the Conservative Party.
	October	Gordon Brown, Chancellor of the Exchequer, specified five economic tests for UK entry into the euro and indicated that the UK would not be ready for entry before the end of the current parliament.
	December	Luxembourg European Council meeting invited Cyprus, the Czech Republic, Estonia, Hungary, Poland and Slovenia to start membership talks in March 1998 with a view to entry to the European Union (EU) early in the next century.
1998	January	UK's six-month presidency of the EU began.
	May	Eleven of the 15 EU states agreed to proceed to the third and final stage of EMU (scheduled for 1 January 1999) with provision for the establishment of a European Central Bank, the fixing of exchange rates and the introduction of a single currency – the euro. Denmark, Sweden and the UK had previously obtained opt-outs from this timetable, while Greece was deemed to have failed to qualify.
	June	End of UK's presidency of the EU.

Index